Russian
Nationalism

Russian Nationalism

Yesterday, Today, Tomorrow

Stephen K. Carter
*Senior Lecturer in Politics and Government,
City of London Polytechnic*

St. Martin's Press
New York

First published in United States of America in 1990

Printed in Gt. Britain

ISBN 0-312-04764-9

Library of Congress Cataloging-in-Publication Data

Carter, Stephen.
    Russian nationalism : yesterday, today, tomorrow/Stephen K.
Carter.
        p.   cm.
    Includes bibliographical references.
    ISBN 0-312-04764-9
    1. Soviet Union—Politics and government—1917-
    2. Nationalism—
Soviet Union—History—20th century.   I. Title.
DK266.3.C37   1990
947.084—dc20   90-31982
                                                              CIP

In memory of her victory over
fascism, this book is dedicated to
Russia's future in a peaceful world

Contents

Figures

Introduction

Since the accession of Mikhail Sergeyevich Gorbachev in March 1985 to the post of General Secretary of the Communist Party of the Soviet Union (CPSU), the pace of change in the USSR, which at first was slow, has accelerated. Until 1986, and after the xxviith Congress of the Party, many Western observers predicted only marginal reform of a basically stable political system, [1] but after the emergence of Gorbachev's book *Perestroika*[2] in 1987, and the xixth Party Conference in the summer of 1988, the world realised that Gorbachev was in earnest about a kind of 'revolutionary' *perestroika*, despite much internal opposition, or at least hidden resistance and inertia. Radical proposals for the reorganisation of the economy, including 'self-financing' of socialist industrial enterprises, have gone hand in hand with proposals for the democratisation of the legislature, local government and the Party. Perhaps the most turbulent changes have been those associated with *glasnost'* or openness, in society and the mass media. Gorbachev appears to place great emphasis on shaking up the Communist Party and its security of tenure, which had helped to create the 'stagnation' or *zastoi* of the Brezhnev period, and in doing so he has sought to involve civil society and the intelligentsia more deeply in public life.

For the West the period after 1985 has been one of hope and some relaxation of tension after the arms race of the late 1970s and early 1980s. The Thatcher and Reagan administrations after 1979–80 took a firm line with the USSR of Brezhnev following its invasion of Afghanistan, its continuing violations of human rights[3] and its threats against Poland during the Solidarity crisis in Poland beginning in 1980.

For a while, the successors of Brezhnev, first Yuri Vladimirovich Andropov, and then Konstantin Ustinovich Chernenko, provided no clear or lasting guidelines on the future shape of Soviet foreign or domestic policy. But the accession of Gorbachev saw a series of attempts to lessen international tensions and to negotiate meaningful reductions in nuclear weapons, culminating, eventually, in the INF Agreements. The late 1980s also saw a significant retreat from foreign adventure and global involvements on the part of the Soviet

Union. In 1989 the USSR withdrew significant forces from Afghanistan, while the Soviet-backed Cuban intervention in Angola was coming to a halt, and Soviet-backed Vietnamese troops were leaving Cambodia.

At the same time, significant changes are taking place in Soviet ideology. Gorbachev's 1986 revision of the Khrushchevite (IIIrd) Party Programme, adopted originally in 1961, reduced references to the achievement of 'Communism' or 'Communist self-government', and stated that the supposedly present stage of 'developed socialism' would last for an historically prolonged period. Thus Gorbachev's USSR has apparently abandoned an important utopian element in Communist thought, and an irreplaceable spur to the political commitment of Communists. Ideologically, the attraction of the Communist path of development for Third World countries seems to be in terminal decline, and its international appeal is rapidly evaporating in the light of its domestic failures. Within the USSR itself, it is now widely admitted that Marxism-Leninism has little popular appeal, and there appears to be a kind of ideological vacuum.

How will Communist ideology and 'Soviet internationalism' adapt themselves to the present adverse conditions? These are important questions for the USSR where the regime is dependent for its continuing legitimacy on the maintenance of Leninism in some recognisable form. It is important in the context of the multinational character of the USSR and its geographical integrity and unity as a state. And it is no less important for the West, which, while hoping for a relaxation of tension and further normalisation of relations, cannot afford to relax its guard while the situation remains confusingly dynamic and uncertain.

Some of the most serious and intractable pressures now experienced by the Soviet political system are those which have been awakened in the national republics of the USSR as a result of the new policies of *glasnost'*. The re-examination of Stalin's annexation of the Baltic states in 1940 has provoked demands for autonomy or at least regional devolution and self-financing among all three national republics. Popular or national fronts have emerged in Estonia, Lithuania and Latvia. Armenian nationalists have laid claim to an enclave of Azerbaidjan, Nagorno-Karabakh. Ukrainian, Belorussian, Kazakh and other nationalisms have made their appearance, often in tandem with the harrowing revelations of Stalin's crimes. As long as the process of de-Stalinisation continues, nationalist movements will continue their political activities. If the USSR is the world's last great empire, then it is now an empire in retreat.

Many Western observers[4] have focused their attention on Soviet nationalities policy, following the shifts in Leninist doctrines relating to nations which should be national in form, but socialist in content. Studies are made of the doctrines relating to the 'drawing-together' (*sblizheniye*) and the supposedly ultimate 'merging' (*sliyanie*) of nations under developed socialism and Communism. Such scholars now also enlarge their studies to include constitutional changes and their probable effects on federal powers within the Soviet machinery of government and local democracy. These studies are likely to become of particular relevance as the nationalities issue rises, as surely it must, to a position near the top of the Soviet political agenda.

However, this book is devoted to the study of this problem from an altogether different, and still much neglected, perspective. It is concerned with Russian nationalism, a complex but very powerful, pervasive and enduring phenomenon, which exerts a very significant influence on Soviet politics in the context of a declining ideology.

Every great nation faced with a retreat from empire, suffers a crisis of identity and a painful but necessary adjustment to new realities. When that nation is a nuclear superpower which has been imbued for decades with a millennial ideology, with expectations (at times fervently believed) of ultimate geopolitical leadership and expansionism, that crisis of identity must indeed be incipiently traumatic. Such an incipient crisis today faces the world's largest state, and within it, the USSR's largest nation – Russia.

Political movements which seek to express, to articulate and to further the interests of a nation are termed 'nationalisms', but nationalism is a very diffuse and ill-defined concept. Anthony D. Smith has recently defined 'nationalism' as 'an ideological movement, for the attainment and maintenance of self-government and independence on behalf of a group, some of whose members conceive it to constitute an actual or potential nation like others'.[5] Smith's ambitious and potentially encyclopaedic treatment of nationalism is focused on newly independent nation-states and nationalism as a means towards independence and modernisation. Russian nationalism, however, has certain characteristics which place it entirely outside this context.

Hans Kohn has defined nationalism in broader, more comprehensive terms as

a state of mind, permeating the large majority of a people and claiming to permeate all its members, it recognises the nation-state as the ideal form of political organisation, and nationality as the source of all creative and cultural energy and economic well-being. The supreme loyalty of man is therefore due to his nationality, and his own life is supposedly rooted in and made possible by its welfare.[6]

Generally speaking, nationalists reject any distinction between 'cultural' and 'political' nationalism, and claim that not only the national economy, but also the national folklore, music, art, literature and traditions have a legitimate claim to protection and furtherance by the creation and maintenance of the political nation-state. Roughly speaking, the 'statist' school of nationalism defines the nation as a territorial-political unit, while the 'ethnicists' see the nation as a large politicised ethnic group, defined by common culture and often alleged descent from a common ancestry. Nationalism therefore turns out to be a cultural movement, since one can have a nationalist movement without a state. Following Herder's argument, I tend to favour an ethnicist view of nationalism, which often stresses language as a crucial uniting and defining factor for nations. Of course, there are many arguments against the universal identification of nations with language groups,[7] but language is a crucial uniting factor in the case of Russian nationalism, which also has at times aspired towards the concept of Russian language as the lingua franca of a much larger geographical unit, namely the USSR. Russian nationalism, then, like nineteenth-century Panslavism, is an ethnocentric nationalism with linguistic, cultural and religious aspirations. It can be either purely 'preservationist' or 'expansionist': like other nationalisms, it has a dual, Janus-like quality.[8]

There have been many attempts to explain and classify nationalism from an historical point of view. Perhaps the most famous of these has been that of E. Kedourie,[9] who depicts nationalism as an unfortunate historical accident dating from the early nineteenth century and giving rise to imperialism, war and ultimately fascism. Other more sociological interpretations explain nationalism in terms of the drive towards modernisation and post-colonial independence, or as an ideology of a ruling class evolved as a means of obscuring class conflict and creating 'false consciousness'.

A very interesting attempt by a political scientist, S. Handman, defined nationalism in four varieties in an article written in 1921.[10] He posited 'irredentism', 'oppression', 'precaution' and 'prestige' as the major types of motivation for nationalism. Handman considered that precautionary nationalism can lead to what he called 'economic state nationalism'. The major purpose of the state is to protect itself and the interests of its members: 'economic state nationalism', says Handman, can evolve into imperialism. 'Prestige' nationalism, on the other hand, is more than a precaution or a protection, since it seeks to redress grievances and arises from 'a perceived lack of esteem for past achievements and unrealised potentialities'.[11] Such prestige nationalism often develops exclusive and Messianic elements, says Handman, which we would surely recognise today as what is popularly identified as fascism.

H. Seton-Weston focused on Western European and American

concepts of nationalism, and distinguished them from nationalism in Eastern Europe and the Balkans. He also, very usefully, separated the independence, irredentist and nation-building movements one from another. His assertion that established nations did not have any tendency towards nationalism is perhaps less valid: 'Nations which are independent, territorially satisfied, and deeply nationally conscious have no need to be nationalist any more.'[12] This is not only prescriptive rather than descriptive but is also, one suspects, very much a prescription in response to his contemporary situation. It is surely a matter of common observation that nation-states with long and well-established identities may, from time to time, be subject to what Anthony D. Smith has called 'preservation' nationalism. According to Smith, in 'preservation' or 'renewal' nationalism, 'a culturally demarcated ruling group aims by a mixture of discriminating and homogenising measures to perpetuate its caste-like rule, while posing as the champion of the whole unit in opposition to the outside world.'[13] This kind of 'preservation' nationalism appeared to be typical of a certain group within the Soviet élite, associated with Mikhail Suslov during the Brezhnev era. Renewal nationalism was also to be found in the years after Stalin's death in 1953, and especially following Khrushchev's revelations about Stalin's crimes at the xxth Party Congress in 1956. As Smith summarises, 'renewal nationalisms occur, by contrast, in culturally homogeneous groups. They usually start . . . outside the main centres of power, and if allied to social discontents, are directed against the incumbent ruler or regime.'[14] This renewal nationalism is typical of the dissident nationalists such as Solzhenitsyn. As Yanov has pointed out,[15] there is a strange kind of symbiotic relationship between establishment and dissident nationalists in Russia, between preservation and renewal nationalists.

Russian nationalism may also have Messianic and prestige elements in Handman's sense. As Gellner persuasively argues, nationalism cannot be dismissed as an unfortunate historical accident, as it is still a real and possibly basic motivation within the political organisation of the modern world, and is present in some attenuated form in many modern industrial countries as well as newly emergent nations of the Third World. However, Gellner admits that there have been many 'false' theories of nationalism, and he would not try, for example, to identify the 'progressive' nationalism of a Mazzini[16] with the amoral militarism of a von Treitschke.[17] Gellner clarifies much about the philosophical origins of nationalism as well as contributing some straight thinking about this notoriously difficult subject.

According to Gellner, there are four kinds of false theories about nationalism. First, the view that every nation has a natural right to national sentiment and self-determination, and that if this is absent, it must be due to outside repression. Second, the 'Kedourie' thesis, namely that nationalism is a regrettable accident which arose as a result of ideas which should never have been taken seriously; an accidental notion which is not at all essential to the modern industrial state. The third false theory, according to Gellner, is what he calls the 'wrong address' theory and which is associated with Marxism. The 'awakening message' of history was delivered to nations, when it should have been delivered to classes. All that is necessary, say the Marxists, is for the wrongful recipient to hand over the message, together with the enthusiasm and political energies associated with it, to the rightful addressee, the working class. Fourth, there is that theory of nationalism popularly associated with fascism, namely, a nationalism of tribe, race, territory and blood. The irrational feelings of aggression, racial purity, the forces associated with 'underground man', are seen by such nationalists as life-enhancing. Gellner calls this theory the 'Dark Gods' theory. He summarises his position by saying, 'none of these theories is remotely tenable'.[18]

Russian nationalism today seeks not only to resurrect ideas which have their origins in Slavophilism and Panslavism as derived from the nineteenth century: it also seeks, in some of its incarnations, to replace Leninist nationalities policy, aptly summarised by Gellner under the heading of the 'wrong address theory'. One variety of Russian nationalism today is a neo-fascist type, with distinctly 'Dark Gods' connotations and is associated with the Pamyat' (Memory) Society. This appears therefore to be a process of substituting one of Gellner's false theories for another equally false theory!

This book concentrates on a history of Russian nationalism and focuses on the twentieth century, seeking to depict the present in terms of the past. It is a broad canvas, painted with an inevitably broad brush, but with an overall structure and argument which will, I hope, stimulate discussion and research as well as (doubtlessly merited) criticism. The book is not primarily about the political theory of nationalism in general, nor about Leninist nationalities policy in particular. Instead, it concentrates on a chronological exposition of the 'Russian Idea'; it is a history of Russia's self-image as it has developed from its mainly nineteenth-century origins to the present day.

The Russian Revolution of October 1917 was carried out by Lenin's Bolsheviks with the conviction that they could establish socialism in Russia and that the revolution would soon become international. The early Bolsheviks were internationalists, politically at the other end of the spectrum in relation to nationalism. However, Lenin's early internationalism had receded by the early years of the regime, technically with the adoption of 'socialism in one country' in 1924. While Lenin's followers no doubt desired a clean break with the tsarist and capitalist past, that peculiarly harsh political and social reality which is Russia was to prove singularly tenacious. Despite the cataclysmic experiences of civil war, collectivisation, industrialisation, world war and Stalinism, Russian nationalism has always survived. Indeed, by Stalin's later years, Soviet patriotism was closely identified with Russian interests and national pride.

Nikita Sergeyevich Khrushchev, like Gorbachev today, attempted to de-Stalinise and to expand the international appeal of the Soviet system. Khrushchev claimed, for example, that the centrally planned economy would catch up with, and then overtake, the capitalist economy of the United States within a relatively few years.[19] Khrushchev's claims very rapidly evaporated in the light of subsequent developments and the ideology of his successors, Brezhnev and Kosygin, was characterised, on the one hand, by a kind of conservative cynicism and repression of dissent, and on the other hand, by a resurgent Russian nationalism, possibly aided and abetted by Brezhnev's chief ideologist, Mikhail Suslov. The dominant literary movement of that era, associated with the 'countryside' writers (derevenshchiki) was also, in its own way, profoundly nationalist. A dissident nationalism also emerged in samizdat writings, including the VSKhSON of Ogurtsov[20] and Veche (Osipov).[21]

In the 1980s a new, tensely defensive and extremist nationalism has emerged in the Pamyat' and Otechestvo societies[22] which originally concerned themselves with the preservation of ancient monuments, but since 1985 have developed anti-Semitic, neo-fascist characteristics. Such groups have a considerable following and could conceivably become politically influential despite the formal restriction on their activities, in the event of the failure of Gorbachev's reforms, possibly in some kind of alliance (probably temporary) with neo-Stalinists in the Party and with the military. The continuing existence of opposition to Gorbachev, of which Russian nationalism is an important part, requires Western policy to be ruled by the head rather than by the heart.

Probably the most important concerns of the Soviet people today are economic ones. Gorbachev's reforms will never be widely accepted unless the economy begins to yield a higher standard of living for the Soviet Union. Leading proponents of perestroika such as the economist Shmelev, have acknowledged this, and they are anxiously urging a diminution of the ubiquitous Soviet queue[23] and radical reform measures such as the introduction of private (co-operative) enterprise. The Soviet worker is now being asked to change his attitude towards work, rewards and socialism. While facing rises in the cost of living, which will be associated with the abolition of subsidies on rented accommodation, meat, bread and other foodstuffs, he is now often deprived of bonuses which he took for granted under Brezhnev because of the activities of *Gospriemka* (State Quality Control). *Gospriemka* often rejected items of low quality from production lines, and the old emphasis on quantitative production which formed a central feature of the planned economy is now gradually being changed.

The bureaucracy involved in State Planning Agencies and the Central Ministries is now under severe attack. Many state and Party officials, used to lifetime tenure under Brezhnev, face radical changes in their lifestyles and their privileges. The Soviet worker is now being asked to become involved in the election of his enterprise manager, and job security, previously a guaranteed feature of the socialist system is being questioned.[24] As yet, the Soviet worker and the Soviet official have little to show for their unaccustomed insecurity, while the queues are lengthening and inflation is rising. There is a deep social unease in the USSR today.

Meanwhile, the intelligentsia, a group much derided during the period of stagnation under Brezhnev, is having a field-day. It is impossible here to summarise adequately the many developments in the arts, cinema, literature and thought, but among the most startling changes has been the publication of Pasternak's *Dr Zhivago* in *Novy Mir (New World)* as from January 1988, and a strongly de-Stalinising trend which has led to the rehabilitation of the leading economist Bukharin[25] who opposed Stalin over collectivisation.

Works by Akhmatova and Mandel'shtam, which for years have been anathematised, have now been published, together with anti-Stalinist novels like Rybakov's *Children of the Arbat*[26] and films like Abuladze's *Repentance*. Monuments to Stalin's victims will be erected in some major Soviet cities.[27] There are signs that the role of Trotsky, for example during the negotiations at Brest-Litovsk, will be more thoroughly investigated. At the same time, myriad informal groups are springing up all over the USSR, many of which support causes to which nationalists are sympathetic, such as the restoration of ancient monuments.

Professor Geoffrey Hosking has pointed out that the Soviet system has certain characteristics which strongly influence the nature of such informal groups. First, they are forming in a society which has been governed until recently by a totalitarian or ideocratic system. Such systems traditionally oppose group formation or 'sub-group autonomy'. Second, there is thus a tendency for small groups to form around a samizdat publication and these groups have inadequate mutual interaction. There are no alternative political parties to the ruling Communist Party, despite attempts to establish these and consequently there is no party political press nor a genuine electoral process involving competitive political parties. The groups form around ideas or culture, rather than being parties in the traditional

Western sense. Third, although systematic terror has not been exercised within Soviet society since the time of Stalin, there is still a legacy of mutual distrust and 'segmentation' which discourages the real exchange of political opinion, so that the Soviet people are politically inexperienced and the levels of political science as a discipline, and political maturity as a social phenomenon, are rather low.

Under such conditions, while the foundations of Soviet socialism are being debated all over the country and new groups are bursting into the political arena, strong passions are being ignited in an atmosphere of confusion and uncertainty. Aspirations have been aroused and expectations for economic and social changes and improvements have been stimulated. Together with the widespread reinvestigation of the Stalin era, there has been a resurgence of national feelings, as already mentioned. In these circumstances the nominally federal structure of the USSR in its present form is under considerable pressure to change. The purpose of this book is to review the reaction of Great Russian nationalism to these developments. If the nationalities policy rises to the top of the political agenda of the USSR, Russian nationalism must surely follow.

In writing this book, I would like to thank in particular Radio Free Europe and Radio Liberty, with special reference to the work of Julia Wishnevsky. I am much indebted to John Dunlop, Alexander Yanov and Darrell Hammer for the inspiration provided by their published work, and to Peter Duncan and Mike Hughes for their comments. The Great Britain–USSR Association provided me with rare Soviet journals and the Pushkin Club afforded me a chance to try out my ideas on its unsuspecting members. I am particularly grateful to Dr Dominic Lieven and to the late Professor Leonard Schapiro of the London School of Economics and Political Science, who have both supervised dissertations of mine on Solzhenitsyn[28] and Dostoevsky,[29] which have contributed to the preparation of this book. I am indebted to the facilities at the Lionel Robbins Library of Political and Economic Science. Its amazingly contemporary information in terms of BBC Caris Reports and other broadcasts as well as its Soviet Press Section was quite indispensable. I should like to thank my father, Douglas Carter CB, for his continuing interest and helpful suggestions.[30] My thanks are also due to Professor Stephen Haseler for his influence and encouragement and to John Spiers and Frances Pinter for undertaking publication. I would like to thank my employers, the City of London Polytechnic, who have allowed me to get on with this book quietly in the background. Last, but not least, my eternal gratitude must go to my wife, Joscelyn, for the long hours she has spent word-processing and correcting proofs on my behalf.

NOTES

1. See, for example, M. McCauley and S. Carter (eds) *Leadership and Succession in the Soviet Union, Eastern Europe and China* (London, Macmillan, 1986), Chapters 1 and 2.
2. M. S. Gorbachev, *Perestroika: New thinking for our country and the world* (London, Collins/Harvill, 1987, 1988).
3. Despite the so-called 'Basket Three' incorporated into the Helsinki Agreement of 1975.
4. For example, H. Carrère d'Encausse, *Decline of an Empire* (New York, Harper Colophon Books, 1981); R. Conquest (ed.), *Soviet Nationalities Policy in Practice* (London, The Bodley Head, Soviet Studies Series, 1967); Carl A. Linden and Dmitri K. Simes (eds), *Nationalities and Nationalism in the USSR: A Soviet dilemma* (Washington, Center for Strategic and International Studies, 1977); G. Lapidus, 'Ethnonationalism and political stability: the Soviet case', in *World Politics*, Vol. 4 (July 1984); Peter Rutland, 'The nationality problem and the Soviet state', in Neil Harding (ed.), *The State in Socialist Society* (London, Macmillan, 1984); Mary McAuley, 'Nationalism and the Soviet multi-ethnic state', in Neil Harding, op. cit.; Rasma Karklins, *Ethnic Relations in the USSR: The perspective from below* (Winchester, Mass. and London, 1986); Brian Silver, 'Soviet nationality problems: analytic approaches', in *Problems of Communism* (July–August 1979); Bohdan Nahaylo, 'Nationalities policy', in Martin McCauley (ed.), *The Soviet Union under Gorbachev* (London, Macmillan, 1987).
5. Anthony D. Smith, *Theories of Nationalism* (London, Duckworth, 1983), p. 171.
6. H. Kohn, *The Idea of Nationalism* (New York, Macmillan 1967), Chapter 1.
7. A. D. Smith, op. cit., pp. 182–5.
8. As Smith summarises, nationalism (the ethnic variety) is both integrative and divisive, both modernising and traditionalist; it tends to have a 'Janus-faced posture' (p. 256).
9. E. Kedourie, *Nationalism* (London, Hutchinson University Library, 3rd edn, 1966).
10. S. Handman, 'The sentiment of nationalism', *Political Science Quarterly*, United Kingdom, No. 36 (1921).
11. A. D. Smith, op. cit., p. 200.
12. A. D. Smith, op. cit., p. 201.
13. Ibid., p. 224.
14. Ibid.
15. A. Yanov, *The Russian Challenge and the Year 2000* (New York, Basil Blackwell, 1987),
16. Giuseppi Mazzini, born in Genoa, exerted an enormous influence on his contemporaries through his political activities on behalf of 'Italia' and through his voluminous writings. His important message was simple and moving: the Italian nation-state, in which he fervently believed, was to be part of the system of Europe and this system, he said, would consist of free and independent nations. They would be the rooms of the house. It would be in the nation, and by the nation, associated with their fellows in its life, that men would rise to the height of their duty to God. No nation could live for itself alone. Each nation owed a duty to others. It should promote peace and a sense of duty to the system of

Europe and humanity at large. Mazzini died in hiding, in Pisa, in 1872, under the assumed name of 'Mr. Brown'. However, the new Italian parliament, by unanimous resolution, expressed the sorrow of the nation for which he had done so much to create. His vision of a world of free and independent nations, living at peace with each other, as good neighbours, helped to inspire the creation of the United Nations Organisation.

17. Heinrich von Treitschke, the son of an army officer, had an entirely different view of nationalism. He rejoiced at the victories of Prussia over the Danes in 1864, the Austrians in 1866 and the French in 1870. He was a university professor of history and politics. His book *Politik* begins:

> It will always resound to the glory of Machiavelli that he placed the State on a solid foundation, and that he freed the State and its morality from the moral precepts taught by the Church, but especially because he has been the first to teach, 'The State is power'.

Elsewhere he states:

> The institution of international and permanent courts of arbitration is incompatible with the very nature of the State. . . . For vital questions there exists no impartial foreign power, and to the end of history, arms will give the final decision. Herein lies the sacredness of war.

He advocated the build-up of the German Army and Navy as the nation's top priority and he depicted Germany as encircled by potential enemies. France was in 'a latent state of war', Russian expansionism was incompatible with Germany's interests, and England, with its Empire and Navy, was Germany's arch-enemy. 'A collision between our interests and those of England is unavoidable,' he stated. He prophesied that both the British Empire and the United States would break up, leaving Germany with undisputed world supremacy. There can be little doubt that von Treitschke's teachings on nationalism contributed to the catastrophe of two world wars in the twentieth century.

18. E. Gellner, *Nations and Nationalism* (Oxford, Basil Blackwell, 1983), pp. 129–30.

19. 'Programme of the Communist Party of the Soviet Union', adopted at the XXIInd Party Congress in 1961. The Programme predicted that the USSR would catch up with, and then overtake the GNP of the United States by the year 1980!

20. VSKhSON was a political organisation, the 'All-Russian Social Christian Union for the Liberation of the People'.

21. The samizdat journal *Veche* was named after a quasi-democratic deliberative body which existed in the city-state of Novgorod.

22. See Chapter 8.

23. See Dmitri Simes, 'Gorbachev: will his economic sums add up?', *The Daily Telegraph* (Monday, 8 August 1988).

24. There is some disagreement here, for example Nikolai Shmelev predicts unemployment of between 13 million and 19 million by the year 2000, while Mikhail Gorbachev says that 'relocation' of jobs is possible.

25. See *Moscow News* (English edition, February 1988).

26. A. Rybakov, *Children of the Arbat* (*Deti Arbata*) (Moscow, Druzhba Narodov, 1987).

27. *The Independent* (Wednesday, 28 December 1988). There are signs that

these memorials, due to be set up under the direction of the 'Memorial Society' are going to be much less ambitious than had been envisaged by some 'Memorial' supporters, such as Yevgeny Yevtushenko.
28. S. Carter, *The Politics of Solzhenitsyn* (London, Macmillan, 1977).
29. S. Carter, 'The political thought of F. M. Dostoevksy' (PhD thesis, London University, 1987).
30. See notes 16 and 17 above.

1 Origins

The Russian poet, Tyutchev, once wrote that one cannot try to measure what is meant by 'Russia', nor understand her only with the mind; one can know Russia by faith alone, and this faith, he implied, will itself assure the brilliant future of that great country.[1] Leskov also predicted that the iron will of Germany, the sharp axe of German aggression, would ultimately be absorbed and lost in the vastness of Russia.[2] Both writers are typical of the consciousness of the nineteenth century, of that period which saw the rise of Russian romantic nationalism, Slavophilism and Panslavism which form the main focuses of this chapter.

However, the national and religious symbols of Russia, many of its folksongs, literature and 'ethnomythology' predate the nineteenth century. Traces of national sentiment may be found as early as *Kievan Rus'* (Kievan *Russia*), and the feeling of homeland, for the people's unity in place, in faith and in language were definitely important from approximately the eleventh century. In the twelfth century, the *Tale of the Host of Igor* was penetrated by a profound national feeling. Despite the Mongol invasions of 1237, and the capture of Kiev and Vladimir after 1240, the divided Russian populations of Galicia and the Suzdal, Moscow and Novgorod regions were united by culture and faith. From the Middle Ages, a political and religious Pan-Russianism was a reality.

The year 1380 brought to the Russians their first great victory over the Tartars at the battle of Kulikovo Field, which formed a further important advance in the growth of the Russian national character. In 1480, Grand Prince Ivan III of Moscow finally abolished the payment of tribute to the Horde. After a further 70 years, the Tartar kingdoms of Kazan and Astrakhan were incorporated into the Russian state, and opened the road to Asia.[3] The building of the cathedral of St Basil the Blessed in 1555, which is illustrated on the front cover of this book, shows that characteristic mixture of Oriental and Russian styles which helped to form the complex Russian culture.

One cannot overestimate the influence of the Russian Orthodox Church in the formation of Russian national consciousness. This church, with its vigorous Greek-style Slavonic script, still in use today, was inherited from Byzantium and the Eastern Empire. It was respected and tolerated by the Mongols and frequently served as a rallying point and focus of loyalty for Russians in distress and times of trouble. When the Council of Florence in 1439 announced the acceptance by the Greeks of papal supremacy over Byzantium, the Greek Isodore was made Metropolitan of Moscow. He attempted to celebrate the Divine Liturgy as the emissary of the Pope. He was arrested after three days and allowed to escape to Poland, while the Muscovites appointed their own Metropolitan. In 1453 Byzantium fell to the Muslims and the Russians interpreted this historical collapse as punishment for the heresy, even apostasy, of the Greeks. The marriage in 1472 between Ivan III and Sophia Paleologue, niece of the last Byzantine emperor, gave Moscow a legitimate right to the Byzantine heritage. Ivan III adopted the double-headed eagle of Byzantium as his symbol, the symbol of Great Russia. It was to become at once a sign of state power and of ecclesiastical supremacy.

As the Russian monk Philopheus summarised in a message to Ivan's successor, Vasilly III,

The Church of the Old Rome fell because of the infidelity of the Apollinarian heresy. The Second Rome, the Church of Constantinople, was hewn down by the axes of the sons of Hagar. And now this Third Rome of thy mighty kingdom, the holy catholic and apostolic church, will illumine the whole universe like the sun. . . . Know and accept, O pious Tsar, that all the Christian kingdoms have come together into thine own, that two Romes have fallen, and that a third stands, while a fourth there shall not be; thy Christian kingdom will fall to no other.[4]

He went on to say that the Russian people were a new Israel, a people chosen by God, the first among all Christian peoples, and called to fulfil the Kingdom of Christ on earth.

In 1610, during the 'Time of Troubles', Prince Vladislav, the heir to the Polish Crown, was elected Tsar of Russia. Latinisation seemed imminent. But a popular movement, sponsored and inspired by Patriarch Hermogen and the Trinity Monastery, and led by Kuzma Minin and Dmitry Pozharsky, resulted in the establishment of the Romanov dynasty in 1613, which set itself the task of returning the whole nation to the ideal of 'Holy Russia'.

The schism of the Russian Church in 1653, caused by the attempt of Patriarch Nikon to 'rectify' Slavonic texts which were at variance with the original Greek, resulted in the formation of fanatically nationalist 'Old Believers' sects, who were persecuted by the official Orthodox Church. The Old Believers resented the apparent theological superiority of the Greek Church, and they stood for the particularism and purity of the Russian faith. Even today, extreme

Russian nationalism has a flavour of the ascetic and puritanical Old Belief.

At the beginning of the eighteenth century, Peter the Great looked towards the heterodox Western world for new technology and its implied cultural superiority. Many Old Believers saw Peter as an Antichrist! The cosmopolitanism of eighteenth-century Russian high society deepened its rift with the masses of the Orthodox peasantry, causing educated Russians much anguish about the identity of their nation and their role in its society. The historian Karamzin lamented, 'We became citizens of the world, but ceased to be Russians.'[5] However, the Great Patriotic War of 1812 and the Napoleonic invasion were to cause a reaction against French culture and Western Europe, while at the same time arousing a profound desire for a modern nationhood.

Following the ignominious retreat of the Grande Armée in 1813, the battle-hardened officers and men of the Russian armies were amazed by what they saw in Western Europe. Its relative freedom and prosperity struck them forcibly at a time when the 'Motherland' was still enslaved and backward. However, on their return to Russia, they could see no hope or sign of reform. Tsar Alexander I withdrew into a kind of mysticism and political indifference while his affairs were in the hands of such men as the militarist Count Arakcheyev, the originator of penal military colonies, camps of rigid discipline which may have been early versions of the Stalinist 'Gulag Archipelago'. In imitation of the German patriotic societies, many Russians formed secret societies such as the Union of Welfare from which, ultimately the Decembrist movement arose.[6] There can be little doubt that the inspiration for the formation of the societies and the romantic nationalism of the Slavophiles of the subsequent generation were originally from Germany. However, many Decembrists were also Freemasons and their organisations were broadly Masonic in structure. While all the Decembrists were patriotic, only a section of them were nationalist; some were drawn to the liberal constitutionalism of the West,[7] while others evolved a kind of extremist Jacobin republicanism.[8] Their insurrection against the autocracy, which in the case of the Northern Society occurred on 14 December 1825, was hardly co-ordinated.

The newly-crowned Tsar, Nicholas I, was badly shaken by this military conspiracy of so many élite officers. He instituted harsh penalties against the conspirators, and established a secret police force, the Third Section, in 1826. For the duration of the reign of Nicholas (1825–55), Russia was subject to a regime of restrictions, conservatism and censorship. Nevertheless, its intellectual, artistic and literary life was to prove exciting and brilliant, apart from the seven years after 1848, when the revolutions of Western Europe drove Nicholas to his last spasm of internal repression.

There was a particularly spectacular flowering of intellectual life in Russia during the decade 1838–48, a period which has been called 'the marvellous decade'. It was preceded by the life and work of Alexander Sergeyevich Pushkin (1799–1837), whose literary genius helped to inspire and facilitate the 'golden age' of Russian literature and the modern Russian language. Pushkin and his successors enabled Russians to become aware of themselves and their society in a way which could not be controlled by the Third Section and the censorship, despite their attempts to do so. Direct political and social commentary was forbidden, but philosophy, literature and criticism enabled the debate about Russia and its place in the world to continue, albeit in a kind of Aesopian manner. Pushkin, Lermontov and the men of the 'marvellous decade' enlightened the mind, heart and spirit of Russia during the gloom and darkness of serfdom and the repression of Nicholas I.

Two events in particular stimulated the controversy which gave rise to the first systematic formulation of Russian nationalism which is called 'Slavophilism'. These events were the publication of 'The First Philosophical Letter' by P. Ya. Chaadayev (1794–1856) in the journal *Telescope* in 1836, and the appearance of the Marquis de Custine's book *La Russie en 1839*. The Marquis de Custine painted an extremely critical picture of the Russian Empire and concluded finally, 'This Empire, vast as it is, is no more than a prison, of which the Emperor holds the key.' Of course, de Custine and other critical observers such as von Haxthausen were foreigners. Chaadayev, however, was Russian, an élite officer, scholar and an aristocrat. His comments exploded into the consciousness of Russian society. As Marc Slonim summarises:

In his letter, Chaadayev said that Russia's past was unbearable, and she had no future. . . . Russia had always lacked the historical, religious, and cultural unity of the West, which was largely based on Roman Law, Christian ethics and the Catholic Church. Belonging to none of the great families of mankind, she was neither of the West nor of the East. . . . From sheer barbarism she had passed to crass ignorance, and then had fallen under the yoke of a brutal foreign invader, who left his impress on all aspects of the Muscovite State. . . . Even Peter the Great had been unable to change this tragic situation: while forcing his subjects to don European garments and manners, he could not destroy the 'dead wall' between Russia and the West. The only salvation for Russia lay in absorbing Western civilisation and setting foot on the high road of the Roman Catholic world.[9]

The head of the Third Section, Count Benckendorff, responded by declaring that Russia's past was glorious, her present magnificent and her future surpassing all expectations! The Education Minister

Count Uvarov formulated the ideology of Russian conservatives in the doctrine of Autocracy, Orthodoxy and Nationality.[10] It is this 'trinity' of Count Uvarov which most profoundly influenced official Russian nationalism of the nineteenth and early twentieth centuries and which is still to be found in the dissident nationalists of today. It postulates that political autocracy is the best form of government for Russia and it suggests that any thought of political development or reform is potentially subversive or destabilising. Thus it also rejects any ideas about the 'separation of powers' or Western constitutionalism, parliamentarianism or the formation of political parties. Proponents of liberal or socialist ideas were therefore seen by Russian conservatives as potentially subversive, un-Russian, unpatriotic. Uvarov's trinity also suggests that the good citizen of the Russian Empire should be Orthodox by religion, so that Protestants or Catholics, sectarians, Jews or members of other religions such as Islam, might be potentially suspect or at least in dangerous error. In later years, and at times of crisis for the tsarist regime, the policy of Russification entailed pressure for conversion, although outright legal restrictions were not always applied. Finally, the non-Russian nationalities of the Empire found themselves potentially second-class citizens because they were not of the right nationality (*narod*). This lowly status applied particularly to Jews, who were restricted to the Pale of Settlement and who were subject to other forms of discrimination, including limited entry to higher education.

Under the influence of Uvarov's formulation, the Russian Empire was to become a kind of 'prison' of nationalities, and it tended endemically towards anti-Semitism, factors which radicalised many able men and women towards the revolutionary Left during the reigns of the last two tsars and gave rise to the belief that the Bolsheviks of 1917 were largely Jews and foreigners.

A more liberal, initially dissident nationalism arose in reaction to Chaadayev, which has been termed 'Slavophilism'. Slavophilism was dissident from the point of view of the government because it claimed that the Tsar's authority had been bequeathed to him from the people. According to the Slavophiles, politics was sinful and un-Russian, but the Tsar had taken it upon himself to rule in the name of the people, to bear the sin of political activity in the interests of Russia. The Tsar should always consult the opinion of the people through the *Zemsky Sobor* ('Land Council'), but he would not be bound by any of the detailed deliberations or legislation of this representative body. The Slavophiles were monarchists and were typically passive in the sphere of practical politics, although active in local affairs. However, even these loyal Russians were at first rejected by the conservatives of the autocracy, who regarded the Tsar's authority as God-given. From their point of view, the Tsar should not take into account any kind of *Zemsky Sobor*, but should be answerable only to God and his own conscience in matters of state.

The Slavophiles included Ivan Kireevksy (1806–56), who was the author of an important article in the journal *Moskvitianin* (*The Muscovite*) in 1845, Alexei Khomiakov (1804–60), an admirer of British Toryism and an original Orthodox thinker, who stressed the 'communality' (*sobornost*) of the Russian people, Konstantin Aksakov (1817–60) and his younger brother Ivan (1823–86). They criticised Chaadayev for denigrating everything Russian and for indicating that only the path of 'Westernisation' could save Russia. They maintained that the nation could proceed along a different path of development, that it had 'its own way of being' (*samobytnost*) which was different from the West, but no less valid.

The Slavophiles were, for the most part, Moscow gentry who stood in opposition to the world of St Petersburg and had their roots deep in the patriarchal soil of peasant Russia. They believed that the system of 'Petersburg Russia' after the reign of Peter I had adopted a style of autocracy that was alien to Russian traditions and they believed that pre-Petrine Russia was the ideal towards which political and social reform should be directed. In this sense, the Slavophiles rejected the Petrine reforms and their ideas may be termed a 'conservative utopia', a concept adopted as a subtitle for the famous book by Walicki about the Slavophile controversy.[11]

In defence of the Slavophiles, it should be remembered that the Russian Empire then still possessed the Julian, as opposed to the Gregorian calendar of the West. Russia used an idiosyncratic system of weights and measures,[12] and was governed by a political system which was self-consciously anti-Western. The intelligentsia were aware of the existence of a disadvantaged proletariat in Western Europe, and deplored its poverty, seeking ways to avoid such a development in Russia. They considered that the traditional Russian peasant commune (*Obshchina*) was a superior form of social organisation to anything found in the West. They thought the West too 'rational', 'mechanistic', too atomised and individualistic, and they considered Orthodox culture and civilisation superior. From the point of view of Slavophiles, the Russian state seemed stable and peaceful internally, while the West was evidently in turmoil and apparently unstable. The year 1848 saw revolutions throughout Western Europe, while in the next generation the struggles for the unification of Italy, the Franco-Prussian War and the formation of Germany coincided with disturbing events in the life of the mind.

In this generation, modern materialism permeated Russia through the works of Feuerbach, Buchner and Marx. Already French utopian socialism (St Simon, Fourier, Cabet) had reached Russia, followed by social Darwinism and a radical questioning of Christian doctrine

(Strauss, Renan). As Sir Isaiah Berlin has pointed out, the Russian mind absorbed these Western ideas with a peculiar fanaticism and reinterpreted many of them so that they underwent a kind of transmutation.[13]

At times, the Slavophiles regarded the West not merely as different in its development, but also as decadent, a series of countries which had passed their peak and were now declining from their positions as 'historical nations', while Russia was a force for the future. This idea was to become a Messianic vision, whose ancestry can be traced back as far as the sixteenth century, to the ideas of Philopheus relating to Moscow as the Third Rome, which have been outlined above. While regarding the West as decadent, the first Slavophile generation were not generally aggressive, since they were socially secure people, who preferred the idea of *samobytnost*, 'one's own way of being', as a kind of moral example to other nations. It was the next generation of neo-Slavophiles, which included such thinkers as Danilevsky and Dostoevsky, who tended towards a kind of expansionist messianism or even military action such as the expansion of the Russian Empire into Central Asia and the seizure of Constantinople. Such aggressive expansionism had overtones of racial superiority and it is a doctrine with more disturbing implications than those of its parent Slavophilism. It is termed Panslavism.

The word 'Panslavism' was first used in 1826 by a Slovak writer, Jan Herkel, in a Latin treatise on Slav philology. At first the Panslavism of Fratisek Palacky and associated thinkers like Kollar and Shafarik was a fairly moderate liberation movement in respect of the rights of Czechs and other Slavs within the Austro-Hungarian Empire. In 1848, Panslavs held a congress in Prague, which achieved little in practical terms but gave the Western Slavs a feeling of self-confidence and cultural identity. However, geographical, religious and national aspirations proved much more difficult to integrate, especially in respect of Catholic Poland.

These divisions facing the Western Slavs did not prevent Russian thinkers from appropriating Panslavism for their own political goals. Among these, Mikhail Petrovich Pogodin (1800–75) was perhaps the most vociferous. At the end of 1838 he composed a 'Letter on Russian History', addressed to Count Stroganov. It was published only in 1867. Pogodin was perhaps influenced by Chaadayev's 'Philosophical Letter', for the tone of Pogodin's comments is diametrically opposed to the anti-nationalism of Chaadayev.[14] The following extract is typical of Pogodin's breathless, exalted narrative:

Russia – what a wonderful phenomenon on the world stage . . . . Which country can compare with its magnitude? Which merely compares with half its magnitude? . . . A population of 60 million people, aside from those who have not been counted, a population that increases by one million every year, and will soon amount to 100 million! . . . Let us add to this multitude 30 million more of our brothers and cousins, the Slavs, who are scattered over the whole of Europe . . .. There we may subtract this number from the population of neighbouring Austria and Turkey and from the rest of Europe, and add it to our numbers. What will be left to them, what will be ours? I cannot think any longer, I am overwhelmed by this vision . . ..[15]

In 1867 a Panslav congress was held in Moscow, with Pogodin and Ivan Aksakov presiding from the Russian delegation. Eighty-four non-Russian Slavs attended, although significantly Poland was not represented. The delegates were received politely, but coldly, by the Emperor, and later by the future Minister of Education, Count D. A. Tolstoy. Tyutchev wrote a poem entitled 'To the Slavs', in which he said that the assembled company was not so much a company of guests, but brother Slavs who were, in effect, at home in Moscow.[16]

The mood of the delegates was buoyant. They proposed to meet every two years and, surprisingly, to found a Panslav University in Warsaw. The Austrian Serb, Mihajle Polit proposed a unification of Western Slavs under Russian protection: 'The creative task of Russia lies not only in Asia, but on what may be called the threshold of her house – the European East . . .. Russia is no longer Russia; it is Slavonia, nay Pan-Slavonia.'[17]

Some of the congress delegates may have felt a little uneasy about the tendency of the Russians to demand that Russian should become the language of all Slavs. To the Russians, Panslavism almost inevitably meant Russification and Orthodoxification. As Louis L. Snyder summarises, 'Cultural Panslavism disappeared in the solvent of Russian nationalism.'[18] Thus, the moderate Panslavism of the Western Slavs of the first half of the century was appropriated by Russian Imperialism in the second half. It was to become a powerful force within Russian society by the late 1870s and may even have been a factor in impelling the Imperial government into war with Turkey in 1877–8. In general, though, 'official' Russia was suspicious of Panslavism. For example, Count Stroganov, in reaction to Pogodin's memorandum, had written, 'Many words, only one new thought (Panslavism) and that too is false.'[19]

Panslavism, then, was a renewal nationalism in Smith's sense of the word, and was supported more strongly outside official circles than within them. It gained a strength in the late nineteenth century, both as a reaction to the growing Pan-Germanism of the period, and as a result of the work of two thinkers in particular, Danilevsky and Dostoevsky.

N. Ya. Danilevsky (1825–85) was a natural scientist by training and had none of the religious interests of the older generation of

Slavophiles. His book, published in 1869, was entitled *Russia and Europe: an inquiry into the cultural and political relations of the Slav to the Germano-Latin world*. Danilevsky asserted that Russia did not belong to Europe naturally, and should not attempt to be accepted as 'European'. Europe had allied herself with Turkey against Russia in 1854, but the European powers had made no move against Prussia when the latter seized Schleswig and Holstein in 1864. Thus the Western powers were conspiring to confine Russia to Asia, being unconcerned which European power came to the fore in the West, as long as it was not Russia. Europe would allow Russia to expand only towards the East, towards Turkestan. European power and civilisation, said Danilevsky, was declining. Like Spengler, Danilevsky believed that the parliamentary regimes of the West, devoid of moral and national ideals, were decaying. Europe had reached the peak of its civilisation in the sixteenth and seventeenth centuries, but was now almost senile, whereas Russia was a young nation with its future on the horizon. The West was the heir of heretical Rome, while the Slavs were the heirs of Byzantium and Greece. Greek philosophy, said Danilevsky, found its highest expression in Orthodoxy, and Greek art found its apotheosis in the Divine Liturgy. Russia was an historical nation, destined to rule over others who would become 'ethnographic material' for Russia. However, to fulfil her destiny, Russia alone was not sufficiently strong. What was required was a Panslav Union under Russian leadership. 'The Panslav Union is the only firm foundation on which can grow an original Slav civilisation. It is the indispensable condition of this cultural development.'[20] The Panslav Union proposed by Danilevsky was to have included the Russian Empire as of 1869 (i.e. including Poland), most of what is now Eastern Europe, Constantinople and Greece. It remains a little unclear why Danilevsky included Hungary and the Magyars in this proposed union.[21]

In order to counteract fears of oppression by Russia, Danilevsky proposed a kind of federation which had Leninist features. Unity between the nations of the Panslav federation could be cemented only by war between the Panslav federation and the West. Danilevsky sounds very like a Marxist when he claims the inevitability of victory over the West.

It is as impossible to fight the historical course of events as it is impossible to fight superior violence. From these general considerations we gain the certitude that the Russian and Slav sacred cause, which is in truth the universal and Panhuman cause, cannot be lost.[22]

Danilevsky surveyed European developments, and concluded that Russia's interests were compatible with those of Prussia, and that

Prussia would need Russia more than vice versa. It is perhaps coincidental that Stalin annexed territory after 1945 which broadly corresponded to Danilevsky's recommendations, excluding Greece and Constantinople, but including Königsberg.

Russian autocracy, said Danilevsky, was superior as a form of government to Western parliamentarianism. The Russian Empire had great cultural and economic potential, and contrary to the Western powers, Russia did not create overseas colonies, but merely advanced and absorbed nations within a territorially unified state. Danilevsky argued that a great people is one which has total self-confidence in its own historical mission, its own religion. The Hebrews had created monotheistic religion, the Greeks had given the world philosophy and art, Rome had bequeathed the idea of the state. Western Europe had made a breakthrough in the field of political economy and economic prosperity. Only the new Russia and Panslav civilisation could now combine all four features in a new synthesis.

F. M. Dostoevsky (1821–81) followed the ideas of Danilevsky with great attention. In March 1869 he wrote to his niece, S. A. Ivanova:

This Danilevsky is an entirely unusual personality. Formerly he was a socialist, an adherent of Fourier, even 20 years ago when he was implicated in our affair, he impressed me as most remarkable; he returned from exile as a true Russian and a nationalist.[23]

Let us follow the evolution of Dostoevsky's ideas in respect of Russian nationalism, since they illustrate very well the duality of this nationalism, the peaceful, moralistic aspirations, as well as the often violent, militaristic implications. Dostoevsky had already shown signs of his incipient anti-Westernism in his *Winter Notes on Summer Impressions* (1862), and under the influence of Apollon Grigor'ev, he began to interpret Russian literature in a prophetic and Messianic fashion. He was incensed by the radicalism and rationalistic utilitarianism of Chernyshevsky, whose novel, *What is to be done?* emerged in 1863. According to Dostoevsky, man is not a rational, socialist being whose future could be envisaged in a utopia. From 1864 Dostoevsky increasingly associated all rational and socialist ideas with Westernism. The answer for the Russian people, he said, lay in the unification of the classes of Russia under the autocracy, a merging of the upper classes and intelligentsia with the peasantry, and a return to the soil (*pochva*). Dostoevsky's followers called themselves *pochvenniki*, and they had many points in common with the Slavophiles, although the *pochvenniki* welcomed the autocracy in its present form and thus the Petrine reforms were endorsed by them.

In 1864–5, Dostoevsky edited a journal under the title *Epokha*, which gradually began to resemble the Slavophile journal edited by Aksakov which was called *Den (The Day)*. As V. S. Nechaeva has pointed out, *Epokha* was troubled by delays and misprints until it finally went under due to the general loss of readership for these 'thick' journals following the collapse of the reform period in the mid-1860s.[24]

Dostoevsky's poverty, ill health and personal misfortunes coincided with a burst of creative activity which included *Crime and Punishment* (1865), *The Gambler* (1866) and *The Idiot* (1867). While he was abroad with his new wife, Anna Grigor'evna, after 1867, Dostoevsky came under the influence of Danilevsky. In *The Gambler* Dostoevsky had contrasted the life-giving force of the Russian protagonists with the arrogant Germans, venal Frenchmen and women and a childishly innocent Englishman. In *The Idiot*, Russian society, already heavily Westernised, was to have been saved by a Russian Christ-figure, Prince Myshkin. However, Myshkin's vocation proved to be a failure. At the end of the 1860s, Dostoevsky was looking for a new direction, a new idea. The publication of Danilevsky's book provided a new synthesis for him.

Dostoevsky believed that the 'world-historical' role of Russia was to bring the Russian Christ, the 'light from the East', to the world, and he expresses these ideas through the mediation of Shatov in his next novel, *The Devils* (1870–2). This novel also contains a vicious lampoon of Western liberals such as Turgenev (Karmazinov) and Granovsky (Stepan Verkhovensky), as well as a warning about the younger generation of terrorists such as Nechaev (Peter Verkhovensky). However, Shatov himself is a victim in this novel, since he is murdered by Peter Verkhovensky and others who are 'possessed' by political fanaticism and Western ideas. Shatov's very name shows him to be uncertain, since it derives from the Russian verb *shatat'sya*, which means to wobble, to vacillate. He does not quite believe in God, as he reveals in his conversation with Stavrogin.[25] This is an important problem for Russian nationalists both yesterday and today: do they believe in Orthodoxy and the Christian religion, or do they instead emphasise Russian Orthodoxy as a crucial cultural influence and emanation of the Russian people? In Dostoevsky's case, it seems that he was not wholly and completely a Christian, but always remained an agnostic.[26] However, he certainly believed in the cultural and racial superiority of Russians over all Western and Asiatic races, Poles and Jews. Thus, in his very last contributions to his journalistic *Diary of a Writer*, he praised the feats of General Skobelev and Russian arms at Geok-Tepe in Central Asia, and predicted a racially superior victory for Russian armies in India.[27] This conclusion appears to contradict his call for peace and brotherhood of nations, which he proclaimed at the Pushkin Memorial Speech in 1880.[28]

Dostoevsky's creative writing is still a source of inspiration for the Russian nationalists of today and it is interesting that many adulatory articles appeared in the Soviet press on the centenary of his death, 1981. Literature is an important medium of expression for Russian nationalists, including Valentin Rasputin, who acknowledges Dostoevsky as an important influence. Russian nationalism as literature is often more impressive, influential and evocative that the nationalism of direct social and political comment.

Less impressive are the works of M. N. Katkov (1818–87), the publisher of Dostoevsky, whose political evolution resembled that of the writer, although Katkov cherished some sympathies for an idealised version of the English gentry, which Dostoevsky would certainly not have shared. Katkov's journal *Russky Vestnik (The Russian Herald)* became a vehicle for the anti-nihilist movement. The nihilists were an eclectic group of thinkers whose works coincided with the period of the Great Reforms in the early 1860s. They rejected contemporary Russian society and the autocracy, and were proponents of materialism and atheism, being portrayed in literature by Turgenev's character Bazarov in *Fathers and Children*. The most famous nihilist was Chernyshevsky, a man who had advocated women's liberation, socialist communes and revolution in his novel *What is to be done?*. 'Nihilism' was a very loose term employed by its opponents, and was used to describe the ideas of such diverse figures as Chernyshevsky, Dobrolyubov and Pisarev. These thinkers were predecessors of the populists (*narodniki*) of the 1870s, and formed an important influence in the Russian revolutionary tradition. For this reason, the conservative nationalists, who were their principal ideological opponents, gained a respectability which might not have accrued to them in other circumstances. 'Anti-nihilism' was also an important spur to the political activities of the conservative nationalists.

Katkov had acquired prominence in 1863 as a result of his comments against the Polish uprising, and in 1866 the attempt on the Tsar's life by the nihilist student Karakozov impelled Katkov to a determined opposition against the intelligentsia in general. He published a Russifying credo in 1867, making an exception with respect to Poland, however. Later, Katkov turned his attention to the subject of the education of Russia's younger generation.

He proposed a strictly classical curriculum in the gymnasia and an end to university autonomy. Surprisingly, he also attacked the bureaucracy for its lack of direction and purpose and even the official diplomacy surrounding the Russo-Turkish War of 1877–8. This reveals, I believe, a certain awareness of the weakness of the system, and his attack on the bureaucracy was at least consistent with this line. However, his wholehearted support for the autocracy, his belief in the possibility of reverting to aristocratic rule in the Russian countryside on the model of the English squirearchy, were surely reactionary and unrealistic.

Another very important conservative thinker of this period was K. P. Pobedonostsev (1827–1907), who was tutor to the last two tsars. As T. G. Masaryk says: 'whoever wishes to know what was going on in Russia under Alexander III and Nicholas II must study . . . the characteristics of Pobedonostsev.'[29] Pobedonostsev published many of his articles in 1896 under the title *Moscow Collection* and this reveals his orientation towards Moscow, which he regarded as the centre of civilisation, the 'Third Rome'. He was undoubtedly influenced by the Slavophiles such as Aksakov and Kireevsky, but he did not believe that the Tsar's power was derived from the Russian people.

Pobedonostsev saw Western Europe as irremediably decadent, and its essential malady was its emphasis on rationalism and its belief in the excellence of human nature. Pobedonostsev taught that man was bad and full of malice, so that any belief in the necessity for representative government was ridiculous and led to demagogy and the corruption which is parliamentarianism. Along with juries, universal suffrage and the press (other than Katkov's), parliaments were seen as 'one of the lying institutions of our time'.

Pobedonostsev, perhaps under Dostoevsky's influence, saw the frequency of suicide as proof of the senseless and unnatural nature of modern life. There are many dangers, he said, in trying to replace the old and tried institutions of social and family life with the egoism and individualism of the modern *raskolniki*.[30]

Pobedonostsev believed in the Orthodox faith, the peasant commune and traditional life. He saw education as dangerous to the simple faith of the masses, even though he acknowledged their superstition and ignorance. He saw the people as a source of wisdom and in their ignorance of the modern world they were showing a healthy lack of any attempt to rationalise. Pobedonostsev, the Procurator of the Holy Synod, also believed in an absolute union of church and state, because the influence of the church could only be spread widely enough by the application of an unmitigated absolutism. This absolutism must itself be preserved at any cost: in 1905, Pobedonostsev argued to Nicholas II that any delegation of power to the Duma or a Constitution would be a betrayal of his divine obligations. It is perhaps for this reason in particular that Nicholas constantly tried after 1906 to 'claw back' powers incipiently promised in the October Manifesto, and to block the development of Russia's 'constitutional experiment' as it has been described by Professor

Geoffrey Hosking.[31] This feature of the last Russian autocrat endeared him to the extreme Russian nationalists of the early twentieth century, the Union of the Russian People, whose activities are described in the next chapter.

The *Moscow Collection* is in fact a very eclectic document, borrowing from Le Playe and de Maistre, while much is also clearly taken from the works of K. N. Leontiev (1831–91). Unlike Pobedonostsev, Leontiev had not been active in public affairs, but retired to a monastery in 1887 after a career which included being an army surgeon, a diplomat in Turkey and a censor in Moscow.

Leontiev accepted, apparently unreservedly, an ecclesiastical Orthodoxy based on Byzantinism, with all its renunciation of the idea of general earthly welfare and the importance of the individual. To Leontiev, love of humanity as such is un-Christian: fear is the proper basis of religion. Autocracy is the logical outcome of this religion of fear, Leontiev believed. He sees Jehovah as the almighty wielder of force. Similarly, mysticism as a true love of God is a science, and negates belief in what he terms mundane science. The peasant who believes implicitly that the world is supported on three whales is no longer a danger to the state, says Leontiev, and popular education would only serve to confuse him. There should be genuine links between the peasant and the educated classes, but these should be based on the principle of inequality and aristocracy. Leontiev was an absolutist who upheld the principle of aristocracy, just as Katkov worshipped (and misinterpreted) the image of the English landowner.

Leontiev idealised the old-fashioned life of the village commune *(obshchina)* and saw aristocracy under the supervision of a caesaropapist autocracy as the salvation of Russia. His philosophy of history was quite simple. He saw the development of mankind and of nations in three phases: childhood, manhood and old age. For Leontiev, Europe had begun to 'decline towards her tomb' in the eighteenth century with the Enlightenment and the spread of rationalism. Quite logically then, Russia must be checked, 'frozen' to prevent her from living and growing old. It is easy to see here an origin of Pobedonostsev's view that Russia should be 'frozen for 50 years'.

Above all, said Leontiev, Russia must not succumb to egalitarian liberalism, which he saw as suppressing natural inequalities and at the same time bearing within itself the seeds of nihilism. Leontiev also regarded the free play of ideas as dangerous and he even eulogised the person who acted as an informer to the police. Interestingly, Leontiev preferred socialism to liberalism, because a socialist order would require a powerful state discipline.

By the beginning of the twentieth century, Russian nationalism had rejected the evolutionary ideas of English conservatism, which were mirrored in the constitutional ideas of the Octobrist party after 1905. They had retreated into a nightmare world of reaction, introspection, fear, suspicion and mental sterility and they had rendered the official doctrine of Orthodoxy, autocracy and nationalism as mechanical, mindless and heartless. Russian nationalism feared political activity and discussion as a Western aberration or even as a kind of subversion. They distrusted modern political institutions and participation, and they suspected Masons and Jews of illicit activity behind the façade of institutions and parties. After the revolution of 1905, when the autocracy was clearly fighting for its life, many Russian nationalists were forced willy-nilly into political activity and organisation of a new kind. Just as the Slavophiles had formulated their ideas in reaction to the challenge of Westernism, the Russian nationalist parties of the Right were formed in reaction to the October Manifesto of 1905, and the Fundamental Laws of the Russian Empire and its attendant Duma of 1906. These groups and parties, in particular the Union of Russian Men (URM) and the Union of the Russian People (URP) had a strong presence in the Imperial Dumas after 1907, and a mass following. Their ideas and activities in the closing years of the Russian Empire form the subject of the next chapter

NOTES

1. Tyutchev wrote in 1860:

    Umom Rossiyu ne ponyat'
    Arshinom obshchim ne izmerit'
    U nei – osobennaya stat'
    V Rossiyu nado tol'ko verit'.

    With the mind, one cannot comprehend Russia,
    One cannot with the usual scale measure her.
    For Russia there's a special way to conceive,
    In Russia, with faith, one must only believe.

2. N. S. Leskov, *Five Tales*, trans. Michael Shotton (London, Angel Books, 1984). The story 'An iron will', pp. 85–185.
3. Royal Institute of International Affairs, *Nationalism* (Oxford, Oxford University Press, 1939), p. 61.
4. M. Agursky, *The Third Rome: National Bolshevism in the USSR* (Boulder, Col., Westview Press, 1987), p. 6.
5. RIIA, *Nationalism*, op. cit., p. 65.
6. The Decembrists were named after their attempt at a military insurrection in St Petersburg on 14 December 1825 (Old Style).
7. The Northern Society of Nikita Muraviev.
8. The Southern Society of Colonel Pavel Pestel.
9. M. Slonim, *The Epic of Russian Literature* (Oxford, Oxford University

Press, 1969), p. 144.
10. It should perhaps be noted that Count S. S. Uvarov submitted this recommendation to Nicholas I in a report on the University of Moscow in December 1832. Education in Russia, he said, should be based on the 'truly Russian and conservative principles of Orthodoxy, Autocracy and Nationality (*Narodnost*) the last anchor of our salvation and the most secure guarantee of the strength and greatness of our fatherland.' Quoted in Hans Kohn, *Panslavism: Its history and ideology* (Indiana, University of Notre Dame Press, 1953), p. 111.
11. A. Walicki, *The Slavophile Controversy* (Oxford, Oxford University Press, 1975).
12. Measures of length included the *arshin* (71cm), the *versta* (1.06km). Measures of area included the *dessyatina* (2.7 acres). Measures of weight included the *pud* (16.38kg).
13. Sir Isaiah Berlin, *Russian Thinkers* (London, Pelican Books, 1979), p. 125.
14. Hans Kohn, *Panslavism*, op. cit., p. 112.
15. Ibid., p. 115.
16. Tyutchev wrote:

> Not in vain did Russia call you to this festival of peace and love. You must know, beloved guests, that you are not guests here, you are at home.

17. Hans Kohn, *Panslavism*, op. cit. p. 141.
18. Louis L. Snyder, *Macro-nationalisms: A history of the Pan-Slav movements* (Westport, Conn., Greenwood Press, 1984), p. 35.
19. Hans Kohn, *Panslavism*, op. cit. p. 119. .
20. Ibid., p. 159.
21. Danilevsky may have believed that Hungary would have wished thereby to avoid becoming 'ethnographic material'.
22. Hans Kohn, *Panslavism*, op. cit. p. 159.
23. F. M. Dostoevsky to S. A. Ivanova, 20 March 1869.
24. V. S. Nechaeva, *Zhurnal M. M. i F. M. Dostoevskikh' Epokha, 1864–65* (Moscow, Izdatel'stvo Nauka, 1975); also A. S. Dolinin (ed.), *F. M. Dostoevsky, Pis'ma*, Vol.1 (Moscow, 1928), p. 353.
25. F. M. Dostoevsky, *The Devils* (London, Penguin Classics, 1953), p. 257.
26. F. M. Dostoevsky to N. D. Fonvizina, 20 February 1854: 'Moreover, if it could be demonstrated to me, that Christ was outside the truth, and really that truth was outside Christ, then I would prefer to remain with Christ rather than with the truth.'
27. F. M. Dostoevsky, *The Diary of a Writer* Geok Tepe, 1881: (London, Peregrine Smith, 1979).
28. Ibid., p. 980.
29. T. G. Masaryk, *The Spirit of Russia*, Vol. 2 (London, George Allen & Unwin, 1968) pp. 197–8.
30. *'Raskol'* means a 'chip' or 'splinter', someone who is cut off from his fellows. A *raskolnik* is a schismatic, with implied connotations of isolation, extreme individualism.
31. G. Hosking, *The Russian Constitutional Experiment: Government and Duma, 1907-1914* (Cambridge, Cambridge University Press, 1973).

2 Russian nationalism 1900–17

According to the theories of the Slavophiles, nationalists and the political right wing, politics was something which only the opposition to the throne engaged in illegally. The Tsar, the court and the government were above such things and therefore Russian conservatives discouraged political organisation. Only a severe crisis of the regime could impel its supporters to organise against the revolutionaries, and when the situation appeared to become more stable, such organisations tended to discontinue effective activity.

At the turn of the century, illegal political parties began to form in Russia.[1] In response to the changing circumstances, a monarchist organisation was formed in St Petersburg in 1900 which was called 'Russkoe Sobranie' (The Russian Assembly). According to Hans Rogger,[2] it had an upper-class membership and its forty founding members included seven generals, twelve senior civil servants and four leading editors and publishers. Its chairman was Prince D. P. Golitsyn, while its deputy chairman was A. A. Suvorin, the editor of the right wing *Novoye Vremya* (*New Time*). Senior clergy were also prominent[3] and later members included P. A. Krushevan, A. I. Dubrovin, V. M. Purishkevich and P. F. Bulastel'. The assembly was founded in order to combat 'the spreading cosmopolitanism of the upper strata of Russian society', by undertaking cultural and educational tasks designed to stimulate national feelings. This society was approved by the authorities in January 1901.

With the expansion of its activities in 1902 it published brochures and a journal, and opened branches in Kharkov (1903), Orenburg, Kazan, Perm, Vilna, Kiev, Warsaw (1904) and Odessa (1905). Many of these branches produced their own journals. The Russian Assembly was popular with the Tsar and its delegations were well received, for example in December 1904, when a 'loyal address' from representatives of the Assembly was delivered.

At first, the Assembly did not have a mass following. However, after the liberal Prince Sviatopolk-Mirsky was appointed Minister of the Interior in August 1904, greater social participation was encouraged and the monarchists began to feel the need of this support. Many conservatives realised the need to develop a movement which would demonstrate that the revolutionaries and reformers did not have the monopoly of virtue and that the Tsar had a myriad of loyal subjects. A demonstration designed to prove this point was mounted by Moscow clergy in January 1905, when they organised a Moscow Society of Religious Banner Carriers. The cataclysmic events of 'Bloody Sunday' (9/22 January 1905) had severely shaken the establishment and at the same time signalled the end of the police-sponsored unions initiated by Zubatov. The social classes which had been represented in the Assembly now sought other ways of influencing the masses and the Tsar.

The editor of *Moskovskie Vedomosti* (*Moscow Lists*), G. A. Gringmut, claimed in February 1905 that victory over Japan and the restoration of law and order would have to precede any reforms. Gringmut formed the Russian Monarchist Party in Moscow in April. At the same time, the revolution was profoundly stirring the masses. A vigilante force, the Voluntary Okhrana, was formed in Moscow, and in response to an inflammatory appeal in *Moskovskie Vedomosti* on 24 February,[4] there arose in the spring and summer of 1905 many vigilante groups with names like The White Flag, People's Union, The League of Struggle against Sedition, Autocracy and Church, For Tsar and Order. These groups were later known as the Black Hundreds and they had a following among the masses which was violent, anti-Semitic and anti-intellectual. These proto-fascist groups were sometimes supplied with resources and weapons (indirectly) by the authorities and engaged in strike-breaking activities and intimidation of the Left as well as pogroms and murder. The police and the Ministry of Justice tended to be passive in the face of these activities.[5] The Black Hundreds gained much notoriety at home and abroad, while causing concern among more moderate nationalists and the general public who feared anarchy and mass violence. There was always a very uneasy relationship between the upper-class monarchists and landowners, on the one hand, and their mass supporters, on the other. Their only real point of agreement on policy was anti-Semitism, since the landowners wished to preserve their property and privileges while the masses favoured radical economic change.

Other organisations which were established in this turbulent and dynamic year of 1905 were The Fatherland Union in St Petersburg (April), The Union of Russian Men (March), and The Union of the Russian People (November). The initial stimulus for the formation of The Fatherland Union was the 'Bulygin' Imperial Rescript of 18 February 1905, which was generally understood as a promise of a future representative assembly. B. V. Stuermer, the future chairman of the Council of Ministers in 1916, suggested that a union should be formed of men with staunchly conservative views. Count A. A.

Bobrinsky became its first chairman. A delegation of The Fatherland Union was received by the Tsar, who always believed that the autocratic principle received strong support from the masses and that only the Jews and the intellectuals were interested in destabilising ideas of political reform. The Fatherland Union presented some detailed plans for a new consultative assembly or 'Zemsky Sobor' (Land Council), to be elected on the basis of social strata. The Union believed that a 'Zemsky Sobor' was compatible with the principle of autocracy and in tune with Russian tradition, whereas a Duma or legislative parliament was not.

Another group which adopted similar Slavophile ideas about a Zemsky Sobor was the Union of Russian Men, founded by Count P. S. Sheremetyev with the assistance of S. P. Sharapov and Prince A. G. Shcherbatov. They advocated a classless union of Tsar and people, but they attacked the bureaucracy, international capital, Count Witte, international Judaism and the Freemasons. They called for a national paper currency which was not tied to the gold standard and a disestablished church. The Orthodox Church would alone retain missionary rights. This programme reflected a desire to appeal to the 'grass roots' of counter-revolution.[6]

The political Right in Russia generally distrusted and disliked any talk of liberalism and parliamentarianism, which they thought would play into the hands of socialist revolution and the Jews. They encouraged the true Russian masses in these tendencies and favoured an undiluted tsarist absolutism. On 15 October *Moskovskie Vedomosti* even called for a military dictatorship. Therefore, the right-wing groups were temporarily nonplussed when the Tsar, at Witte's instigation, issued the famous October Manifesto of 17/30 October, promising an elected Duma.

On 24 November a conference of 300 Monarchist delegates met in Moscow, calling for the formation of fighting detachments to quell the revolution and to undertake strike-breaking activities. In St Petersburg, the group or party which was to prove most important also emerged in November: the Union of the Russian People. Devoted to the restoration of absolutism (*samoderzhavie*), the URP dominated the right wing for many years, despite its subsequent splinter groups and divisions. It was founded by Dr A.I. Dubrovin, a former physician, and V. M. Purishkevich, a former assistant to Interior Minister von Plehve. Dr Dubrovin had received encouragement from the Grand Duke Nikolai Nikolaevich and the Head of the Police Department Political Section, P. I. Rachkovsky, who knew of the many informal groups already forming in Moscow and St Petersburg and realised their counter-revolutionary potential. After some preliminary political meetings, at which the major officers of the new party were apparently in agreement,[7] the URP was launched at a meeting hall provided by the St Petersburg Russian Assembly. Dubrovin became head of the URP Directorate and Purishkevich became one of his deputies. It had many intellectuals among its members, such as B. V. Nikol'sky, a law lecturer, and A. A. Milyukov, son of the famous poet. Adventurers and mercenaries also joined,[8] and one of its leading ideologists was G. V. Butmi, a publisher of the notorious anti-Semitic forgery, *The Protocols of the Elders of Zion.*

Dr Dubrovin supported and armed the Black Hundreds and may have been involved subsequently in the murders of Jewish deputies of the Kadet and Trudovik Parties. Testimonies of witnesses from the URP, given to the Provisional Government, show that Dubrovin was subsidised by the Ministry of the Interior[9] and the URP received subsidies as a registered party under Stolypin. Nevertheless, Stolypin was suspicious of Dubrovin and preferred to deal with Purishkevich after 1908, when the latter formed his own group, 'The Union of the Archangel Mikhail'. Later, in 1911, N. E. Markov II took over the organisation of the URP, while Dubrovin continued with a rival organisation of the same name and the URP newspaper *Russkoye Znamya (Russian Banner)*, which was financed in the end only through a rich benefactress.[10]

The policies of the URP included opposition to the Duma, violent anti-Semitism and a radical economic and agrarian programme, as well as support for Autocracy, Orthodoxy and Nationalism. It is very significant that on 23 December 1905 a delegation to the Tsar presented him with the Union's insignia, which he accepted on behalf of himself and his heir. The Tsar declared, 'Unite, Russian People, I am counting on you.'[11] There is no doubt that the Union had great influence with the Tsar, who received many telegrams from its members, and that he tended to regard the URP as a voice of the otherwise inarticulate Russian people, the 'silent majority'. For this reason, the relative neglect of the URP and nationalist groups by Western scholars seems surprising and may reflect the prevailing Kadet view of history[12] which is still fashionable in the West.

The first congress of right-wing organisations met in St Petersburg in February 1906, when thirty groups were represented, including the URP. They resolved that the October Manifesto should not be regarded as a prelude to a constitution and that the forthcoming Duma should not be accepted as a parliament. They feared that the Duma's new freedoms might be exploited by revolutionary forces, but they did not wholly dismiss the idea of participating in the Duma, since it could eventually be reduced to a consultative Zemsky Sobor. Rogger considers that this conference may have influenced the final draft of the Fundamental Laws of the Russian Empire, which appeared on 23 April and which so disappointed the liberals. The question may also be asked whether the abrupt dismissal of Count Witte was influenced by the virulent attacks of the right wing on Witte as an agent of foreign capital, Jews and Freemasons.

What is the source of the universal anti-Semitism of the Russian Right? One very important source and one which has resurfaced today in the hands of D. Vasil'ev of the Pamyat' Society is *The Protocols of the Elders of Zion*. *The Protocols* were based largely on a fictional work by Hermann Goedsche entitled *Biarritz*, published in Berlin in 1868–70. The novel contains a chapter 'On the Jewish Cemetery in Prague', in which, according to Goedsche, the Sanhedrin meets once every hundred years at the grave of Simeon bar Yehuda and discusses in great detail the Jewish plans for world domination. One of the first to use this fictional passage was Theodor Fritsch, who attributed it to an English gentleman named John Retcliffe, without revealing that this was Goedsche's pen-name.[13] In 1901 the 'Speech of the Chief Rabbi' was reprinted in Germany and the Russian authorities had it translated and widely distributed. Two Russian publishers of this speech were G. V. Butmi (1905) and S. A. Nilus (1911, 1917). W. Laqueur summarises *The Protocols* as

an alleged verbatim record of 24 secret sessions of the heads of the world Jewish conspiracy. . . . Their declared aim is the overthrow of all existing states and the building of a Jewish world empire, with an Emperor from the seed of David. Various secret organisations are required for this purpose, such as Masonic Lodges, but their main tools are democracy, liberalism and socialism.[14]

Laqueur goes on to say that according to *The Protocols*, all revolutions are the work of the conspirators; strikes and political assassinations are their speciality and they induce workers to become alcoholics, while they consciously create chaotic conditions by increasing food prices and spreading infectious disease. The Jews already have a powerful international organisation which is an embryonic world government, but since they do not as yet possess sufficient power, they incite peoples against each other with the aim of provoking world war. While *The Protocols* prescribe support for revolutionary movements and class struggle in their tactical theory, the 'Elders' are far from being democratic in their own house. They demand blind obedience to authority and only a small section of the population will receive education in the future Jewish world order. It is the honourable duty of citizens to spy on one another and to inform the police of any subversion. The Elders of Zion will also eventually put down their co-conspirators such as the Freemasons, others being expelled to penal colonies overseas. A network of underground railways will enable the conspirators to blow up capital cities, government buildings and so on, if the plot is discovered in advance.[15] This extraordinary document, which bears some resemblance to the tactics and aims described in Dostoevsky's novel *The Devils*, literally has to be read to be believed.

This strange world outlook influenced certain nationalist groups, some members of the court and the Tsar himself. For example, the electoral programme of the Russian Assembly of 1905 contains the following articles:

Article 8: National questions in Russia must be resolved consistently with the degree of readiness of the individual nation to serve Russia and the Russian people in the carrying out of the tasks of the state as a whole. All attempts at the division of Russia under any guise whatsoever is inadmissable.

Article 9: The Jewish question must be resolved by laws and measures which are separate from the other national questions, in view of the continuing elemental hostility of Judaism towards Christianity and non-Jewish nationalities, *and the aspiration of the Jews towards world domination.*[16] (My emphasis)

The extent to which the Tsar himself believed the main outlines of *The Protocols* remains a matter for conjecture, but he certainly favoured the Union of the Russian People and in 1907 he sent them a telegram which stated, 'Let the Union of the Russian People be my support, serving in the eyes of all and in everything as an example of legality and order.'[17] According to S. W. Baron, the Tsar actually subscribed to the printing and distribution of *The Protocols*.[18] It is no exaggeration to say that in certain circles a kind of pathological Judeophobia was present in the last years of Nicholas II. An example of this is the famous Beilis case of 1913, in which a Jewish factory employee, Mendel Beilis, was charged with the murder of a Christian boy in 1911 by ritual means. As Rogger summarises,

Although it was established quite early in the criminal investigation that the supposed victim . . . had been killed by a gang of thieves, the judicial and police authorities of a great empire, headed by the Minister of Justice, I G Shcheglovitov, persisted for two years in trying to prove Jewish fanaticism and depravity in a court of law.[19]

In view of the above, it is surprising that Western scholars have generally concentrated on the radical Left and the crisis of the moderates in Russia,[20] rather than the influence of anti-Semitism and nationalism which, apart from the work of Robert Edelman, has been relatively neglected.[21] Nor should the lunatic world of *The Protocols* be dismissed without careful thought. After the Bolshevik seizure of power in October 1917, many White officers and men were to seize upon the 'explanation' proffered by *The Protocols* and to continue believing this explanation in the many places of White emigration.

However, it is extremely difficult to assess the precise influence of anti-Semitism, nationalism and Panslavism on the policy of Nicholas II and his government. In the field of foreign policy, perhaps the most perceptive analysis in recent years has been that of D. C. B. Lieven[22] in his account of the forces and personalities which were operational in St Petersburg during the period immediately prior to the First World War. Lieven summarises the influential voices as being representatives of an old ruling class which was very aware of its ancestors' achievements and a military ethos. He adds:

To the limited extent that public forces had begun to make an impact on state policy their influence was . . . not in general for moderation or restraint. The dominant parties in the third and fourth Dumas shared the ethos of the ruling class, to which most of their members belonged. In addition, they sometimes tried to make a nationalist or pro-Slav policy a major weapon in their party's political arsenal.[23]

Lieven attributes the policies of the Russian Empire in the years leading to the First World War, to many influences within an authoritarian political system, including· the Duma parties of the Right. He argues that if the Duma, after 1907, had been predominantly Kadet (Constitutional Democratic Party), or further to the Left, nationalist and pro-Slav policies would have been less easy to follow.[24] For this reason, it is appropriate to investigate the structure of the parties to the Right of the Kadets and their response to the actions of government.

As a result of the Stolypin *coup d'état* of 3 June 1907, there were 148 Octobrists in the Third Duma elected in November. Their leader was A. I. Guchkov, a man of great energy and political stature, but whose individualism was not always congenial to his party. Moreover, the Octobrists, or more precisely, the Union of 17 October, was never a really coherent grouping. Its members were usually connected with the liberal traditions of the gentry and their zemstvo background inclined them towards constitutionalism. However, their economic interests were really those of the landowner and thus their relative political liberalism was not clearly matched by their inherent inclination towards the economic status quo within the context of a land-hungry Russia. Because of the restricted franchise of the 3 June system, they neither needed nor possessed a large and coherent organisation in the regions. Their amorphous party was unused to the necessary parliamentary discipline of a modern party. Moreover, their leader Guchkov took a special interest in military and naval affairs, areas of power which the Tsar considered particularly his own. By underlining Duma aspirations to control military budgets, Guchkov alienated Nicholas II and insult was added to injury when Guchkov criticised the competence of the Grand Dukes and the naval staff.

The Union of 17 October believed that the Tsar should honour the detail of his pledges given in the October Manifesto of 1905. They were loyal monarchists and their nationalism had a distinctly Panslav dimension, so that in some respects they were more nationalist than the pragmatic nationalists to their Right. Stolypin at first sought a working relationship with the Octobrists, who were often referred to in the press, misleadingly, as the 'government party'. In so far as the Octobrists recognised the reality of the Tsar's autocratic power, but supported the Duma, theirs was apparently a realistic renewal nationalism. However, the lack of real 'grass roots' organisation, which sometimes led to embarrassing election results, tended to mean that Octobrism became what its leaders said at any particular time. The party was also undermined by the vacillating attitude of the government towards the Duma in general.

In addition to the Octobrists, there were about 150 deputies further to the Right. Seventy of these formed a 'moderate Right', while another twenty-three under the leadership of Prince A. P. Urusov formed a 'national group' a few months later. Both groups distinguished themselves from the URP, which openly opposed the institution of a 'parliamentary' Duma and was often disruptive of its proceedings. The moderate Right was sometimes known as 'the national party', whose leader was P. N. Balashev. It contained many remarkable figures, including V. V. Shulgin, who regarded pogroms and the activities of the Black Hundreds as a precedent for social anarchy and the destruction of civilisation. According to R. Edelman, the historian of the national party, it was a well organised and modern political party, designed to protect local interests rather than having a well-defined ideology. It had good lines of communication between its deputies and its localities, which were largely in the western provinces. Edelman points out that the national party was a party of 'gentry politics', but at the same time it set out to guard its interests (that is, the interests of Russian landlords) against the Polish landlords and the often very numerous local Jewish populations of the towns and cities. The nationalism of the national party was therefore a preservation nationalism, based on hard-headed self-interest in an area of commercial farming. In general, the national party was not interested in Panslavism or military conquest. They were a conservative group, loyal to the Tsar and Russia, anti-Polish and anti-Semitic, yet distinct from the *pravye* ('political Rights') and the URP. According to Rogger, the URP had only about 11.5 per cent of the seats in the Third Duma,[25] but as I have argued, its particular brand of nationalism was unfortunately close to the 'anti-preservation' fantasies of the Tsar and his court.

After 1909, it was with the national party that Stolypin sought a working relationship, and Edelman interprets the determination of Stolypin to get his western zemstvo legislation through the State Council in this light. The establishment of zemstva (organs of local government) in the western provinces, with a weighted representation in favour of Russians, would strengthen the hand of the nationalist party. They would thus support Stolypin in his grand design of achieving a working relationship with the Duma and with Russian society. Stolypin overturned the adverse vote of the Upper House by persuading the Tsar to suspend sittings of both chambers and so alienated the Tsar and certain important right-wing figures as well as Guchkov and the Octobrists. However, as Edelman shows, the result of the zemstvo elections in the western provinces, elections boycotted by the local Polish landlords, did produce the result Stolypin had hoped for and the basis for a renewed period of co-operation with the nationalist party. However, Stolypin's bold attempt to ally himself with the moderate preservation nationalism of the nationalist party was doomed by the bullet of a mysterious assassin at the Kiev Opera House on 1 September 1911. The 'Stolypin reaction', as it is referred to in some Soviet historiography, was in fact a realistic attempt within the fragmented confines of political institutions to overcome the regime crisis of the autocracy. Unfortunately, as Professor Geoffrey Hosking points out, Russia's élites were by this time so divided by mutual suspicions and antagonisms that they had no real chance of surviving the severe stresses and strains which the First World War was about to impose upon them.[26]

It is unfortunate that Edelman's detailed and devoted study did not extend to the URP and the *pravye*. In the Fourth Duma, elected in 1912, there were sixty-four *pravye* and URP, which compare in number with the sixty nationalists and twenty progressive nationalists. It has often been said that the URP and the *pravye* were the fringes of Russian politics, with uninteresting ideologies and a penchant for street violence. It is argued that the URP mass membership declined after 1905-6, while its strength in the Third and Fourth Dumas reflected the very restricted franchise of the 3 June system. Moreover, since a big national representation was no longer dependent on mass membership after 1907, the following of the URP declined dramatically after the days of turmoil from 1905 to 1907 and its influence, it is said, accordingly lessened. It is also true that the leaders of the URP quarrelled and factions formed under Dubrovin, Purishkevich and Markov II. This typically Russian *krugovshchina* ('the curse of factionalism') was thought to have weakened the party.

However, these arguments, which are repeated endlessly by respectable historians whose sources are limited, while they understandably recoil from the grisly doctrines of the URP, are based on the application of Western style criteria to a non-Western political system. The pogroms, inspired by the URP and often passively supported by the police,[27] were important channels for counter-revolutionary violence and provided scapegoats for the masses. Many ministers, such as Nikolai Maklakov and Ivan Shcheglovitov, were members of the URP and may have influenced the Tsar, for example when they advocated the relegation of the Duma to purely consultative status. The URP's chosen technique of sending telegrams to the Tsar directly from his 'loyal subjects' appealed to the mystical beliefs of the Emperor, which discounted representative institutions in the manner of Pobedonostsev and favoured notions of the direct communication between Tsar and 'the people'. The Tsar read the conservative *Novoe Vremya* avidly, but in general he believed that the popular press was irrelevant, as was the Duma, with its clever lawyers and 'Jewish' Kadets. However, as far as I know, there has been no systematic study of the URP in English, nor its messages to the Tsar nor his known responses to them.

The ideological hostility of Nicholas towards the Duma and public opinion may have been strengthened in 1915 by the fact that the largest faction of the national party under Balashev and the URP and *pravye* stayed outside the 'progressive bloc' and resisted demands for a 'government of public confidence'. Despite the detailed and ingenious work of G. Katkov,[28] we have little hard evidence about the formation or otherwise of a 'black bloc', or the role of Durnovo and Balashev in its conception. However, the advice of Goremykin to the Tsar to suspend the Duma in the face of its majority demands may have been influenced by the existence of an anti-Duma faction to the Right of the progressive nationalists. Many historians believe that it was the steady shift of the autocracy towards the extreme Right which was a crucial factor in its eventual downfall. After November 1916, when Purishkevich made his famous speech attacking the 'dark forces' surrounding the Tsar, even the extreme Right became alienated from the throne.

The story of the Russian Right after the revolution is a sad one. Purishkevich escaped to the south and established a People's State Party in Rostov, while Vostokov set up a Brotherhood of the Creating Cross. Black Hundred journals and newspapers appeared, including a brochure entitled *V Moskvu (To Moscow)* which even General Denikin described as a 'pogromist document'. The main organisation of the extreme Right in the south was The Union of Russian National Communities and another Russian Assembly headed by Zamyslovsky and Kommissarov.[29] In the last resort, these groups believed in 'Autocracy, Orthodoxy, Nationality', and the slogan 'Bei Zhidov, Spasai Rossiyu' ('Beat the Jews, Save Russia'). They proved very popular with officers and men of the White armies, who were often totally confused about the collapse of the old order and for whom the 'explanations' offered by *The Protocols* seemed convincing.

This, then, has become an important part of the legacy of the White emigration. Like many Russian political ideologies, the ideology of the Right required a total world outlook, a satisfying explanation of the entire socio-economic scene, which also acquired an absolutist, quasi-religious status. Russians who now look back over their turbulent past and seek, as is only natural, to restore the national memory (Pamyat') after the depredations of Stalinism and the disasters of seventy or more years of Soviet rule, are bound to search with nostalgia among the documents, memoirs and myths of the White cause in Russia and the emigration. There will, therefore, be those who find therein an 'alternative' ideology of a lost age, an age in which the uglier aspects are now forgotten and to which the golden glow of nostalgia may afford respectability.

Purishkevich, anti-German to the last, died in 1920, but Markov II went over to the German right wing, as did many Russian *émigrés*, so that a Russian fascism, allied to the axis powers emerged in the 1930s and 1940s. Their story is a shameful one, but their theories need not concern us here, for they sought to impose a Nazi social order on Russia with the help of a foreign power. Such beliefs and actions cannot be termed 'nationalist' since they are self-negating. However, the influence of Russian *émigrés* on the German Right and the formation of its ideology under Rosenburg and others, might be explored with profit. An odd feature of contemporary Russian extreme nationalism is its acknowledged debt to Adolf Hitler.

Many of the politically less extreme nationalist *émigrés*, who had at first opposed the Bolshevik revolution and had even fought with the White armies, soon began to think again about the nature of the new regime which was consolidating its hold over what was left of the old Russian Empire. Were perpetual emigration and opposition to the Soviet Union the only possible options for those displaced by the revolution? Many *émigrés*, some of whom were as far Left as the Kadet Party, began to consider the merits of Bolshevik power as a means to consolidate the might of the Russian state. This development, which became particularly strong after the adoption of NEP and the policy of 'socialism in one country' in the 1920s, forms the subject of the next chapter.

In 1905 the Tsarist system, informed by an exceptionally inflexible nationalist ideology, faced a severe regime crisis which was contained only by reluctant concessions and the use of force. The nationalism of the Tsar and some of his ministers, inspired by the doctrines of Pobedonostsev and Uvarov, was not even a preservation nationalism. Its ideology was based on shaky foundations and was divorced from reality, while the political system itself was divorced from society. Slavophile, or Octobrist nationalism was a dissident renewal nationalism, while the more solidly empirical claims of the National Party were the basis of a 'preservation' nationalism. After 1907 the best chance of survival and political development by the regime lay in co-operation with Octobrists and nationalists, as Stolypin realised, on the foundations of an agrarian reform and constitutional development. Russian nationalism itself in some form was bound to predominate, since the Left stood for revolution and the Kadets' maximalist demands for a ministry answerable to the Duma were unrealistic. Stolypin was trying to bring about a workable relationship between society and the state and it is Russia's tragedy that he failed.

A third kind of nationalism was that of the aggressive Union of the Russian People, which proclaimed the doctrines of racial purity, Russian dominance, anti-Semitism and anti-intellectual violence. Their variety of fascism could be described in Handman's terms as 'prestige' nationalism. Unfortunately, the Tsar and many of his influential ministers were attracted to the apparently populist nature of the URP, whose influence has been underestimated. As a result of this tendency, the Russian conservatives adopted a line of total inflexibility towards Jews and non-Russian nationalities and perpetual intransigence towards Russia's constitutional experiment. These policies alienated a large proportion of the Russian Empire's population and brought dishonour to the autocracy both internally and internationally. Exposed as incompetent by the severe stress of the First World War, the tsarist system collapsed in the February Revolution of 1917, having lost the confidence of even the extreme Right. The nationalists and the URP were uncertain allies. Despite subsidies from the Ministry of the Interior, these groups were subject to constant splintering and divisions. Even the URP itself had three separate factions by 1911. The social support of these groups was thin, despite their artificially large representation in the Dumas, in which after 1907 1 per cent of the population controlled 300 seats out of 442.[30] The Tsar was not in touch, as he apparently thought, with the voice of a mass of loyal Russians, but with a peripheral fringe which was controlled by a few charismatic leaders.

It seems, then, that the regime crisis of 1905 could have been overcome, once order had been restored, by the kind of coalition of moderate nationalists envisaged by Stolypin. Instead, the autocracy, when subjected to the harsh test of the First World War, faced a full-blown systemic crisis (revolution) in 1917, partly as a result of the influence of the anti-Western, anti-Semitic and anti-constitutional prestige nationalism of the extreme Right. This influence blocked any possible chance of co-operation and communication between society and the state and finally brought about a cataclysmic conflict between them.

NOTES

1. Erwin Oberlander, 'The role of the political parties', in G. Katkov et al. (eds), *Russia enters the 20th century* (London, Methuen, 1973), pp. 74–5.
2. Hans Rogger, *Jewish Policies and Right-Wing Politics in Imperial Russia* (Berkeley, Calif., University of California Press, 1986), Chapter 7.
3. W. Laqueur: *Russia and Germany: A century of conflict* (London, Weidenfeld and Nicolson, 1965), p. 84.
4. Hans Rogger, *Jewish Policies,* op. cit., Chapter 7.
5. A. Chernovsky (ed.), *Soyuz Russkogo Naroda* (Moscow, Leningrad, 1929), p. 42.
6. Hans Rogger, *Jewish Policies,* op. cit., Chapter 7.
7. A. Chernovsky (ed.), *Soyuz Russkogo Naroda,* op.cit., p. 32. See also evidence of M. N. Zelensky.
8. V. Levitsky in L. Martov, P. Maslov, A. Potresov (eds), *Obshchestvennoe dvizhenie v Rossii, v nachale XX veka,* vol. 3, Book 5 (St Petersburg, 1974).
9. A. Chernovsky (ed.), *Soyuz Russkogo Naroda,* op. cit., p. 32.
10. A. Chernovsky, ibid. Evidence of Y. A. Poluboyarinova, 28 June 1917.
11. *Moskovskie Vedomosti,* No. 12, 1906.
12. For example, Raymond Pearson, *The Russian Moderates and the Crisis of Tsarism* (London, Macmillan, 1977), p. 4.
13. W. Laqueur, *Russia and Germany,* op. cit., p. 95.
14. Ibid., p. 98.
15. Ibid., p. 99.
16. V. Levitsky, 'Pravye Partii' in L. Martov, P. Maslov and A. Potresov, *Obshchestvennoe dvizhenie v Rossii v nachale XX veka,* op.cit., p. 358.
17. Thomas Riha, 'Constitutional developments in Russia' in T. G. Stavrou (ed.), *Russia under the Last Tsar* (Minn., University of Minnesota Press, 1969), p. 98.
18. S. W. Baron, *The Russian Jews under the Tsars and Soviets* (London, Macmillan, 1976), p. 61.
19. Hans Rogger, *Russia in the Age of Modernisation and Revolution 1881-1917* (London, Longman, 1983), p. 206.
20. Raymond Pearson, *The Russian Moderates and the Crisis of Tsarism, 1914-1917* (London, Macmillan, 1977), *passim.*
21. Robert Edelman, *Gentry Politics on the Eve of the Russian Revolution: The Nationalist Party 1907-1917* (New Brunswick, NJ, Rutgers University Press, 1980), *passim.*

22. D. C. B. Lieven, *Russia and the Origins of the First World War* (London, Macmillan, 1983), Chapter 3.
23. Ibid., p. 64.
24. Ibid.
25. Hans Rogger, *Jewish Policies*, op. cit., Chapter 8.
26. G. Hosking, *The Russian Constitutional Experiment: Government and Duma 1907–1914* (Cambridge, Cambridge University Press, 1973), p. 246.
27. M. McCauley *Octobrists to Bolsheviks* (London, E. Arnold, 1984), pp. 209–10. Testimony of N. S. Khrushchev in Strobe Talbot (ed.), *Khrushchev Remembers* (London, Sphere Books, 1971).
28. G. Katkov, *Russia, February 1917* (London, Fontana, 1967), Chapter 8.
29. W. Laqueur, *Russia and Germany*, op. cit., p. 88.
30. S. N. Harper, *The New Electoral Law for the Russian Duma* (Chicago, 1908).

3 Stalinist realities

The collapse of the tsarist system in 1917 and its eventual replacement by Lenin's Bolsheviks seemed initially to destroy the hopes of Russian nationalists. As E. H. Carr has written, 'never in any previous revolution had the break in continuity seemed so absolute.'[1]

Lenin was an internationalist and his followers were very largely non-Russian, a feature which may have reflected the revolutionising effects of tsarist nationalities' policy and its incipient anti-Semitism. The Bolshevik Party was the home of Trotsky, Radek, Zinoviev, Kamenev, Ordzhonikidze, Djugashvili, Dzerzhinski and had many Jewish and Latvian members.

The revolutionary situation both at home and abroad seemed promising at first. Lenin declared in January 1918:

We have never cherished the hope that we could finish it [the revolution] without the aid of the international proletariat. We have never had any illusions on that score. . . . The final victory of socialism in a single country is of course impossible.[2]

However, in France, Germany, Poland and the rapidly disintegrating Austro-Hungarian Empire, there seemed fleetingly to be a chance of working-class seizure of power among the war-weary masses of Europe.

In March 1919 Lenin was still playing the same tune when he declared that

Complete and final victory . . . cannot be achieved in Russia alone; it can be achieved only when the proletariat is victorious in at least all the advanced countries, or, at all events, in some of the largest of the advanced countries. Only then shall we be able to say with absolute confidence that the cause of the proletariat has triumphed, that our first objective – the overthrow of capitalism – has been achieved.[3]

It was in fact in March 1919 that thirty-five delegates voted in the Kremlin to constitute the Third (Communist) International. There were only five delegates from the Russian Communist Party (*bolsheviki*) present, namely Bukharin, Chicherin, Lenin, Trotsky, and Zinoviev, who became the Chairman of the Comintern. The Russian Bolsheviks were then deeply engaged in the trials and tribulations of civil war, but they had cause for hope that at least the German Party might seize power. By the time of the Second World Congress of the Comintern (July–August 1920), there were 217 delegates from sixty-seven organisations in some forty countries. The Red Army was near Warsaw. The right-wing *Kapp putsch* had just been defeated in Germany, while the factory occupations continued in Italy. Zinoviev's statement had some apparent plausibility for those present when he declared at this time: 'I am deeply convinced that the Second World Congress of the Communist International is the precursor of another World Congress, the World Congress of Soviet Republics.'[4] However, it was also at this Congress that certain stringent conditions were imposed on the participating parties of the Comintern, the so-called Twenty-One Conditions, and these restrictions gave considerable power to the dominant Communist Party of the International, namely the RKP(b).

The revolutionary tide ebbed in 1921 and the 'Theses on the World Situation' adopted at the Third World Congress in 1922 admitted, 'a series of working-class risings have ended in partial defeat.'[5] In Poland the Red Army had been turned back from Warsaw, while in Italy the rise of Mussolini had checked the Italian factory workers after September 1920. German Communism suffered a severe defeat in March 1921, and in Russia itself, Lenin had been compelled to adopt the New Economic Policy (NEP), a partial restoration of capitalism, at the xth Party Congress. Although the Fourth World Congress of the Comintern (November–December 1922) had an impressive 343 voting delegates from fifty-eight countries, all the practical experience and real power lay with the RKP(b).

The year 1923 was a crucial one for the USSR and the Comintern, with Lenin out of active politics and the beginnings of a power struggle among his successors already in progress. It was, as E. H. Carr has said, 'a sort of intermediate period, a truce or interregnum in party and Soviet affairs'.[6] There was a real chance of power for the German Communists in October 1923, but after the failure in Germany, a much more 'realistic' and bureaucratic form of power began to assert itself in the USSR. This new kind of Communist bureaucracy, led by the Party, adopted the slogan of 'socialism in one country' during the following year. Zinoviev, as Chairman of the Comintern, opposed this policy until at least December 1924, but after this date the Comintern itself became more and more an instrument of its dominant Communist Party. The Comintern, in other words, began to operate as a transmission belt for the execution of Soviet foreign policy objectives. 'Bolshevisation' became the watchword of the Fifth Congress of the Comintern in the summer of 1924.[7]

What had been the post-revolutionary experience of the RKP(b) and how did this begin to change the character of Lenin's early internationalism? As E. H. Carr has pointed out, revolutions do not in themselves resolve the tension between continuity and change. Historical continuity always tends to assert itself, because a revolution is made within certain material and environmental constraints by men who have been politically socialised within specific national conditions. Moreover, government or the principle of ordered rule is the antithesis of revolution. A new order must eventually emerge and the Jacobins will replace the monarchy. The new order will be opposed by the anarchists who were at first prominent in the revolution and by the revolutionaries' more consistent supporters. By 1921 the Left of the Bolshevik Party, or Workers' Opposition, were defeated at the xth Party Congress and all other parties of the Left were already banned. The new government which emerges after the consolidation of power will have features and even personnel inherited from the former administration. A new Communist autocracy may be said to have replaced the old tsarist autocracy.[8] Finally, there will inevitably be a need for the new state to develop a foreign policy, which will of necessity be limited by immutable geographical and economic factors. E. H. Carr considers that the Peace of Brest-Litovsk in 1918 was the first real compromise made by the new government as wielder of state power.[9]

In addition, these general characteristics quickly brought about the reassertion of Russian national tradition against Western encroachments. The leaders of the Russian Revolution believed at first that as an exclusively Russian phenomenon, the revolution had for them, 'no meaning, no validity and no chance of survival'.[10] But, as E. H. Carr points out, the very belief that Russia's revolution was itself dependent on a much more important German, European and eventually world-wide proletarian revolution, was itself an extreme version of the belief that Russia would need to learn from and imitate the West. There is another aspect of the Russian Revolution which is typical of political change in Russia, namely its imposition from above: Lenin's new order was a programme of social transformation imposed upon the anarchic revolutionary masses. The transition from the Communist policy of forcible expropriations of grain from the peasantry (War Communism) to the New Economic Policy of 1921 was also a 'traditional' spasmodic shift of policy, typical of Russian political change in that it was unexpected and uneven.

As a result of the failures of internationalist perspectives after 1921, the Russian Communist Party developed a latent anti-

Westernism, which enabled its followers to merge their Communist messianism with an older Russian messianism. The Third Rome became the Third International. However, the Third Rome and the new Advent were indefinitely delayed and the new Marxist-Leninist ideology, like early Christianity, had to make its peace with the state. Revolutionary Bolshevism had to compromise with Russian state power.

A sign of the gradual merger of Bolshevism with the more traditional Russian 'statism' was the belief at an early stage of the civil war that Bolshevism and Communism were not the same thing. Bunin recorded a conversation between Red Army men in 1919, which may be summarised as follows: 'Everything evil comes from the Jews, they are all Communists, but the Bolsheviks are all Russians.'[11] The names of Trotsky and Zinoviev were connected in the popular mind with the Communists, but Lenin's name was not so intimately connected. It is said that during the Kronstadt rebellion of 1921, the revolutionary sailors destroyed portraits of Trotsky and Zinoviev, but not those of Lenin. A similar residual reverence for Lenin is still to be found today within the ranks of the Pamyat' Society.

In 1920 Lenin wrote a pamphlet entitled 'Left wing Communism: an infantile disorder', which urged upon Communists the necessity for intelligent compromise with their national political conditions and other working-class parties, with a view to becoming the dominant national party of the Left. A group of German Marxists coined the phrase 'national Bolshevism' at this time, perhaps in response to Lenin's seminal ideas. The concept also came to the attention of a former Kadet and supporter of Kolchak, Professor Nikolai Ustryalov. He came to the conclusion in the early 1920s that true Russians should not fight against the Bolsheviks. He had never liked the way in which the Whites were dependent on the allies and he distrusted the West. He was also strongly influenced by the ideas of Danil'evsky, believing in the historic destiny of Russia and the incipient decay of the Western world in general. After Russia's initial period of weakness and suffering, said Ustryalov, she would rise to the status of a great power in her new Soviet incarnation. Ustryalov considered that the introduction of the NEP in 1921 prefigured a new period of Soviet rule, which should be supported by loyal Russians at home and abroad. Professor Ustryalov and others such as Lukyanov and Klyuchnikov, published a collection of essays in Prague in 1921 which was entitled *Smena Vekh (Change of Landmarks)*, echoing in this title the famous collection by Russian liberal conservatives in 1909, which had been called *Vekhi (Landmarks)*. In the original collection of essays, several leading Russian thinkers had made their peace with the forces of law and order as a prelude to further more realistic political reforms. Berdyayev, for example, had criticised the Russian intelligentsia for their devotion to ideology rather than to truth. The central place in *Change of Landmarks* was taken by Ustryalov's article 'Patriotica', in which he summarised his position as follows:

No, neither we nor 'the people' can properly evade our direct responsibility for the present crisis, for its dark, as well as its bright aspects. It is ours, it is genuinely Russian, it is rooted in our psychology, in our past, and nothing like it can or will happen in the West even in the event of a social revolution copied in external forms from it. And even if it is mathematically proven, as not altogether successful attempts are now being made to prove, that 90% of the Russian revolutionaries are non-Russians, for the most part Jews, this does not in the least refute the purely Russian character of the movement. . . . It is not the non-Russian revolutionaries who govern the Russian revolution, but the Russian revolution which governs the non-Russian revolutionaries.[12]

For Ustryalov, the Bolsheviks were a kind of cement with which a newly powerful Russian state could be held together. This new idea provided the *smenavekhovtsy* with a potential focus of loyalty. Klyuchnikov, for example, even went as far as to criticise the original *Vekhi* writers for their attachment to Orthodoxy. He wished instead to substitute a kind of mystique of the Russian state. Writers such as Boris Pilnyak also favoured the idea of support for the Communist regime in so far as it stood for a newly renascent Russia. Pilnyak stated:

I am not a Communist and therefore do not acknowledge that I ought to be a Communist or write as a Communist. I acknowledge that the Communist power in Russia is determined not by the will of the Communists, but by the historic destinies of Russia; and insofar as I want to follow, according to my ability and as my conscience and mind dictate, these Russian historical destinies, I am with the Communists – that is, insofar as the Communists are with Russia, I am with them. . . . I acknowledge that the destinies of the Russian Communist Party are far less interesting to me than the destinies of Russia.[13]

Strictly speaking, the *smenavekhovtsy*, Ustryalov and Pilnyak were 'fellow travellers' of the Communists. Ustryalov, for instance, was a supporter of the New Economic Policy, which gave rights to private traders and the peasants after 1921. For the Communists, NEP was a kind of strategic retreat from full Communism and Ustryalov called it 'an economic Brest-Litovsk'. He regarded the NEP as a sign that the regime was becoming more liberal and sensible and he advised the Russian middle classes to support the Bolsheviks. As he later summarised: 'In the Bolsheviks and through Bolshevism, the Russian intelligentsia overcomes its historical apostasy from the people and its psychological apostasy from the state.'[14] Naturally, the regime liked this conclusion and welcomed some of the *smenavekhovtsy* back to the USSR, but of course with reservations. Those reservations were connected with the fact that the *smenavekhovtsy* regarded the transition to NEP as a return to normality. In 1922 Lenin admitted that the *smenavekhovtsy* 'express the mood of thousands and tens of thousands of bourgeois and all sorts of Soviet officials who participate in our New Economic Policy'.[15]

The *smenavekhovtsy* also had many followers in the Red Army and among the specialists (*spetsy*) who were directing Soviet industrial enterprises. The Soviet journal *Krasnaya Nov (Red Virgin Soil)* called these people 'national Bolsheviks' although this term had not previously appeared in the collection *Smena Vekh*.

The *émigré* scholar M. Agursky defines 'national Bolshevism' as

The Russian statist ideology that legitimises the Soviet political system from the Russian *étatiste* point of view, contrary to its exclusive Marxist legacy. . . . I would like to define *étatisme* as a powerful form of nationalism. . . . National Bolshevism does not reject Communist ideology though it strives to minimise its importance to the level necesary for legitimacy. However, its objectives are different from those of Communist ideology. National Bolshevism in its original form strove for world domination, conceived as the universal Russian Empire cemented by Communist ideology. It is not excluded that in some circumstances national Bolshevism might limit itself to the *étatiste* concept of a Russian superpower.[16]

Agursky makes much of the influence of smenavekhovism on the *émigrés* and literary figures, *spetsy*, the Red Army and indeed on almost every conceivable section of society including the so-called 'living church' movement within Orthodoxy. Agursky says that the People's Commissar for Education, Lunacharsky, supported a variant of smenavekhovism which was termed 'Red patriotism' and there was even some sympathy for smenavekhovism within the Party itself. It can be shown that in 1922–3, Trotsky, Steklov and Lenin were ready to exploit smenavekhovism, whereas the Left and the Communists from national minorities, such as Sultan Galiev and the Ukrainian Skrypnik, were understandably opposed to support from traditional Russian nationalism. The main opposition to any form of national Bolshevism came from Zinoviev and Bukharin.

Apparently there were even some Russified Jews who supported national Bolshevism, such as the critic I. Lezhnev. He even went as far as to declare: 'Russian imperialism (from ocean to ocean), Russian messianism (*ex oriente lux*), and Russian Bolshevism (on the world scale), are all magnitudes of the same dimension.'[17] Lezhnev is typical of the kind of man who passionately sought a foothold in Russian identity, although he naturally excluded Russian Orthodoxy. He turned to Marxism and the Party in 1933–4 and gained prominence in the Soviet press right up to his death in 1955. It is interesting that he condemned the Pyatakov–Radek group during the show-trials in terms borrowed from Dostoevsky. He accused them of 'Smerdyakovism', claiming that like the illegitimate son, Smerdyakov, who murdered his father Fyodor Karamazov in Dostoevsky's famous novel *The Brothers Karamazov*, the defendants were guilty of a visceral hatred of the Russian people.[18]

In May 1922 Zinoviev closed down a Soviet journal *Novaya Rossiya (New Russia)* in Petrograd on account of an article by Lezhnev, 'Emancipation of the Soviets'. The Politburo under Lenin revoked this decision of the Petrograd Soviet, but apparently Zinoviev refused to compromise. Lezhnev had to move the journal to Moscow, where it was published under the title *Rossiya*.[19] At the xIIth Party Congress in August 1922, Lenin was absent through illness and Zinoviev, apparently with Stalin's support, attacked the *smenavekhovtsy*. The Ukrainian national Communist Skrypnik complained that the Red Army were being supported by the *smenavekhovtsy* as bearers of 'the Russian national idea'.[20] Trotsky, however, supported the *smenavekhovtsy* and the continuing subsidies to the journal *Rossiya*.

In time, the consolidation of state power by the CPSU(b) and the Soviet government led to the acquisition by Party and state of national characteristics. The Party was under pressure from a variety of sources which Agursky summarises as 'neopopulism, Scythianism, Red patriotism, Smenavekhovism, anti-Semitism.'[21] By 'neopopulism' he meant support for the peasant interests of the Russian majority and his reference to 'Scythianism' relates to a supposedly prophetic poem by Alexander Blok which compared the new Bolshevik state to an all-conquering barbarian horde. After Lenin's death in 1924, and the adoption of the policy of 'socialism in one country', Stalin became more and more associated with the trend towards national Bolshevism, while Trotsky seemed to move in the opposite direction, towards support for the doctrines of internationalism, especially after losing his post as Commissar of War in 1925.

After Lenin's death, the 'Lenin enrolment' of new members into the Party brought in a strongly Russian element, which tended to support Stalin against Trotsky. Stalin's position in respect of national Bolshevism was, however, a little ambiguous. This ambiguity may be illustrated by Stalin's attitude towards a play by Mikhail Bulgakov entitled *The White Guard*, a dramatisation of his novel *Days of the Turbins*. Bulgakov's play paints a sympathetic picture of the Turbin family in Kiev at the time of the revolution, German occupation and the civil war. The Turbins are an old Russian Orthodox family and its members are White Guards or sympathetic to the White cause. However, at the end of the play, some of the Turbin family and their close friends seem to accept the coming of the Bolsheviks as a restoration of law and order after the turmoil of the previous years and the ephemeral rule of Petlyura and his violently anti-Semitic Ukrainian nationalists. Stalin liked the play and saw it several times. However, when Bulgakov wrote a successor entitled *Flight* (1926), which glorified a former general of Wrangel' who returned voluntarily to Russia, Stalin demanded several changes on ideological grounds, which Bulgakov refused to make. It seems therefore that Stalin the Marxist-Leninist was at this stage stronger than Stalin the Russian nationalist. Stalin was ready to use nationalism for his own purposes, but it cannot be maintained that he was already simply a nationalist as Agursky seems to argue. The influence of Ustryalov's national Bolshevism on Soviet thought is also quite difficult to assess.

However, Agursky is surely correct when he says that the influence of national Bolshevik ideas was considerable in these formative years of the Party. In 1927 Bukharin complained:

'One must realise that smenavekhism's 'national Russian' aspect was in its time, at a certain stage of our development, a.bridge which enabled part of our intelligentsia to become reconciled with the Soviet system, which they had previously sabotaged. The fact that we Bolsheviks had gathered Russia together in the fashion of Ivan Kalita was regarded by the smenavekists in a positive light. We tried to use them, direct them, lead them. . . . However, it happens that according to Lenin's expression, the steering wheel is slipping from our hands. This is clearly manifested in our literature. A very considerable part of it is now howling in a genuine Russian fashion, though it is usually dressed in a Soviet cap for decency, decorated with Soviet trinkets and disguised as Communism.[22]

Nevertheless, it may be doubted that the final triumph of 'national Bolshevism' was guaranteed by Stalin's decision to launch the industrialisation–collectivisation drive and the First 5-Year Plan, since this would surely overestimate the power of Ustryalov's ideas and ideology in general. There must have been many factors impelling Stalin towards the social transformations of 1928–32, including the drive to 'build socialism' in a backward country, to expand the class basis of support for the Party, to break the hold of the peasantry over the towns, to modernise the country for war production, to build Stalin's own political power and so on. The destruction of a traditional peasant culture in Russia itself during the 5-Year Plans has today given rise to the emergence of a critically anti-Soviet Russian nationalism and these tumultuous years were typified by a powerful 'Sovietisation' rather than the triumph of national Bolshevism as such, still less of smenavekhism, which could logically apply only during the relatively limited period of NEP. However, the Sovietisation of the Stalin period did contain a powerful Russifying element, which became particularly obtrusive after the introduction of the Stalin Constitution of 1936 and especially after the experience of the Great Patriotic War.

As J. N. Westwood has summarised, 'after about 1936, Stalin's policy was to Russify the political institutions of the nationalities. The purge trials of 1938 made victims of many so-called "bourgeois nationalists" among the leaders of the national Communist parties.'[23] The doctrine of Lenin, namely that the Soviet republics should be national in form but socialist in content, was expanded in the personnel sphere to mean that a member of the local nationality would occupy the ostensibly senior position, while a Russian would occupy the actually more powerful position of deputy. The Second Secretary of a republican Communist Party would usually be a Russian, who had direct access to the security services (OGPU, NKVD, MVD or KGB). In this way, new national élites were created by the time of Stalin's death and it was hoped that they would prove both loyal and proficient, extending their influence throughout their national communities. The peoples of the Soviet Union would thus begin to adopt Russian culture and language to their own advantage. In this connection the use of the Russian language was naturally of great importance. In one of his last theoretical works, Stalin condemned the linguistic theories of Marr, who had suggested that a revolutionary social system would eventually produce a new language. In the early 1950s, Stalin claimed instead that the new Soviet socialist system would use the language of its dominant member, Russia. Russia, said Stalin, was the 'older brother' of the entire Soviet family. In post-war Eastern Europe and the USSR the Russian language became a compulsory subject in all schools, institutions of higher education and in Soviet administration, while Russians themselves were slow to learn the languages of the national republics and other socialist countries.

During the years 1941–5 of the Second World War, the Soviet authorities led, and took credit for, the upsurge of patriotism among the people. Stalin's speech of 3 July 1941 addressed his listeners as 'Brothers and Sisters, dear Fellow Countrymen. . .', using the language of Orthodoxy and Russian national tradition rather than that of Communism. At the Red Square parade of 7 November 1941, Stalin reminded his listeners of the deep crisis of the Red Army in 1918, but also he spoke of pre-revolutionary traditions, including the names of Alexander Nevsky, Dmitry Donskoi and Mikhail Kutuzov. As Geoffrey Hosking summarises, Stalin 'evoked the warfare of nations, not of classes.'[24] Soviet soldiers went into battle with the cry 'For the Motherland! For Stalin!'. Ideological slogans were partially subordinated to patriotic slogans and a kind of concordat with the Orthodox Church was reached. Subsequent interpreters of the Second World War have often stressed the Russian nationalism and patriotism of the heroic defenders of Leningrad, Moscow, Stalingrad and other Soviet cities. The defence of Mother Russia and the subsequent drive to Berlin was seen by Tarkovsky, for example, in terms of the defence and triumph of Orthodox Russia and her loyal sons, in his film *Ivan's Childhood*.[25]

Just as the Bolshevik Party may be said itself to have acquired characteristics of autocracy in its struggle against tsarism, so the Soviet state under Stalin may have acquired some of the characteristics of Hitler's Reich during the period 1941–5. The system became dictatorial, nationalist and anti-Semitic. However, the nationalist element was decked out in the guise of 'Soviet patriotism', which was particularly harsh in the border areas of the USSR that had been under German occupation for some time. The Crimean Tartars were deported in 1943–4, while similar action was taken against the Volga Germans, the Baltic nationalities, Greeks, Turks, Ukrainian nationalists and others.

As the Cold War gathered momentum in 1946, the Soviet system became increasingly xenophobic. As Heller and Nekrich point out:

The campaign against 'antipatriotic' elements began a few months after a speech by Stalin at a gathering of voters in February 1946. He did not make any references to socialism and Communism; instead the state, the Soviet social system and the greatness of the Motherland were the main themes of his speech.[26]

In the post-war period, the Stalinist system reached its final incarnation, its consolidation. This was to prove the 'classic' structure from which all future attempts at reform and evolution had to start and to which the system has hitherto tended to revert. After Khrushchev's reforms of 1953–64, the Soviet Union under Brezhnev reverted to a kind of neo-Stalinism. It remains to be seen whether Gorbachev's reforms and *perestroika* will radically break the Stalinist mould.

As Geoffrey Hosking has summarised:

Stalin's last years marked the nadir of intellectual and cultural life in the USSR. Both Marxism and Russian nationalism were raided to produce a crude, reductionist and paranoid view of the world, which was made obligatory for every artist, scientist and scholar, indeed, for anyone who wanted to get into print. Yet, like all paranoid visions, it had its own internal consistency and its own compelling logic.[27]

The 'ministerial' system of central economic planning was consolidated, while agriculture was once again ruthlessly socialised and exploited. A reassessment of national liberation struggles was undertaken, in particular that of Shamil in the Caucasus against tsarist Russia in the nineteenth century. The orthodox Marxist view had been that Shamil's attempts to resist Russian colonialism had been 'progressive'. But after some fairly tortuous arguments, it was now concluded that Shamil had been a British agent and his actions therefore comparatively reactionary. In Kazakhstan, Azerbaidjan, Kirghizia, Yakutia and Dagestan, 'national Communists' were expelled from the Party. It was formally stated that nearly all anti-colonial struggles against tsarism had in fact been reactionary.[28] This discussion then transformed itself into an ideological attack on 'rootless cosmopolitanism', 'bourgeois objectivism' and 'the whitewashing of American imperialism'. There were many victims. In January 1949 *Pravda* condemned 'antipatriotic' theatre critics, while Simonov alleged a conspiracy of these 'rootless cosmopolitans'.[29] Others, such as Anatoly Safronov, echoed these attacks, while writers were denounced in the Soviet press with their (Jewish) names being published alongside their Russified pseudonyms. Former members of the Jewish Anti-Fascist Committee, Lozovsky and Mikhoels were assassinated. The 'Doctors' Plot' disgraced the final year of Stalin's life, as did his plans for the Jewish population of the USSR.

Literature, the arts, architecture, science, genetics, all suffered from the catastrophic *Zhdanovzhchina* of Stalin's last years, as indeed did Zhdanov himself[31] and many of Stalin's henchmen. But the case of Yevgeny Varga, Director of the USSR Academy of Sciences Institute of World Economy, illustrates particularly well the nature of the weird variant of Russian national Bolshevism which afflicted late Stalinism. Varga had attempted to show that capitalism could recover from its critical recession of the 1930s and post-war difficulties. He was dismissed and many of his colleagues were arrested or denounced in specially convened meetings of the Institute. At one such meeting, Varga was denounced as having 'the blood of the Russian people' on his hands. His son had been killed in the Second World War.[32]

As I have said, the Stalinist system, for all its evident ideological decomposition, was the starting point from which all attempts to reform have begun and to which, in albeit muted and modified forms, it has tended to revert. However, the revelations about the Stalin era under Gorbachev now appear to be irreversible. Amid the ideological confusion and debate of today, it remains an open question whether a section of the Party might attempt a kind of neo-

Stalinist 'reversion to type', perhaps in league with Russian nationalists.

NOTES

1. E. H. Carr, *A History of Soviet Russia,* Vols V-VII: *Socialism in One Country* (London, Macmillan, 1958), p. 4.
2. V. I. Lenin, *Collected Works* (Moscow, Politizdat, 1963-70), Vol. 26, pp. 465 *et seq.*
3. V. I. Lenin *Collected Works,* op. cit., Vol. 29, p. 58.
4. D. Hallas, *The Comintern* (London, Bookmarks, 1985), p. 29.
5. Ibid., p. 54.
6. E. H. Carr, *A History of Soviet Russia,* Vol. IV: *The Interregnum* (London, Macmillan, 1969), p. 5.
7. D. Hallas, op. cit., p. 106.
8. I owe the concept of 'Communist autocracy' to the late Leonard Schapiro.
9. E. H. Carr, *Socialism in One Country,* op. cit., p. 6.
10. Ibid., p. 8.
11. M. Agursky, *Ideologiya Natsional-Bolshevizma* (London, YMCA Press, 1980), p. 60.
12. E. H. Carr, *Socialism in One Country,* op. cit., p. 56.
13. B. Pilnyak, 'Pisateli ob isskustve i o sebe', (1924)
14. N. Ustryalov, *Pod Znakom revolyutsii* (2nd edn. 1927), pp. 257-8.
15. V. I. Lenin, *Collected Works,* op. cit., Vol. 27, p. 243.
16. M. Agursky, *The Third Rome: National Bolshevism in the USSR* (Boulder, Col., Westview Press, 1987), p. xv.
17. Ibid., p. 286.
18. M. Agursky, *Ideologiya Natsional-Bolshevizma,* op. cit., p. 116.
19. M. Agursky, *The Third Rome* op. cit., p. 292.
20. Ibid., p. 300.
21. Ibid., p. 305.
22. Ibid., pp. 330-1.
23. J. N. Westwood, *Endurance and Endeavour: Russian history 1812-1986* (3rd edn, Oxford, Oxford University Press, 1987), p. 377.
24. G. Hosking, *A History of the Soviet Union* (London, Fontana, 1985), p. 273.
25. The Russian title of this film is *Ivanovo Dyetsvo.* Its hero, the orphan Ivan, dedicates his young life to the defeat of fascist Germany.
26. M. Heller and A. Nekrich, *Utopia in Power: A history of the USSR* (London, Hutchinson, 1986), p. 486.
27. G. Hosking, *A History of the Soviet Union,* op. cit., p. 312.
28. M. Heller and A. Nekrich, op. cit., pp. 491.
29. *Pravda,* 28 January 1949.
30. M. Heller and A. Nekrich, op. cit., pp. 503-4.
31. G. Hosking, *A History of the Soviet Union,* op. cit., p. 313.
32. M. Heller and A. Nekrich, op. cit., p. 491.

4 Khrushchev's 'revisionism'

Nikita Sergeyevich Khrushchev became First Secretary of the CPSU in 1953 and proved himself to be one of the most vivid and innovative politicians to emerge within the Soviet political scene. He has been compared with Gorbachev himself, and his period of rule, which terminated in October 1964, has been compared with the radical changes which have taken place during the late 1980s. Khrushchev's political skills were extraordinary and he was able not only to eject Beria from his apparently unassailable position at the head of the security apparatus in 1953, but also to undermine Malenkov by the year 1955; to rout the Stalinist 'anti-Party group' in 1957 and acquire the post of Chairman of the Council of Ministers, in addition to his Party leadership, in 1958.

In some ways, Khrushchev served his people well. By ridding the Soviet Union of Lavrenty Beria and subsequently bringing the KGB under Party control, he freed people of the ever-present fear of arbitrary arrest and incarceration in the Gulag Archipelago. He helped to restore the norms of Party life and was personally responsible for the rehabilitation of millions of Stalin's victims. He did a great deal for the rehabilitation of Soviet law, especially after the revision of the Criminal Code in 1958. Despite his politically motivated attacks on Beria's supposedly liberal nationalities policy and Malenkov's consumer goods programme, he helped clarify the record in respect of deported nationalities, such as the Crimean Tartars and he improved living conditions for many, particularly Soviet farmers. The Khrushchev years saw a beginning of foreign tourism, improved availability of housing and consumer goods, a relaxation in the arts and the doctrine of 'peaceful coexistence', first enunciated at the xxth Party Congress in 1956.

However, as Roy Medvedev,[1] Edward Crankshaw[2] and others have shown, Khrushchev's early life and political experience had confirmed him as an uncritical Marxist. He believed implicitly that the centrally-directed economy of the USSR was superior to the supposed 'anarchy of capitalist production'. Schooled in the period of Stalinist 5-year plans and encouraged by the powerful growth rates of that period, he believed that there were no fortresses which could not be stormed. 'Impossible' planning targets had been approximately achieved before and they could be achieved again. All that the USSR needed was enthusiasm, a reformed planning structure and reliable cadres. To this end, Khrushchev embarked on his 'Virgin Lands' scheme in 1954, producing the characteristic mixture of sensible reforms (with respect to pay and pensions for farmers) with ill-considered drives for quick success in Kazakhstan and elsewhere. Spectacular results in the harvests of 1956 and 1958 were not maintained, as soil erosion and ecological damage ensued. The harvest of 1963 was a disaster. Similarly, in making absurd claims for Soviet meat and milk production, Khrushchev undermined his credibility.

Khrushchev's enthusiasm for agriculture knew no bounds. He interfered in crop designations, earning himself the title of 'the maize man' and tried to decentralise the Ministry of Agriculture. His Marxist enthusiasm for eliminating the distinction between town and country prompted him to propose the provision of urban-type dwellings for the peasants, the 'agro-town' scheme. Such ideas served to hasten the already catastrophic decline of the traditional Russian village. In 1962 Khrushchev attempted to divide the local Party organisations into industrial and agricultural sections, a move which was as hated as it was impractical. After 1958 Khrushchev insisted that the Machine Tractor Stations, which had supplied machinery to the collective farms, should sell equipment to the already impoverished localities, where that equipment was often inadequately maintained. His campaigns in the Virgin Lands at harvest time and in respect of the 'chemicalisation of agriculture' are well known.

In the sphere of industry, the same kind of hectic reforms and innovations took place. The Sixth 5-Year Plan (1956–60) quickly proved unworkable and was replaced by a 7-Year Plan (1959–65), itself subsequently replaced by a Seventh 5-Year Plan (1961–5). In 1957 Khrushchev split the planning system into 'councils of national economy' (*sovnarkhozy*) or more precisely 105 different planning regions. These regions did not themselves exactly correspond to the local political (*oblast'*) divisions of the country. The role of the central state planning agency, Gosplan, was downgraded but it became very quickly evident that excessive vertical integration was taking place in the *sovnarkhozy* and managers were unusually reliant on the services of unofficial traders known as *tolkachi* or 'pushers' to obtain the necessary inputs. Within a few years, a central planning agency, the All-Union Sovnarkhoz, had to be created to provide coordination.

All kinds of 'quick solutions' began to emerge through the medium of an increasingly Khrushchevite press. Mathematical economists such as Kantorovich and Fedorenko posited computer determination of prices throughout the system, known euphemistically as 'objectively determined valuations', while Professor E. G. Liberman proposed cash incentives for overfulfilment of plans. His ideas were published in *Pravda* (9 September 1962), but were sabotaged by the excessively bureaucratic methods proposed for the distribution of the 'profits' or 'money values of surplus products'. Meanwhile, the problem of falling growth rates and what Professor Wiles has called 'the multiplication of priorities' beset the economy. At the same time, Khrushchev made more and more promises and predictions. In 1961 at the XXIInd Party Congress, he promised that the USSR would catch up with, and then overtake, the GDP per capita of the United States by the year 1980. This would have involved a fivefold increase for the USSR and the figures were, unfortunately, published in the Party Programme of 1961. This Programme was to form the basis of what may be termed 'Khrushchevism'.

The Communist Party at the time of Stalin's death has been described as a Byzantine bureaucracy of slothful incompetence. Its members were cowed into submission and fearful obedience to every twist and turn of the 'Party line' as enunciated by Stalin. Far more important than the Party were the Central Ministries, and above all, the sinister Ministry of Internal Affairs under Lavrenty Beria. Khrushchev reversed this position, at first with the help of another 'pillar' of the Soviet State, the armed forces.

It has already been said that Khrushchev restored the 'norms of Party life' and 'socialist legality'. Under Stalin, there was not even a Party congress between 1939 and 1952. This is a measure of his personal dictatorship, which may readily be compared with that of Adolf Hilter. Khrushchev was no doubt expressing the will of the majority of the Soviet élite when he abandoned these methods and restored some degree of confidence and tenure to his followers. After the execution of Beria and his closest associates, no Soviet politician was sent before the firing squad or imprisoned in the Gulag. The 'anti-Party group' were merely retired on a pension or demoted and sent into a kind of administrative exile. Khrushchev himself after his fall from power was retired on a pension and availed himself of this opportunity to write his fascinating memoirs before his death in 1971.[4]

Khrushchev used the Party as his primary path to power and it has subsequently become an institutional feature of the Soviet state, so that the General Secretary of the Party effectively rules the USSR. Another 'lesson' of the Khrushchev era also seems to be that a General Secretary confronts or undermines the Party at his peril. The Party members, now numbering over 19 million are the élite of the Soviet system and stand most to gain from the continuation and stability of the system, especially if they hold the senior *nomenklatura* posts. However, Khrushchev's simplistic political ideology led him to believe that Party membership should be widened as far as possible, and in an almost populist sense he relaxed the rules of entry,[5] as well as insisting on a regular turnover of top personnel.[6]

Khrushchev defined the Party's 'leading role' in Soviet society and claimed that it would continue to have an important cultural and moral function even after the 'withering away of the state' which he predicted for the period of Communism. He promised that the younger generation living in the Soviet Union in 1961 would actually experience the Communist society. He proclaimed that all class conflict had been eliminated from the USSR and that the state was therefore a 'state of the whole people'. Finally, he promised a new constitution for the USSR, although this was not to emerge until 1977, under his successor Leonid Ilyich Brezhnev.

Having taken advantage of his close links with the military in order to defeat both Beria and the 'anti-Party group', Khrushchev at first promoted the Minister of Defence, Georgy Zhukov, to the Praesidium of the Party, only to demote him again a few months later. Following his declaration of the doctrine of peaceful coexistence in the nuclear age, he demobilised about 30 per cent of the regular officers and men in the armed forces, creating extensive problems of social readjustment and considerable hostility. His educational reforms, designed to instil the practical work ethic into Soviet teenagers, were also unpopular with parents and educationalists, while his insistence on increased political education may have further alienated a generation of students.

In 1954 Ilya Ehrenburg published a novel entitled *The Thaw*, a name which has been applied more generally to Khrushchev's period in the artistic and literary fields. Vladimir Dudintsev's novel, *Not by Bread Alone*, published in 1956, praised the 'small man' whose innovatory ideas finally triumph over a passive bureaucracy. Some splendid poetry by Yevtushenko and Vosnezensky appeared at the time, much of it very popular with young people, including Yevtushenko's *Baby Yar*, *Zima Junction* and *The Heirs of Stalin*. Much of this literary renaissance was inspired by Khrushchev's de-Stalinisation campaigns, which began at the xxth Congress in 1956 and the famous 'Secret Speech'. A revision of the Party History followed in 1959 and an even more anti-Stalin version in 1962. The immediate reaction to the 'Secret Speech' denouncing Stalin (and cleverly implicating Khrushchev's rivals for power) was one of anger and confusion. Upwards of a million Soviet citizens were rehabilitated after the xxth Congress, including an obscure physics teacher from Ryazan, Alexander Solzhenitsyn. In Poland and Hungary there were extensive political changes, which in the case of

Hungary included demonstrations against followers of the Stalinist dictator Rakosi, and the physical destruction of Stalin memorials. Under their new leader, Imre Nagy, the Hungarians threatened to leave the Warsaw Pact. The 'popular uprising', as it is now known, was crushed by Soviet forces in the autumn of 1956. In retrospect, the 'Secret Speech' may be seen as a nail in the coffin of Marxism-Leninism in the USSR and Eastern Europe.

As a result of the disorders following the Secret Speech, Khrushchev was forced to soft-pedal for a time on his de-Stalinisation campaign and in 1957 he ordered the suppression of Pasternak's novel *Dr Zhivago*, which after its publication abroad (in Italy) won its author the Nobel Prize for Literature. Pasternak was hounded by the Soviet authorities and forced to repudiate the prize. This was one of the most shameful episodes of the Khrushchev years, and shows one striking aspect of Khrushchev, his inconsistency. However, in 1962, following the removal of Stalin's body from the Red Square Mausoleum, he allowed the publication of Solzhenitsyn's *One Day in the Life of Ivan Denisovich* in *Novy Mir*, the journal edited by Tvardovsky. This story is a downbeat account of an ordinary day in the life of a peasant prisoner (Ivan Denisovich Shukov) in one of Stalin's labour camps. Its publication awakened a sympathetic chord in the Soviet people, giving rise to a veritable stream of 'camp literature' and memoirs and placing Solzhenitsyn in the front ranks of Soviet literature. In the same year, Yevtushenko's poem, *The Heirs of Stalin* was published in *Pravda*. The heirs of Stalin, those who had staffed the camps or received promotion during Stalin's era must have been dismayed indeed. As always, however, there were limits to Khrushchev's 'liberalism'. The following year, he crudely attacked Neizvestny for his modernist sculptures and other works of modern art.

Khrushchev failed to understand that significant domestic reform must be matched by a co-ordinate foreign policy. Despite his doctrine of 'peaceful coexistence', he did not for one moment contemplate peace in the arena of ideology. In newly independent countries such as India and Egypt, he was very active and he attracted a client state in the shape of Cuba after Castro's coup against Batista in 1959. Khrushchev's attempt to install nuclear missiles in Cuba in 1962 very nearly provoked a world war. In Berlin, Khrushchev was partially responsible for the erection of the famous Wall designed to prevent the 'leakage' of qualified personnel from the East. This again was a source of enormous political and military tension and remained a symbol of the division of Europe even in these days of our so-called 'common European home', until November 1989.

Khrushchev's simplistic vision of the future of Soviet socialism is contained in his (Third) Party Programme of 1961, adopted at the xxiind Congress. It is an immensely boastful and somewhat repetitive document, which predicted that social organisation could replace the state apparatus (Communist self-government) in the era of Comunism, scheduled for 1980. Tedious discussion appeared in the Soviet press on the subject of 'the new Communist man', while Khrushchev defined the meaning of the 'age of abundance' which, he said, was just around the corner. It included the promise that every married couple in the USSR would have their own flat. Religious beliefs were dismissed as a 'fantastic world outlook' and a huge number of Russian orthodox churches and other places of worship were literally destroyed.

In the field of nationalities policy, Khrushchev's earlier liberalism with respect to deported nations was replaced by a very destructive and simplistic doctrine. Nationalism was declared to be a 'bourgeois' survival from a previous age and it was suggested that the nations and ethnic groups of the USSR would undergo a 'drawing together' (*sblizheniye*) and then a complete 'merger' (*sliyaniye*) under Communism, so that a new type of internationalist ('new Soviet man') would emerge. These were not new doctrines, but what was new under Khrushchev was the insistence on the ultimate goal of 'merger' (*sliyaniye*), based on a facile economic determinism which is typical of Khrushchevism as a whole.

Prior to the age of Gorbachev, Khrushchev's was the first attempt to 'update' the Stalinist world outlook and give it some international respectability in the age of post-colonialism. The materials of the xxiind Congress were published under the title *The Road to Communism*. In the light of subsequent events, Khrushchev's revisionist Marxism looks slight and superficial. There is no doubting Khrushchev's sincerity, but time and chance wait for few men and the dynamic progress of thought, like that of technological change, seemed by the early 1960s to be moving in directions wholly uncharted by the ideologists of the Party. Modern people had been shocked by Khrushchev's revelations about Stalin and the doctrines of dialectical materialism themselves were under increasing scrutiny and doubt in both East and West. Russians in particular were increasingly concerned to uncover the truth about their past, to find the solid foundations on which to base their lives in the future, to reinterpret the terrible experiences of collectivisation, the purges, war and the Cold War. Increasingly they were turning towards the solidity of Russian cultural history and Orthodoxy. As for Khrushchev, he was finally ousted by a 'palace coup' in October 1964, while *Pravda* summarised his passing in the following fashion:

The Leninist Party is the enemy of subjectivism and drifting in Communist construction, of harebrained scheme-making, of half-baked conclusions and hasty decisions and actions taken without regard for realities. Bragging and phrase-mongering, bossiness, reluctance to take account of scientific achievement and practical experience, are alien to it. . . . It is only on the Leninist principle of collective leadership that it is possible to direct and develop the increasing creative initiative of the Party.[7]

Despite the successes, *Sputnik*, Yuri Gagarin, nuclear ice-breakers, improved living standards, the 'thaw' and limited de-Stalinisation, Khrushchev and above all Khrushchevism were failures. New ideologies, some of which were based on ideas which were far from new, were emerging to fill the vacuum created by these failures. Among these were the doctrines of Russian nationalism, articulated most fully and strikingly, although not at first clearly, by Alexander Isaevich Solzhenitsyn.

NOTES

1. R. Medvedev, *Khrushchev* (London, Chalidze Publications, 1986).
2. E. Crankshaw, *Political Leaders of the Twentieth Century – Khrushchev* (London, Pelican Original, 1966).
3. *Pravda*, September 1962.
4. N. S. Khrushchev, *Khrushchev Remembers* (ed. Strobe Talbot) (London, Sphere Books, 1971).
5. *CPSU Party Rules* (1961), Rule 4.
6. *CPSU Party Rules* (1961), Rule 25.
7. *Pravda*, 17 October 1964. Quoted in J. N. Westwood, *Endurance and Endeavour: Russian history 1812-1986* (Oxford, Oxford University Press, 1987), p. 389.

5 Alexander Solzhenitsyn and the New Right

Clearly one of the most important dissidents of the entire Soviet period, Solzhenitsyn has nevertheless puzzled and exasperated many commentators schooled in Western traditions of political science. At the same time, he still enjoys an enormous following in the Soviet Union and among the Russian *émigrés*. His uncompromising Russian nationalism, combined with an unyielding personality in the traditions of the Old Believers, reminiscent of the Archpriest Avvakum, is uncongenial to Western liberals, giving rise to an unmerited neglect of his continuing influence in Russia today.

At first, Solzhenitsyn concealed his true beliefs in the hope of having his works published while he was still resident in the USSR. Later, however, his ideas have been clarified by Stephen Carter,[1] Michael Scammel[2] and others, following the publication of such works as *Nobel Prize Lecture, Lenin in Zurich, The Oak and the Calf*, 'Warning to the Western world', *The Mortal Danger, From Under the Rubble, Gulag Archipelago* and *Letter to Soviet Leaders*, Solzhenitsyn's ideas have apparently evolved while he has been living in the West after his enforced exile in 1974. I therefore begin with his most explicit pre-exile manifesto which was published in 1973, the *Letter to Soviet Leaders*.

Solzhenitsyn's *Letter* was concerned above all with the fate of the Russian and Ukrainian peoples, having a sense of urgency in view of the (then) apparently possible war with China, and the ecological dangers associated with attempting to follow a rapid rate of economic growth. In order to avoid war with China, he proposed that Soviet leaders should abandon any claims to lead the world Communist movement, but instead concentrate on Russian national concerns to the exclusion of Soviet-style empire-building and world-wide ideological influence. Proposing a programme of renewal, he reminded his readers that during the Second World War, Stalin exchanged ideology for 'the old Russian banner – sometimes, indeed, the standard of Orthodoxy – and we conquered!' Solzhenitsyn apparently believed that the legitimacy of the ruling Party would not be adversely affected by the renunciation of Marxism-Leninism. He

suggested that there was no real threat to the USSR from the Western world, and proclaimed it to be weak and divided:

the Western World, as a single, clearly united force, no longer counterbalances the Soviet Union, indeed has almost ceased to exist . . . the catastrophic weakening of the Western world and the whole of Western civilisation . . . is . . . the result of a historical, psychological and moral crisis . . . of humanitarian western culture and world outlook'.

However, an ecological crisis does indeed threaten both East and West unless mankind renounces a 'civilisation of "perpetual progress" now choked and . . . on its last legs'. Russia could avoid the path of capitalism by Marxist industrialisation: 'And herein lies Russia's hope for winning time and winning salvation, in conquering the Northeastern spaces (of Siberia). These spaces allow us to hope that we shall not destroy Russia in the general crisis of Western civilisation.'

Solzhenitsyn's position is therefore that of a Slavophile, based on a concern for the Russian soil. His followers have therefore accurately named themselves *pochvenniki* or the 'followers of native soil' movement, a philosophy founded by Dostoevsky and Grigor'ev and mentioned in Chapter 1. Like all liberal or Slavophile nationalists, Solzhenitsyn advocates a policy of peace, retrenchment and reform. He suggests cutting arms expenditure and the 'irrelevant' space race and he says that support for 'national liberation movements' in the Third World is a waste of money and effort by a nation which needs time to heal its wounds and recover its strength. He also believes that the USSR should not try to hold nationalities in the border lands or the satellites of Eastern Europe against their will.

Like all Slavophiles, Solzhenitsyn advocates an emphasis on moral and personal development as opposed to political change and activism:

The considerations which guide our country must be these: to encourage the inner, the moral, the healthy development of our people; to liberate women from the forced labour of money earning – especially the crowbar and the shovel; to improve schooling and children's upbringing; to save the soil and the waters and all of Russian nature; to re-establish healthy cities.

What kind of social, as opposed to political, action is required for these changes? Solzhenitsyn did not espouse the ideal of democratic change, although he advocated passive resistance to any enforced ideology, resistance to 'the lie'. Indeed Solzhenitsyn believed that Russia was not ready for democracy and the result of any multiparty democracy in Russia would be 'turbulence' or even anarchy, just as it had been in the months between February and October 1917:

So should we not perhaps acknowledge that for Russia this path was either false or premature? That for the foreseeable future, perhaps, whether we like it or not, Russia is destined to have an authoritarian order? Perhaps this is all she is ripe for today? . . . It is not authoritarianism itself that is intolerable . . . but arbitrariness and illegality . . . Let it be an authoritarian order, but one founded not on an inexhaustible 'class hatred' but on love of your fellow men.

Solzhenitsyn did not, apparently, realise that his political philosophy suffered from the inherent weakness of all Slavophilism, namely the divorce from political maturity and practice which makes it impossible for his lofty aims to be realised in the context of an authoritarian government against which there are inadequate checks and balances and legal guarantees. His world is the illusory world of total social harmony and the absence of conflict of interest. For this reason, the *pochvenniki* and other Russian nationalists tended to diverge from the mainstream of the human rights movement, and in some cases they edged imperceptibly towards the non-Marxist authoritarian right wing.

Nevertheless, Solzhenitsyn did call for the release of political prisoners and those who had been incarcerated for political reasons in psychiatric hospitals. He advocated an end to censorship and a free debate of all political, artistic and especially religious and literary tendencies. He wanted freedom of ethical, economic, social and scientific research, while at the same time proclaiming that freedom of thought or discussion was not an end in itself, but only a means of discovering the truth, which presumably he believes will be found in Russian orthodoxy.

As Ludmilla Alexeyeva summarises:

The *Letter* became a sort of platform for the entire Russian nationalist movement, from the most democratic to the most conservative participants. The program Solzhenitsyn proposed was accepted by Osipov and Shafarevich, former participants of the Social Christian Union, and even by Skuratov. Only Shimanov rejected it as 'too liberal'. But it also provoked a deep rupture between the adherents of this movement and human rights activists, for whom, in the majority of cases, a just democratic government was the ideal.[3]

Sakharov cast doubt on the viability of any non-democratic ideal for Russia and the USSR, and he consistently argued against any social, economic or technical isolationism from the Western world. He was deeply concerned about the emergence of a new Great

Russian chauvinism and considered that Solzhenitsyn, for all his 'legal Slavophilism' would be used by Russian fascists for their own purposes.[4] Nevertheless the 'legal Slavophiles' did gain some important footholds in the Soviet literary journals, especially around the 600th anniversary of the Battle of Kulikovo (1380) and received a strong following abroad, in the National Labour Union (NTS) for example and Russian *émigrés* grouped around the journal *Possev*, published in West Germany.

Solzhenitsyn also developed an extremely penetrating criticism not only of Stalin and Stalinism (a feat which had endeared him to Khrushchev), but also of Lenin and the entire Communist episode. This penetrating criticism deserves closer analysis, since it retains its hold on a considerable section of public opinion both within the USSR and abroad. The main works in which these anti-Leninist conclusions are developed are *Lenin in Zurich* (1975) and *The Gulag Archipelago* (1973–6). It must be said at the outset that Solzhenitsyn's depiction of Lenin in Zurich and during the emigration period immediately preceding the February revolution is tendentious and emotionally involved. Lenin is depicted as fanatically dedicated to revolution, politics and civil war, and on occasion he is even depicted as the very devil incarnate. The Russian tradition of interpreting political events through the medium of literary creation is very evident here, and the carefully marshalled facts and sources are mixed with literary and artistic licence. The account of Lenin is taken from three 'knots' or studies of the First World War and the first revolution, namely one chapter from *August 1914*, seven chapters from *October 1916* and three chapters from *March 1917*.[5] For this reason the book *Lenin in Zurich* is something of a patchwork, but it does contain a coherent interpretation.

Solzhenitsyn's first point is that Lenin was anti-patriotic. He welcomed the First World War as a means whereby he could realise his revolutionary aims and discredit the Second International whose members had almost unanimously voted for war credits. He planned from the beginning to convert the 'imperialist war' into a civil war in all the belligerent countries. He is seen as an internationalist and doubtful about the prospects of a purely Russian revolution, dreaming of international revolution based on Switzerland or Sweden in a way which now appears obsessive or even absurd. He is shown as Machiavellian and amoral, ready to deal with Parvus (Helphand) and Imperial Germany in order to realise his revolutionary goals, ready to 'use' his socialist comrades and to use the most dubious financial means to further the aims of his Party. Lenin is portrayed as a Jacobin who always insists on the need for ideological unity under his leadership, an inveterate 'splitter' who bullies, cajoles and demands discipline in the name of his version of revolution on behalf of the proletariat.

As Lenin summarises in Solzhenitsyn's account: 'The majority is always stupid, and we cannot wait for it. A resolute minority must act – and then it becomes the majority.'[6] Lenin admired Zwingli and his militant attacks on the established church, his statue which depicted him holding a book and a sword. Theory must be a guide to military action, as found in Clausewitz' thesis 'On War'; war is an extension of politics by other means. This philosophy gave Lenin grounds for developing a whole theory of war, and appeared to substantiate his claim that the class struggle in Russia could and should be converted into a civil war in the post revolutionary period. The First World War would provide the necessary revolutionary situation in Russia, so that Lenin

always looked for these figures [of Russian losses at the front] and made a nail-mark by them – with surprise and satisfaction. The bigger the figures, the happier they made him: all those soldiers killed, wounded, or taken prisoner were stakes falling out of absolutism's fence and leaving the monarchy weaker.[7]

Once again, Solzhenitsyn here harps upon Lenin's 'anti-patriotism' and his inhumanity, his Machiavellian *realpolitik*. Lenin feared that Nicholas II would sign a separate peace with Germany, and that this would help to preserve his regime and avoid a revolution. Solzhenitsyn is clearly taking a swipe at Lenin for the subsequent Brest-Litovsk Treaty of 1918, at which Bolshevik Russia ceded enormous amounts of territory to Germany in a (successful) effort to preserve the revolution. Lenin's major fault, in Solzhenitsyn's eyes, was that he was essentially un-Russian: 'Why was he born in that uncouth country? Just because a quarter of his blood was Russian, fate had hitched him to the ramshackle Russian rattletrap.'[8] In casting doubt on Lenin's patriotism and 'Russianness', Solzhenitsyn echoes a typical complaint of Russian nationalists, that Lenin and the Bolsheviks were really foreigners. Lenin is also seen as a machine-like politician, who treats his colleagues with suspicion and contempt, while being a poor judge of character. Yet his assessment of the political situation in Russia after the abdication of the Tsar is well portrayed, together with his determination to seize power for the Bolsheviks alone.

Solzhenitsyn is quite clear that the exercise of this power by Lenin laid the foundations of Stalinism. The arguments which lead up to this conclusion are to be found most fully stated in *The Gulag Archipelago*. This work mainly concerns the Soviet prison camps from 1918 to 1956, but includes some information about the Brezhnev period, thus covering a time interval from Lenin to the

1960s. It is based on the testimony of 227 witnesses as well as Solzhenitsyn's own experiences. Many people have testified to its overall accuracy and truth, including R. Medvedev[9] and A. Sakharov,[10] as well as today's Memorial Society, a society formed for the purpose of erecting a memorial to Stalin's victims in the USSR.[11] Solzhenitsyn traces the origins of the camps to the first Soviet concentration camp on the Solovetsky Islands in the White Sea, and to practices originating in the civil war period under Lenin and Dzerzhinski. Solzhenitsyn reports that it was Lenin who wrote to Kursky, People's Commissar of Justice, in May 1922, 'It is also necessary to extend the practice of execution by shooting.'[12] It was Lenin, in August 1918, who wrote to Yevgenia Bosh, 'Lock up all the doubtful ones in a *kontslager*.'[13] It was Lenin who amended the Criminal Code in 1922 to raise the number of capital crimes from six to twelve and advocated the use of terror as a means of persuasion.[14] An important part of Lenin's proposed amendments to the Criminal Code was the section which later became part of Article 58: 'propaganda or agitation, or participation in an organisation, or assistance (objectively assisting or being capable of assisting) orga- nisations or persons whose activity has the character of being anti- Soviet.'[15] Solzhenitsyn points out that under such a formulation it would be possible to find literally anyone guilty and that the law was specifically used for this purpose.

Solzhenitsyn traces the origins of Soviet law under People's Prosecutor N. V. Krylenko, who apparently stated that the govern- ment (VTsIK) 'pardons and punishes, at its own discretion, without any limitation whatever'.[16] He dismissed ideas of the separation of powers as bourgeois, and went on to state that revolutionary courts are both creators of law and a political weapon. Krylenko went on to pile the lethal judicial concepts one upon another: 'A tribunal is an organ of the class struggle of the workers directed against their enemies.'[17] 'Class expediency', it seems, was the vital factor, not proof of guilt. The concept of guilt was an old bourgeois concept (said Krylenko) which had now been uprooted.[18] He went on to say:

And it must be borne in mind that it was not what he had done that constituted the defendant's burden, but what he might do if he were not shot now. We protect ourselves not only against the past but also against the future.[19]

Solzhenitsyn's point is that neither Krylenko (who fell victim to Stalin's purge in 1938) nor any jurist who upholds these principles can protect himself in the future, for if the courts have such powers, literally no one is safe. Solzhenitsyn takes his readers through many of the famous trials of the 1920s and 1930s in order to show how features of Soviet practice developed under the influence of both Marxist legal theory and Krylenko's formulations. In discussing the judicial practice of Soviet Union as it evolved in the pre-war period, it is necessary not to overlook the extra-judicial practices of the secret police. The Cheka was set up by Lenin and Bonch-Bruevich in December 1917, and was the forerunner of all subsequent organs of extra judicial repression in the Soviet Union, namely the GPU, the OGPU, the NKVD, the MVD and the KGB of today. In Lenin's 'Regulations for Revolutionary Tribunals'[20] we find that the Cheka was empowered to execute prisoners for belonging to the 'exploiting class' or merely to 'deter the enemies of the revolution'. Such enemies could be located and shot at the behest of the Chekist's 'revolutionary conscience'.

The *Gulag Archipelago* is an account of a massive machinery of repression against the peoples of the Soviet Union, an account which the Western mind finds almost impossible to envisage or grasp in its entirety. In 1929–30, we are told, 15 million kulaks were deported in the collectivisation campaign and forced to work in camps in the tundra and taiga of Siberia. Solzhenitsyn also describes the wave of arrests in 1937–8 as a 'Volga' of national grief. And afterwards 'came the stream of 1945–6, as big as the good Yenisei: whole nations were forced through the sewage pipes, along with million upon million of others who . . . had been in prison, had been deported to Germany and then returned.'[21]

Solzhenitsyn refers here to the deportation of such nations as the Crimean Tartars and the Volga Germans, and to Soviet troops imprisoned in Germany, all of whom were suspected by Stalin of collaboration with the Nazis. Judicial persecution and the extra-judicial repression did not alter fundamentally in the post-war period and the 1950s and 1960s – despite Khrushchev's limited de-Stalinisation. Solzhenitsyn says the rehabilitations of 1956 and the changes in the Criminal Code in 1958 were only partial. Changes in terminology, for example calling political prisoners 'criminals',[22] do not really amount to reform. Solzhenitsyn states that the whole edifice of courts and trials is really a façade in important political cases, for the real decisions are taken by the Party, and courts and prosecutors are merely the obedient servants of the Party. Solzhenitsyn concludes: 'A powerful State towers above its second half century, embraced by hoops of steel. The hoops are there indeed, but not the law.'[23]

Solzhenitsyn points out that public opinion in the USSR has little belief in the system of courts and the KGB as they are now constituted. His opinion is apparently echoed by the Soviet authorities under Gorbachev, himself a former graduate from the legal faculty of Moscow State University. In 1989 it was reported that the journal *Novy Mir* would begin publication of *Gulag Archipelago*, as

part of the continuing campaign of *glasnost'*. This admirable development, designed to improve the legality of the Soviet system and
impress the world with the seriousness of the reform movement, is
most welcome. However, it is surely controversial from the point of
view of the legitimacy of the existing regime and may prove
dangerous to its long-term political power.

Solzhenitsyn is a liberal nationalist who seeks the regeneration of
his people after the fall of Communism. Like all such *vozrozhdenets*
nationalists, his vision is anti-Communist and there is no logical way
in which Solzhenitsyn can be accommodated to any new 'federal'
Soviet constitution. His book *The Mortal Danger*, published in 1980,
makes this abundantly clear:

All the peoples of the Soviet Union need a long period of convalescence
after the ravages of Communism, and for the Russian people, which
endured the most violent and protracted onslaught of all, it will take
perhaps 150 to 200 years of peace and national integrity to effect a recovery.
But a Russia of peace and national integrity is inimical to the Communist
madness. A Russian national reawakening and liberation would mark the
downfall of Soviet and with it of world Communism. And Soviet Communism is well aware that it is being abrogated by the Russian national
consciousness. For those who genuinely love Russia no reconciliation with
Communism has ever been possible or ever will be.[24]

In the light of comments such as these, it is strange that Western
sources reported in 1988 that Solzhenitsyn was seriously considering
accepting an invitation to return to his homeland, from which he was
forcibly expelled in 1974. The return of Solzhenitsyn to his country
would be extremely significant but there would always be a suspicion
that the authorities were seeking to use him in some way, just as
Maxim Gorky was used by Stalin in the early 1930s.

Solzhenitsyn's nationalism is that of cultural restoration and
rebirth based on orthodox Christianity It is non-militant and anti-
colonial, allowing for the secession of border republics and a policy
of 'repentence and self-limitation'.[25] However, Solzhenitsyn still
believes in the necessary moral influence of Russian culture and
orthodoxy and in this sense he is a believer in the 'light from the east'.
His nationalism is that of Herder and the Slavophiles, as indicated in
his *Nobel Prize Lecture*, while in the speech he delivered at the City
of London Guildhall, 'The Templeton Address', he comes near to
repudiating post-Petrine Russia and the modern world in its entirety.
Solzhenitsyn's powerful message is modified by his nostalgia for a
ravaged past, as is much of the work of the so-called 'countryside
writers' or *derevenshchiki*, which forms the subject of Chapter 7.
Particularly influential as a seminal story, both in terms of structure
and theme, was 'Matryona's Home', first published in the USSR

shortly after the appearance of *One Day in the Life of Ivan Denisovich.*

'Matryona's Home' is a touching story, based on Solzhenitsyn's own experience after his miraculous recovery from cancer in 1953. As he says, 'I just wanted to creep away and vanish in the very heartland of Russia – if there was such a place.'[26] He found an area where the villages had names like Chaslitsy, Ovintsy, Spudni, Shevertni, Shestimorovo, which he said 'wafted over me like a soothing breeze. They held a promise of the true, legendary Russia.'[27] He expresses here a truly romantic Slavophile longing for his homeland. In contrast, he criticises Soviet appellations like 'Peatproduce' as a violation to the Russian language. Ending up in the village of Tal'novo, he lodged with an old lady called Matryona, a widow whose children had died, yet she was still happy and active, in tune with nature. We are told that the living things in Matryona's home, including the plants, were 'silent yet alive, they filled the loneliness of Matryona's life.'[28] She is the victim of an injustice with respect to her pension, and the authorities are seen as inhuman and inaccurate in dealing with her, as they are also inefficient in respect of the local economy. Matryona is a folk-heroine, perhaps idealised from the outset into a kind of iconographic figure. She criticises the local women and 'the system':

They waste time arguing about the hours they've worked, who's on and who's off. Now to my way of thinking, when you work, you work – no gossiping, but get on with the job, and before you know where you are it's supper time.[29]

The skilfully crafted story gives the reader a clue as to the tragic fate awaiting Matryona as she expresses her fear of the rapid express trains passing through the region.[30] Her relatives are scheming to lay their hands on a timber extension to the property, as building timber was locally scarce. In late winter of the year in which the narrator is resident, the brother-in-law arrives with a tractor and his 'gang' rapidly dismantle the outhouse, driven by greed and, of course, the promise of moonshine liquor when the job is done. Matryona helps them in her usual saintly fashion, even earning a scolding from the narrator for wearing his favourite quilted jacket. Later that night, a blizzard delays the work, which is only later completed with the aid of a 'borrowed' tractor and sledges.

Solzhenitsyn suggests obscurely that the 'rape' of the cottage is ill-starred, as suggested by the delays and obstructions to the completion of the work. Eventually, the team of dismantlers, well-oiled with liquor, drag the whole consignment of timber away in the gathering darkness. Their makeshift sledges and tractor, we learn, including Matryona herself, are destroyed at an unmarked level crossing by an unlit express.

Solzhenitsyn remembers his last, reproving words to the saint, in a scene reminiscent of one of the 'confessions' found in the early part of Dostoevsky's novel *The Idiot*. His moral crisis, among the brutal and unfeeling relatives at the subsequent 'wake', precipitates a profound insight into Matryona's character, and a spiritual conclusion which is worthy of patristic writings or traditional hagiography. Essentially Slavophile, this story praises the 'much-suffering' Russian villager and her moral qualities, denigrates modern technology in a manner similar to Kireevsky or Leo Tolstoy and advocates handicrafts and traditional methods. At the same time, the story is profoundly critical of Soviet 'production villages' and pronounces them unnatural and often violent places, as compared with older, more 'organic' settlements. Finally, this story is permeated throughout by a deeply orthodox consciousness, despite the considerable emendations to the original text which were apparently thought necessary by Tvardovsky and *Novy Mir*. As Solzhenitsyn concludes: 'None of us who lived close to her [Matryona] perceived that she was that one righteous person without whom, as the saying goes, no city can stand. Nor the world.'[31]

'Matryona's Home' was an influential work in that it created a genre eminently suitable to the Soviet 'thick' journal, having ostensibly socialist realist elements. In the sense that the story is about the life of the common people, it has what Russians call the quality of *narodnost*. It is critical of 'bourgeois' materialism and alcoholism, and it is ecologically conscious. At the same time, it elevates moral qualities above 'class consciousness' and politics, and carries unusually religious undertones throughout. It is therefore quite clear that Solzhenitsyn's brand of Russian nationalism, as implicitly conveyed in this story, can never be accommodated within any kind of adaptation of Leninism

Another type of nationalism emerged during the Khrushchev years, especially after the xxth Party Congress in 1956. This was the neo-Stalinist nationalism of Fetisov, which had the character of a kind of Russian fascism. A. Fetisov was one of a group including M. Antonov, V. Bykov and O. Smirnov who were incarcerated in mental hospitals in Leningrad and Kazan in March or April 1968. Fetisov had resigned from the Party shortly before his arrest, saying that he had always opposed the de-Stalinisation of 1956, and that he considered Brezhnev's limited re-Stalinisation feeble and ineffective. Fetisov put forward the novel hypothesis that the Jews had been responsible for chaos in civilisation and that the totalitarian regimes of Stalin and Hitler were the desirable and 'historically inevitable' means whereby the 'healthy' populations of Russia and Europe had tried to restore order. Fetisov and his group dreamed of the restoration of the peasant commune and patriarchal peasant society in European Russia, with the transfer of all industry to Siberia. Some of Fetisov's colleagues were architects and had drawn up plans for the restoration of the Russian countryside and new villages to replace those destroyed during collectivisation. When a Fetisov associate presented his higher degree dissertation on this subject to the Institute of the Theory and History of Architecture, he was refused a degree, whereupon he claimed in his appeal that his examining board had been almost wholly Jewish.[32] Fetisov also distinguished himself at the time of the trial of Sinyavsky and Daniel by exclaiming that the dissident writers should have been shot.[33]

Ludmilla Alexeyeva believes that Fetisov and his group were followed directly in their political line by the samizdat journal *Word of a Nation* (*Slovo Natsii*), in which the authors accused Russian liberals of pursuing or advocating policies which would destroy the purity and vitality of the Russian race. They opposed 'random hybridisation' and wanted to revive the great 'single and indivisible Russia' with Russian orthodoxy as the state religion.[34] These ideas were developed in an even more extreme form by Gennady Shimanov, whose prolific works are studied in Chapter 8.

In conclusion, Khrushchev's reforms did not immediately improve the international reputation of the Soviet system, as they were intended to do. While creating some amelioration in the living standards of the Soviet people, the reforms also aroused hopes and made claims that could not be fulfilled, and at the same time helped to engender an anti-Stalinist, liberal Russian nationalism, as well as a neo-Stalinist chauvinist nationalism. The anti-Stalinists sought to rectify a ravaged past and perhaps also recreate a 'lost' world in the manner of the Slavophiles. This school of thought was best expressed towards the end of Khrushchev's period by Alexander Solzhenitsyn. The neo-Stalinist chauvinists gathered round 'patriotic' societies with names like Rossiya and Rodina (Russia and Motherland)[35] and a genuine fascism emerged in the person of Fetisov and his group by 1968. The lines of demarcation between the various types of Russian nationalism are blurred and they overlap in several places, but the two major streams of thought are fairly clear. On the one hand, the Slavophile or *vozrozhdenets* nationalism is genuinely religious, liberal, anti-colonial and anti-Communist. On the other hand, the fascist or chauvinist Great Russianism is anti-Semitic, authoritarian and imperialist in tone. The relationship between this fascist nationalism and Stalinism remains ambiguous. There is no doubt that many Stalinists in the Party under Brezhnev would have sympathised with Fetisov in his verdict on Sinyavsky and Daniel, and with his anti-Semitism. On the other hand, Fetisov's desire to restore the

Russian village, and the patriarchal way of life in European Russia based on Orthodox worship and culture, thus diminishing the industrial muscle of the USSR, would seem too utopian to Stalinists and at the same time implies strong criticism of Stalin's collectivisation programme of 1929–32. However, there can be little doubt that there are more points of contact between the Stalinists and the new fascists than there are between the Stalinists and *vozrozhdenets* nationalists.

As I have argued above, an alliance of convenience between Gorbachev and the reformers, on the one hand, and 'liberal nationalism' on the other, might be dangerous for the Communists, although the patriotism and Slavophile apoliticism of a Solzhenitsyn, and his emphasis on cultural concerns, could conceivably serve the interests of moderates. However, any putative alliance between Stalinists and the new fascists would surely work to the advantage of the latter, especially as the political position of Stalinists has been so thoroughly undermined by the revelations of the Gorbachev regime.

NOTES

1. S. Carter, *The Politics of Solzhenitsyn* (London, Macmillan, 1977).
2. M. Scammel, *Solzhenitsyn: A biography* (London, Hutchinson, 1985).
3. Ludmilla Alexeyeva, *Soviet Dissent* (Conn., Wesleyan University Press, 1987), p. 444.
4. A. Sakharov, 'On Alexander Solzhenitsyn's letter to Soviet leaders' in Meerson and Shragin (eds), *Political, Social and Religious Thought*, (Belmont, Mass., Nordland, 1977), pp. 291–301.
5. A. Solzhenitsyn, *Lenin in Zurich* (London, The Bodley Head, 1976).
6. Ibid., p. 57.
7. Ibid., pp. 87–8.
8. Ibid., p. 89.
9. R. Medvedev, in L. Labedz (ed.), *Solzhenitsyn: A documentary record* (London, Pelican, 1974), pp. 372–3.
10. A. Sakharov in L. Labedz, op. cit., p.364.
11. *The Independent*, 31 October 1988.
12. I. Szenfeld, *Radio Liberty Research Bulletin* (15 March 1974) p. 11.
13. A Solzhenitsyn, *Arkhipelag GULag*, Parts III–IV, (Paris, YMCA Press, 1974), p. 17.
14. V. I. Lenin, *Sobranie Sochinenii*, Vol. 39 (Moscow, Politizdat, 5th edn, 1963) pp. 404–5.
15. A. Solzhenitsyn, *The Gulag Archipelago* (London, Fontana Books, 1974), p. 354.
16. N. V. Krylenko, *Za Pyat Let* (1918–22), p. 13.
17. Ibid. p. 73.
18. Ibid. p. 318.
19. Ibid. p. 82
20. V. I. Lenin, *Sobranie Uzakonenii*, Vol. 13 (1919), Chapter 7, para. 22.
21. I. Szenfeld, *Radio Liberty Research Bulletin* (15 March 1974), p. 10.
22. A. Solzhenitsyn, *Arkhipelag GULag*, Parts V–VII (Paris, YMCA Press,

6 The Brezhnev years, I: Russian nationalist thought

Future historians will probably date the death-throes of Soviet Marxism-Leninism to the late Khrushchev period, for his superficial, messy 'revisionism' fulfilled none of its promises. The questing mind of mankind continually seeks a world outlook which is both intellectually and spiritually whole and creative, and which shows the way forward in political and socio-economic policy. Khrushchev's repetitive, boastful, boring and trivial Party Programme of 1961 could hardly begin to answer such demands. Nevertheless, Khrushchev's successors, after engineering a highly risky 'palace coup' against him in October 1964, tried very hard to salvage the system from the wreckage. They tried to restore the privileges of the Party by immediately reversing the dangerous innovations of Khrushchev. They abolished the infamous 'Rule 25' which stipulated the rotation in office of Party cadres and they abolished the division of the Party, while restoring the central 'Ministerial' planning of the economy. A partial rehabilitation of Stalin was attempted at the xxiiird Congress in 1966, when the Stalinist terminology of 'Politburo' and 'General Secretary' were restored.

A modest statue to Stalin was erected behind the Red Square Mausoleum, and in 1969 a new Party History was issued with offending comments about Stalin simply removed from the text. At the same time, limited reforms of the economy were attempted by Premier Kosygin in 1965, only to be abandoned by the early 1970s.

The dissidents were more severely controlled and the literary and cultural 'thaw' was brought to an end by the trial of Sinyavsky and Daniel in 1965. Brave attempts by Russia's younger generation to continue the process of democratisation were stifled, leading to the trial of Ginsberg and Galanskov in 1967 and the continuing persecution of a samizdat journal, the *Chronicle of Current Events*, founded in 1968. Solzhenitsyn's 'Open Letter to the Fourth Writers Congress' protested about the continuation of literary censorship, but this resulted in renewed persecution of the great writer and began the process which eventually led to his enforced exile from his homeland in 1974. Lithuanian and Ukrainian nationalists, hopeful for political change in the early 1960s were crushed, while the 'Prague Spring' of Alexander Dubček in Czechoslovakia, the struggle for 'socialism with a human face', was terminated in August 1968 by Soviet and Warsaw Pact troops. An ensuing demonstration led by Pavel Litvinov, Natalya Gorbanevskya and others in Red Square was suppressed.

In retrospect, the invasion of Czechoslovakia in 1968 was the crucial event which terminated all hope of political reform within the Soviet Union. Democratisers within the Party, such as the historian Roy Medvedev, were persecuted, and the only significant trends within the CPSU which remained were either neo-Stalinist or bleakly conservative. This repressive and cynical conservatism, embodied by General Secretary Brezhnev, was to become predominant in the years following 1968. It led to an incipient crisis of ideology and stagnation in the economy and society. Agricultural subsidies amounting to 27 per cent of entire investments[1] did nothing to reinvigorate agriculture, while growth rates fell catastrophically between 1970 and 1980. The regime nevertheless decided to seek a way out of its dilemma by embarking on a policy of *détente* with the West, which was also connected with its worsening relations with China. At home, the regime initiated a policy of repression of all political dissent, to be carried out by the KGB under the dynamic chairmanship of Yuri Andropov.

The retreat of the United States in Vietnam and a kind of 'moral paralysis' in the West allowed the Soviet leaders to make significant progress in foreign policy. President Nixon's 1972 visit to Moscow was followed by the SALT I Agreement of 1973, while the Helsinki Agreement on European Security in 1975 seemed to acknowledge the status quo in Europe and the USSR gained access to many technology transfers and other trade concessions from the West. Promises made in respect of human rights ('Basket Three' of the Helsinki Agreement) were hardly honoured by the USSR, while outside Europe and in the field of arms development, the USSR made significant gains. Brezhnev's seizure of the Presidency of the Supreme Soviet Praesidium of the USSR in 1977 coincided with the promulgation of a new Constitution and a 'cult of personality' surrounding the General Secretary. The Constitution bore a striking resemblance to the 'Stalin' Constitution of 1936, although it clarified the leading role of the Party (Article 6) and seemed more protective of civil liberties, while at the same time ignoring the necessary means whereby these liberties could be safeguarded in an independent court of law. It also pledged the USSR to support 'wars of national liberation' in the developing world (Article 28). More a manifesto than a constitution, this document personified the mendacity and stagnation of the Brezhnev era.

However, with the failure of SALT II in 1979 and the invasion of Afghanistan, the period of *détente* came to an abrupt end. Having lost all credibility in Western eyes, the regime allowed the KGB to move in on dissidents including the 'Helsinki monitoring groups' and Jewish refuseniks, who had previously been somewhat protected in the interests of Soviet credibility abroad. A dissident Orthodox priest, Father Dmitri Dudko, was forced to make a public apology for his activities, while Academician Sakharov was sent into internal exile. At the time of the Moscow Olympics in 1980, many dissidents or potential critics of the regime were rounded up.

By 1980, as Heller and Nekrich put it, 'everything was on the decline'.[2] Over Brezhnev's 18-year period of rule, annual increases in national income had fallen from 9 per cent to 2.6 per cent and industrial growth rates had fallen from 7.3 per cent to 2.8 per cent. Agricultural productivity in the same period went into negative figures, while labour productivity also fell significantly. Social statistics showed some worrying trends, with infant mortality rising to 40 per 1,000, compared with 13 per 1,000 in the United States and Western Europe. Since 1956, male life expectancy had declined by an average of four years. Alcohol consumption had risen dramatically: for example in Lithuania, annual consumption of vodka per head of population rose from 8 litres in 1963 to 28.5 litres in 1973.[3] These were grim years for the Soviet people. In 1980 Academician Sakharov summarised the situation in the Soviet Union as follows:

A country living for decades under conditions in which all means of production belong to the state is suffering serious economic and social hardship. It cannot feed itself without outside assistance; and it cannot make progress in science and technology on the contemporary level without using the benefits of *détente*.[4]

In 1983 a samizdat report was circulating in Moscow, attributed to the leading economist Tatyana Zaslavskaya, which stated quite clearly: 'the centralised-administrative form of management has exhausted its possibilities . . . the social mechanism for the development of the economy was inclining towards the suppression of useful economic activity among the population.'[5] In short, the period of 'stagnation', as it is now officially described, was indeed a period of crisis or at least pre-crisis. In the field of ideology it had nothing to offer, although it claimed to be a period of 'real socialism', a phrase without clear meaning. It attempted a limited re-Stalinisation, while at the same time introducing a marked element of 'anti-Zionism' as a kind of outlet for aggression and a scapegoat for systematic failure, comparable perhaps to the campaigns against free-traders (NEP men) in the 1920s and 'wreckers' and kulaks in the 1930s. This anti-Zionism (for which, read anti-Semitism) was to have serious consequences for the development of Russian nationalism, as we shall see.

The first openly anti-Semitic book to be officially published in the Soviet Union was *Judaism without Embellishment*[6] by T. Kichko, published in 1964. It was illustrated with cartoons lifted from the Nazi periodical *Der Stürmer* and reprinted in the 1970s. Another factor affecting the intensity of Soviet anti-Zionism was the Six-Day War of 1967, after which it became possible for 'ordinary' Soviet citizens to express their hostility to Zionism. In the late 1970s, a crudely anti-Semitic publication, *Danger, Zionism* was published by Yuri Ivanov in a large print-run, while anti-Semitic novels by Shevtsov, Pikul and others made their appearance.[7] One of the greatest victories for Soviet propaganda in the late 1970s was the UN resolution which described Zionism as 'racism'. In this way, say Heller and Nekrich, 'Anti-Zionism became the proletarian internationalism of the era of real socialism'.[8]

The truth is that the conservatives of the Brezhnev years offered no really convincing ideological innovations of any kind. They met ideological dissent with the institutionalised repression of the Fifth Chief Directorate of the KGB, while stifling any real discussion about the way forward even among their loyal supporters. Brezhnev's years were the years of gerontocracy, not only in terms of the physical age of the leaders, but in terms of the life of the mind. Brilliantly encapsulated by the ironic pen of Alexander Zinoviev, the Soviet Union became the land of 'Ibansk' in *The Yawning Heights*.[9] This satire portrayed the failure of the 'radiant' (*siyayushchie*) heights of Communism and their replacement by the 'yawning' (*ziyayush-chie*) social and economic conditions of real socialism under Brezhnev. Paradoxically, the younger generation of leaders in Communist systems in the USSR and elsewhere have been encouraged by the apparent stability of Zinoviev's awful 'Ibansk', as Boris Kagarlitsky[10] has pointed out: it seemed to promise that somehow the privileges of the Party could be retained.

At the same time, the tide of public opinion and the beliefs of Soviet intellectuals were turning decisively away from official ideology. Totally new areas of thought and discussion were opening up, new political and social activisms were evolving. Among the most important, vital and genuine in the world of the dissident movement was the mighty, variegated stream of Russian nationalism. It should, of course, be remembered that political dissidents in the Brezhnev era worked in conditions of extreme difficulty. Their honesty and convictions cannot be doubted, but they had to operate in secrecy with limited resources at their command, within a context in which political thought had stagnated for decades. Owing to the disillusionment which afflicted almost every variety of Marxist reformism, Russians turned to their pre-revolutionary traditions for guidance, including a reappraisal of the party politics of the Duma period, White Guard literature and even the Slavophile–Westerniser debate of the nineteenth century. A country in which indigenous traditions and religious life had been ruthlessly and unnecessarily persecuted in the pursuit of rapid and ecologically disastrous industrialisation, now awakened to the desire for the reconstruction of its ravaged past. In the light of fragmentary glimpses of that pre-revolutionary past and in comparison with the falsifications of the Stalin era and the half-truths of Khrushchev, the pre-revolutionary period seemed to be surrounded by an attractive aura.

In addition to the above considerations, the political traditions of the pre-revolutionary intelligentsia were still powerfully felt, despite the rejection of the pervasive atheism and materialism of those distant days. As the Russian philosopher Berdyaiev had pointed out in an earlier generation, political thought in Russia always tended towards moral or even eschatalogical absolutism, secrecy, total dedication, conspiracy, martyrdom. The characteristic discerned by Berdyaiev in his book *The Russian Idea*[11] was actually praised by the author, although to Westernisers, it is traditionally seen as a defect of Russian thought, a factor which diminishes the status and effectiveness of political and social action in Russia and undermines the autonomy of political science.

A group appearing as early as Khrushchev's last year in office (1964) and which was strongly influenced by Berdyaiev and others, was the first conspiratorial Russian nationalist group to emerge in the period under discussion. It was the All-Russian Social Christian Union for the Liberation of the People (VSKhSON), which had as its aim the removal of the existing Communist regime by military *putsch* and its replacement with a dictatorship composed of clergy and 'representatives of the people' elected for life. At the time of their arrest, there were twenty-eight members and thirty candidates. This very significant organisation had its own rules, programme and methods of agitation and recruitment.VSKhSON was led by a very remarkable ascetic and saintly figure, Igor Ogurtsov, a man of towering moral authority; Mikhail Sado, a very experienced organiser who was of non-Russian nationality; Yevgeny Vagin, chief of the ideological division and an admirer of Dostoevsky, Berdyaiev and Leont'ev; Boris Averichkin, the group's archivist; and others such as Leonid Borodin, who was at the time principal of Serebriansk High School in Leningrad Province. Like Solzhenitsyn, this group believed that Communism had proved itself anti-national, hostile to Russian interests. Members of VSKhSON believed that the Party had no real following among the population at large, so that the manifesto published by the group claimed: 'The Communist world is disintegrating. The peoples have found from bitter experience that it brings poverty and oppression, falsehood and moral decay . . . [the regime's] utter defeat is predetermined.'[12] The political beliefs of the group were authoritarian, being based ultimately on a kind of theocracy, but at the same time contained the Slavophile demand that the legislative body of the new government should be 'social, representative and popular'.[13] There would be local self-government and a legislature which contained representation of peasant communes, major trade unions and national corporations. This legislature would have strongly circumscribed powers, since its legislation could be vetoed by the 'Supreme Council', a body which would consist of clergy (one-third) and life-tenured representatives (two-thirds) from outstanding citizens. This Supreme Council would elect a Head of State, to be confirmed by popular vote in the 'Popular Assembly', itself elected from 'village and urban communes on the basis of proportional representation. It should also be elected from industrial and commercial corporations, associations of the free professions and from the organisations of political movements.'[14] The Supreme Council would have the right to veto 'any law or action which does not correspond to the basic principles of the Social Christian Order'.[15]

Part 2 of the VSKhSON Programme consists of a section dealing with the basic principles of Social Christianity and an eighty-five-point embryonic constitution. Declaring Communism to be the 'sickly offspring' of materialistic capitalism, it asserts that Social Christianity is based on the spiritual value of the human personality and that human rights must be based on certain inalienable rights which spring from this view of mankind. The Programme tries to establish a balance between state, society and the individual and rejects the totalitarian model which, it says, subverted society to the interests of the state. Social Christianity elevates the family and private property to a high level and asserts woman's role within the family as opposed to her inalienable right to work within the economy as a whole. The church, it is claimed, should be free of the state and encouraged to pursue its goal of 'global unity'. This section finishes with the statement:

In its cultural policy, Social Christianity affirms that living culture is a means of national self-knowledge and self-expression and that it can flourish only in an atmosphere of freedom. At the same time, Christian culture bears an inherently supra-national character which will play a decisive role in our era in the task of bringing peoples together into one pan-human family.[16]

The embryonic constitution (Sections VII–XV) sketches out such matters as property rights, land ownership, industry, credit and banking arrangements, culture, science, health, education, law, state institutions and lastly, rights of humans and citizens. It suggests that this constitution would apply to all citizens of Great Russia,[17] thus implying that the nationalism of VSKhSON is a 'liberal' nationalism applying only to the Slav republics. It envisages a mixed economy, with state, communal and personal property. Most commercial and industrial activity would, it seems, be of a co-operative kind, while the land would be divided into personal farming, communal and state-owned land. The state would retain control of energy, mining, transport and military industry, while at the same time monopolising credit, foreign trade and having extensive powers of *dirigiste* planning. The Programme suggests the adoption of a gold standard, but would apparently allow substantial private banking and credit institutions. Private schooling, university autonomy and private health provision should be allowed, together with a 'free' press, subject to the law.

A constitutional lawyer would perhaps be struck by the very brief sections on law and state matters, which follow a section on religion and the church, but which precede the sparsely articulated section on rights of humans and citizens. While trial by jury is demanded, we are told that 'judges must possess moral authority, which gives them the moral right to dispense justice'.[18] The powers of the Head of State seem to be almost monarchical, as he can appoint or remove the entire administration and is supreme commander of the armed forces. He can also appoint the Prime Minister and 'on his recommendation' members of the Cabinet. However, we are told (ambiguously) that the government must be 'responsible to the Popular Assembly and the Head of State'.[19] Western observers will perhaps be forgiven for questioning the workability of such sloppy formulation. We are informed that 'Points of contention between the government and a corporation, the government and an individual, a corporation and an individual and between corporations must be resolved by a Constitutional Court.'[20] However, the composition of this Constitutional Court and the manner of its appointment are not clarified. Nevertheless, this document does allow for the protection of 'the rights of humans and citizens' by recourse to courts of law.

In general, this document reflects the traditions in which it was formulated. It reflects the low status of constitutional law in the USSR today and the internal inconsistencies of constitutional provisions which are to be found in the 1936 (and the 1977) Constitutions of the USSR. It mixes political manifesto with constitutional law, even stating in its preamble that in order 'to achieve complete victory, the people must have an underground liberation army which would overthrow the dictatorship and destroy the oligarchy's security forces.'[21] It was presumably for this clause that the Soviet regime imposed exceptionally heavy penalities, particularly on Ogurtsov, after the group's arrest and trial in 1967. After the arrest of VSKhSON, any aspiration to political conspiracy by Russian nationalists remained dormant for many years, but the themes and ideologies adumbrated by VSKhSON continued to have many followers. These themes seem to be:

- a disillusionment with the record of Communism in the USSR and internationally;
- a lack of interest in Marxism-Leninism;
- a suspicion of Western democracy and capitalism combined with a marked lack of knowledge of, and sophistication about, political science in general and Western political systems in particular;
- an insistence on the need for government which is 'moral' and supported by a consensus, so that party politics is ruled out;
- a strongly religious flavour, with Orthodoxy predominating;
- a preference for strong authority and a powerful Head of State; and
- neo-Slavophile utopianism which predominates over political pragmatism.

As John Dunlop has summarised, the 1960s and 1970s saw a prolonged development of 'an ascendant neo-Slavophilism'.[22] In 1964 a group of Moscow students founded the 'Homeland' ('Rodina') society after making a pilgrimage to the ancient Russian towns of Zagorsk, Suzdal' and Vladimir. By 1965 the 'Rodina' society had 500 members. The year 1964 also saw the appearance of Andrei Tarkovsky's film *Andrey Rublev*, which dealt with the life of the great icon painter of the period of the Tartar yoke and the foundations of the Russian state and culture from the point of view of renascent Russian patriotism. By 1965 the All-Russian Society for the Preservation of Historical Monuments (VOOPIK) had 3 million members, with an estimated 7 million by the early 1970s. The All-Russian Society for the Protection of Nature boasted an even greater membership – over 19 million by the year 1971. The Russian Orthodox Church has a still broader base in Soviet society. One cannot fail to be impressed by these figures, which, for all their amorphous inscrutability, indicate a real and growing movement for national renewal which is based in the masses as well as the intelligentsia and which is genuinely felt and acted upon by the populace.

During the period 1967–70, neo-Slavophilism, provided it confined itself to cultural themes, was tolerated and even encouraged by the regime. The same years saw the revival of neo-Slavophilism in literature, with the publication of such works as Soloukhin's *Black Boards* and other 'countryside' themes (see Chapter 7). In 1971 some

50 million Soviet citizens (twice the number in 1964), visited ancient Russian towns and cultural centres for their holidays. This renewed interest showed itself in official journals such as *Molodaya Gvardiya* (1968–70), *Nash Sovremennik* (*Our Contemporary*) (1980–2) and in samizdat literature such as *Veche*, named after the ancient and supposedly democratic assembly in the city of Novgorod and which produced ten editions before its demise in 1974. After this date, the predominant trend in unofficial Russian nationalism seemed to become authoritarian rather than 'liberal'. I shall deal with the themes developed by the 'official' journals first.

By 1969 Stalinist and Russian-nationalist editors had joined forces in their shared opposition to Tvardovsky's *Novy Mir* and the liberal intelligentsia in general. In November 1969 eleven conservative writers blamed *Novy Mir* for its supposedly anti-patriotic and anti-Communist themes. This claim appeared in the form of a letter to the then conservative journal *Ogonyok* and it seems that it was a signal for the dismissal of Tvardovsky from the editorial board of *Novy Mir* and a purge of the editorial board in 1970. The present chief editor of *Molodaya Gvardiya*, Anatolii Ivanov, was among the signatories of that famous letter. In August 1970 an article by Sergei Semanov appeared, entitled 'Concerning values relative and eternal', which presaged an ultranationalist and Stalinist 'general line' for *Molodaya Gvardiya*. From 1970, then, an alliance between Russian nationalism and neo-Stalinism, which has been indicated above as a distinct possibility within the historical evolution of the Soviet system, was already emerging in a certain area of centrally published Soviet journals. It is rumoured that Brezhnev's chief ideologist Mikhail Suslov may have been the instigator of this trend, as he realised that Russian nationalism could perhaps be 'harnessed' to official ideology, that nationalism was a real and vital force within important sections of the armed forces and society, and that it could give life and moral content to a greatly enfeebled Marxist-Leninist theory.

Russian nationalist themes first appeared in *Molodaya Gvardiya* with articles by Mikhail Lobanov ('Educated shopkeepers') in April 1968, followed by Viktor Chalmaev's essay, ('Inevitability'), in September 1968. It may be significant that these essays appeared during the crisis in Czechoslovakia, where Dubček's Prague Spring had been provoked by the need for reform in the economy. The 'educated people' who put material or economic matters first were the target of Lobanov's attacks and it may be that Lobanov was acting as a mouthpiece for a regime which felt itself under fire from intellectuals such as Sinyavsky, Galanskov and others.[23] Lobanov, it seems, was articulating a populist initiative by the leadership to ally itself with 'simple Russians' against the Westernised and privileged intelligentisia.

The true source of Russian culture, said Lobanov, had always been the people (*narod*), whom he contrasted with the intelligentsia. The latter, it seemed, were always critical of everything Russian. They had the mentality of the *meshchanstvo*, the merchant stream of pre-revolutionary times, that is to say a narrow, money-grubbing attitude. The intelligentsia were guilty of an 'Americanisation' of the spirit, which emphasised rising standards of living above all else. These 'educated shopkeepers', as Lobanov called them, were becoming a mass phenomenon alien to the people and threatened to destroy the very foundations of national culture.[24] Their horizons were limited by a kind of bourgeois pettiness: 'They have a mini-language, mini-thoughts, mini-feelings', and sought to replace even the concept of the Motherland (*Rodina*) with the mini-ideal of material satiety, 'the pleasures of the stomach'.[25] Lobanov attacks the Americanisation of the spirit and supports in its place Russification. His prescription for policy is that the social orientation of the regime should be based on the common people, not the educated groups, that its aim should not be material prosperity alone and that its foreign policy should be based on Russification. He implies opposition to *détente* and Western influences in Russian life.

A subsequent article by Victor Chalmaev ('Inevitability') created a storm of controversy and developed many of Lobanov's themes still further. Chalmaev declared:

In the efforts of Peter I and Ivan the Terrible and in the attempts of the church reformers to modify for the good of the Motherland the Byzantine idea of the denial of the earthly world as man's greatest achievement, there is something majestic, which is an inspiration for our thought, too.[26]

Chalmaev saw the entire sweep of Russian history as a continuum. The awakening of Russian national consciousness found expression in the victories of Alexander Nevsky over the Teutonic Knights, of Prince Dmitry Donskoi over the Tartars at Kulikovo, of Peter the Great over the Swedes at Poltava, of Alexander I over the French at Borodino, of Stalin over the Germans at Stalingrad. Chalmaev predicted an impending new 'Stalingrad' for the Russian people, whose greatness passed from one stage to another by a series of crises or battles, by evolution or revolution. In this sense, Lenin is compared implicitly with one of the great anchorites of the church and the Soviet era is compared, on a continuum of historical events, with the consolidation of the Muscovite state or the reforms of Peter the Great. Like the reformers of the Russian Church such as Patriarch Nikon, or even the 'anchorite patriarch', St Sergius of Radonezh, the Communists had fired the imagination of the Russian people towards new achievements for their state and society.

Chalmaev's programme thus glosses over the militant atheism of Lenin and the abrupt historical discontinuity of 1917. The crucial continuity of the entire sweep of Russian history had been the power and glory of the Motherland (*Rodina*). It was essential, therefore, to oppose anyone who attacked the concept of the Motherland, and the struggle against these attacks was the 'historical inevitability of our time'.[27]

Chalmaevism became the object of a Central Committee investigation devoted to 'Young Guardism' and the editor-in-chief of *Molodaya Gvardiya*, Anatolii Nikonov, was fired. Chalmaev was also attacked in print by the Marxists, in particular by Dement'ev in *Novy Mir* and Alexander Yakovlev in *Literaturnaya Gazeta*. However, the dismissal of Nikonov and the attacks of the establishment had puzzling outcomes. For example, despite the sacking of Nikonov, *Molodaya Gvardiya* did not radically alter. Dement'ev and *Novy Mir*, however, were defeated and the entire editorial board changed. Yakovlev was banished for several years to an elegant exile as Soviet ambassador in Canada. The politics of these decisions can only be conjectured, but they strongly suggest that a section of the establishment was not at all opposed to the anti-Western Russian nationalism of Chalmaev. As Alexander Yanov summarises:

[Nikonov's] place was ultimately taken by his former deputy, Anatolii Ivanov, an even more faithful henchman of Chalmaev's. Brezhnev's patience continued to be tried by church bells and onion domes on TV. 'Chalmaevism' in poetry and prose continued to dominate *Molodaya Gvardiya* and a new magazine of Chalmaevist tendency, *Nash Sovremennik* appeared. Its editor-in-chief, Sergei Vikulov, did not even try to disguise this sympathies.[28]

Before we turn out attention to the progress and beliefs of *Nash Sovremennik* (*Our Contemporary*), it is necessary to investigate Alexander Yakovlev's famous article in *Literaturnaya Gazeta* of 15 November 1972, entitled 'Against anti-historicism'. Yakovlev became a member of the Politburo under Gorbachev. He is also the object of vicious attacks by the more extreme Russophiles of today, the notorious Pamyat' Society. Yakovlev's two-page article represented a well-thought out and systematic attack on Russophilism, which he detected in the arts, poetry, literature, historiography and even in *The Great Soviet Encyclopaedia*. Yakovlev stated quite clearly that there was a deviant ideology behind this trend and that it was reactionary in that it eulogised ways of life existing before the revolution.[29] He claimed that the Russophiles of today had attacked both Chernyshevsky and Lenin. Obviously this was a very serious charge from the then acting head of the Central Committee's Propaganda Department. Given the apparently orthodox Marxist position of Yakovlev's article, his subsequent demotion and appointment as ambassador in Canada is very odd. Powerful forces within the Brezhnev leadership, we conclude, must have been supporting the Russophiles. While Yakovlev was demoted, the editorial board of *Molodaya Gvardiya* remained virtually intact, and by the late 1980s the journal was described by Julia Wishnevsky (one of the West's leading experts on Russian nationalism) as 'a Stalinist and extreme Russian-nationalist Soviet monthly journal. . . . Indeed *Molodaya Gvardiya* seems to have assumed the role of opposition journal *par excellence vis-à-vis* the line of the present Soviet leadership.'[30]

During the last two years of Brezhnev's rule the journal of the RSFSR Writers' Union, *Nash Sovremennik*, published a series of articles with a strongly nationalist flavour. Issue 6 for 1981 even appeared with the motto 'Russia – my homeland' on the inside cover. The Russian Orthodox writer Soloukhin, author of such works as *Black Boards*, wrote some aphoristic remarks called 'Pebbles in the palm of the hand', among which he categorically stated his belief in the existence of God.[31] Vadim Kozhinov, writing in Issue 11 about the 600th anniversary in 1980 of the battle of Kulikovo, interpreted the battle as a triumph of the Russian state over the dark forces of the 'aggressive cosmopolitan armada'.[32] The term 'cosmopolitan' carries anti-Semitic overtones in Soviet writing. Sergei Semanov, writing in Issue 7 for 1981 reviewed a book about Trotsky, in which he castigated Trotsky's policies in respect of fomenting international revolution by force and his fanatically extreme plans for 'direction of labour' by a Party élite. Semanov referred to Trotsky as 'Bronshtein', drawing attention to his Jewishness. Trotsky had 'tried to support his belief in revolutionary war between Soviet Russia and international capitalism with practical actions. Thus in 1919 he recommended that 30,000 or 40,000 cavalry be sent to India.'[33] Surely this was an attack by implication of the recent invasion of Afghanistan? Semanov was also perhaps attacking the Andropovites, who at that time appeared to be candidates for power. As John Dunlop points out, Andropov himself was not entirely Russian and seemed to stand for labour discipline at home and an aggressive foreign policy.

Other articles in *Nash Sovremennik* at the time included strong criticism of alcoholism, the break-up of the family and high divorce rates. Vasilii Belov produced articles about traditional peasant life and customs, including the baptism of infants and converts. The illustrations in the journal were frequently patriotic ones: birch-groves and pictures of the Russian countryside of Yesenin-like nostalgia for peasant Rus'. Soloukhin attacked the destruction of churches and their use as museums of atheism and planetaria. Articles which strongly attacked environmental pollution appeared frequently.

However, in January 1982 Mikhail Suslov died. The belief that Suslov could have been the *de facto* protector of the nationalists is strengthened by the fact that immediately after Suslov's death, the official journal *Kommunist* attacked Soloukhin for his tendency to 'flirt with little god'.[34] The next issue of *Nash Sovremennik* was shorn of its slogan Rossiya – Rodina Moya, but Issue 3 contained another unrepentantly religious 'pebble' from Soloukhin. Issue 4 contained the slogan again, but Issue 5 appeared with a considerably changed editorial board. Vikulov was retained as editor-in-chief, apparently having been compelled to apologise on behalf of Soloukhin in the pages of *Kommunist*. However, the first deputy editor, Seleznev and another deputy editor, Ustinov, were removed. The editorial board had five new appointees. Clearly the journal was under attack, for it had articulated views which were out of favour with the Andropov leadership. These views were broadly related to Westernisation, the environment, the attitude towards 'wars of national liberation' and Soviet adventures abroad, religious freedom and the record of Marxist materialism, the restoration of peasant life and the role of Russia within the Soviet Union as a whole. The nationalists had been strong enough in the later Brezhnev years to have the support of the Party Second Secretary, Mikhail Suslov, who had apparently sensed the weakness of traditional Marxism among the 'masses' and had experimented with a form of 'national Bolshevism' based on an alliance between Party conservatives and Russian nationalists. *Nash Sovremennik*, Issue 12 for 1982 welcomed the new General Secretary coldly and published some effusive praise for the departed Brezhnev.

If the era of the nationalists seemed to have passed, they had nevertheless raised issues which captured the minds and hearts of many people and the questions posed by them were now very firmly on the political agenda for the 1980s. However, the evolution of both 'official' and dissident nationalists during this period seemed to be away from the liberal nationalism of earlier times and towards a more extreme kind of chauvinism and anti-Semitism. This evolution is illustrated by the fate of the journal *Veche* and its successors, and the emergence, after 1985, of the famous Pamyat' Society, which will be outlined in Chapter 8.

NOTES

1. M. Heller and A. Nekrich, *Utopia in Power: A history of the USSR from 1917 to the present* (London, Hutchinson, 1986), p. 632.
2. Ibid., p. 695.
3. Ibid., p. 644.
4. A. D. Sakharov, 'Trevozhnoe Vremia', in *Novoe Russkoe Slovo*, 14 June 1980.

7 The Brezhnev years, II: The 'countryside writers'

Literature has always played a special part in the formulation of social and political thought in Russia and the USSR. The close relationship between literature and politics has both advantages and disadvantages. For while literature may be studied with profit in order to follow trends in intellectual matters and to gain insight into Soviet conditions, which would otherwise be unavailable to Western scholars, as a result writers acquire enormous importance in Soviet life and this encourages them towards a didactic role which is at the same time ambiguous.

In Russia, literature is often used as a means of political opposition[1] and 'cultural politics' often lies at the heart of national decision-making. This fact encourages famous writers to take a prominent part in opinion formation, while at the same time the reader is not certain about the dividing line between fact and fiction in their works, between poetic licence and ideological innuendo. What is the dividing line between an imaginative work of literature which features real historical figures and genuine history? If one reads Mikhail Sholokhov's *Quiet Don* or *Virgin Soil Upturned*, for example, the answer to this question remains obscure.

Similarly, political pressure is often applied in Soviet literary life, from the dismissal of 'liberal' editors of journals (Tvardovsky) to interference with literary texts. It is thought that Khrushchev successfully persuaded Sholokhov to change the ending of his sequel to *Virgin Soil Upturned* in order to make it more compatible with his version of Soviet history in the aftermath of the xxth Congress.[2]

However, despite the many ambiguities and methodological difficulties involved, a close study of serious Soviet literature remains an indispensable necessity in Soviet conditions. The 'countryside writers' (derevenshchiki) are no exception to this rule.

In the 1950s Khrushchev encouraged writers such as Ovechkin and Dorosh[3] to turn their attention to the life of the neglected Russian peasantry. These early works, often referred to as *Ocherki* ('sketches'), inspired a whole stream of rural themes in Russian and Soviet writing which continues to this day. Perhaps the most influential single work in this genre was Solzhenitsyn's short story, 'Matryona's Home', in which he explored an aspect of the life of the common Russian villager which is far removed from the compulsory 'socialist realism' of Communist ideology. Matryona herself, as mentioned in Chapter 5, was a deeply religious old lady, whose qualities are hardly those of the ideal Communist shock-worker. True, she has always worked hard for the community, but her chief merits are Christian humility and an ability to get on with the task in hand, often despite the activities of the authorities. Her major contribution is that she is 'that one righteous person without whom, as the saying goes, no village can stand. Nor any city. Nor the world itself.'[4]

As Vladimir Soloukhin says in one of his delightful sketches from *A Walk in Rural Russia*, the countryside writers were in effect 'wanderers returning to our native land'.[5] D. C. Gillespie lists the names of the major countryside writers as follows: S. Zalygin, V. Tendryakov and G. Troepol'sky in the 1950s, followed by V. Belov, B. Mozhaev, F. Abramov, V. Astaf'ev, Ye. Nosov, V. Likhonosov, V. Lichutin, V. Soloukhin and V. Shukshin in the late 1960s and 1970s and places special emphasis on the work of V. Rasputin in the 1970s and 1980s. In this chapter I propose to focus on Abramov, Belov, Soloukhin, Shukshin and especially Rasputin, since in my view, these writers in particular illustrate themes that are recurrent among Russian nationalist writers. Their works are also pervaded with concerns which have little to do with the 'official' doctrines of socialist realism. In the words of Professor Geoffrey Hosking, they are generally *Beyond Socialist Realism*,[6] which is also the title of Hosking's pioneering work on this subject, to which I am much indebted.

The countryside writers are concerned above all with historical re-evaluations. They critically investigate that politically distorted and socially disrupted experience which transformed the Russian countryside during the Stalinist collectivisation/industrialisation drive after 1929. They seek to assess the mortal wounds of the Second World War, to understand the values of the older generation in its suffering and its victory and to counterpose these values with those of the younger generation, which are judged to be comparatively superficial and damaging, both morally and ecologically. The countryside writers are generally 'mature' writers, full of psychological insight and true to the complexity of life, often rough and ready in externals, yet internally probing, metaphysically rich and often disturbing, even apocalyptic and pessimistic in tone. They are indeed far removed from the compulsory optimism of Soviet socialist realism. As Gillespie summarises, both neo-Stalinist and countryside writers 'are guided by conservatism and chauvinism in their cultural tastes and political ideals and it is significant that, unlike their more adventurous and questioning fellow writers of the "youth prose" movement, none of them have forsaken their native land.[7]

Perhaps the father of the *derevenshchiki*, a man of great, gaunt, morally elevated stature, the veritable Aeschylus of Russian village prose, was Fydor Abramov, whose four-volume *Brat'ya i Sestry* (*Brothers and Sisters*) tells the story of a northern Russian village from the war years to the 1970s.[8] At the Sixth Writers Conference in 1976, Abramov summarised:

And so today, when the village is living out its last days, we look with particular rapt attention at the type of person created by it, we look at our fathers and mothers, our grandfathers and grandmothers. . . . The extensive discussion in our literature about people of the preceding generations is an attempt to appreciate and retain their moral experience, the moral potential, the moral forces, that brought Russia back from the brink during its gravest ordeals.[9]

Abramov draws realistic pictures of the life of a collective farm and seems to blame human nature almost as much as the insensitivity of the authorities for the neglect and poverty which typified the Russian villages. He is less optimistic than Soloukhin about the effect of administrative changes, such as the salaries and pensions which were introduced by Khrushchev to replace the Stalinist 'workday' system. However, he praises the women of the kolkhoz for their tenacity in the face of back-breaking labour and the shortage of manpower caused by the war and he upholds the 'small deeds' of the kolkhoz chairman who saves the winter fodder by taking a personal initiative.[10]

The cataclysmic disruptions of Soviet life and its very rapid industrialisation have clearly created a kind of schizophrenia among the mass of the Soviet public, for the peasant origins are often very recent.

Professor Hosking quotes a very good example of this problem in Yury Kazakov's story *The Smell of Bread* (*Zapakh Khleba*), in which a daughter who had lived for decades in town returns to her native village to sort out her mother's estate after the funeral. At first, the relaxing peace of rural Russia is a welcome holiday for the daughter; but she breaks down at the sight of her mother's grave and sobs uncontrollably when the smell of home-made bread in her mother's house reminds her of the life – and the soil – which she has for so long neglected.[11] As Belov relates:

Although we leave our native parts, we return to them again and again, however susceptible we may be to the charms of other abodes. For one cannot live cut off from one's roots; a human being cannot be happy without that corner of the greater homeland that cradled him . . . the Motherland is felicity, a blessing never to be renounced, however rigorous and ungentle she might be.[12]

Very much the same sentiment has been displayed by a whole generation of Russians in the 1960s and subsequently. Soloukhin related that he was literally amazed at the reaction of the reading public to *A Walk in Rural Russia*, based on a holiday he took in the rural Vladimir region. A similarly enthusiastic reception greeted his Russia-centred *Letters from a Russian Museum* and the novel about the discovery of ancient Russian icons, *Black Boards*.

This very great nostalgia for Mother Russia is perhaps expressed most poignantly in an interview given by Vasily Shukshin whose family home was in the remote Altai region of Siberia: 'It is hard to comprehend,' said Shukshin,

but whenever anyone mentions the Altai, it makes me start, an immediate flame of feeling licks my heart, to the point of pain; and in my memory, invariably, are those . . . beds [known locally as *polati*]. When I die, if I'm conscious, at the last moment I will think of my mother, of the children and of the place where I was born, that lives on in me. There is nothing dearer to me.[13]

Shukshin also illustrates another abiding theme of the countryside writers, namely a concern for the protection of the environment and the preservation of tradition. In his film *Pechki-Lavochki* (*Stove-Benches*), Shukshin tried to depict the life of the Siberian peasant in the days of his grandfather, while at the same time suggesting that modern two-storey brick buildings in the Siberian villages are ugly and poorly constructed in comparison with the 'convenient, under-standable and indispensable village houses of the past'.[14]

The ecological theme is perhaps most strongly pursued in the writings of Rasputin, such as *Farewell to Matyora*, which is dealt with in detail below, and in his direct action to save the waters of Lake Baikal. The ecological issue is now very high on the political agenda of the Soviet Union, from debates about the proposed diversion of Siberian rivers to the arid lands of Central Asia, to the disaster surrounding the Aral Sea. The Chernobyl nuclear catastrophe figures strongly in the nation's consciousness and provides a major platform against the authorities for many critical organisations, such as Belorussian and Ukrainian nationalists. The countryside writers dwell deeply on this theme, often symbolically as in Soloukhin's story of the nightmarish elk-hunt, 'A Winter's Day'. After pursuing their wounded quarry over the snow for several kilometres on foot, Soloukhin's hunting party find the stricken elk and cut steaks from its corpse, a meal which subsequently makes them sick. They intended to go back in the morning to claim the rest of the meat, but during the early hours of the morning they hear the sound of 'the hungry, yellow-toothed wolves . . . gathering for the feast'. Destruction of nature leads to sickness, corruption and waste. There is a topical comment here, for poaching within the USSR is rapidly acquiring the dimensions of a natural disaster.[15] In more general terms, the countryside writers have definitely cast doubt on the naïve optimism of earlier Soviet generations, who believed fervently in the possibility of man's subjugation of nature.

Another near-universal aspect of the work of the countryside writers is their suspicion of women's liberation. This, I suspect, is an extremely emotive issue in contemporary Soviet life and it produces surprisingly strong reactions in writers such as Soloukhin and Belov. In his story 'The guests were arriving at the *dacha*', Soloukhin is at his most intolerant:

A woman's strength is not in her mathematical abilities or trade-union activity. Her strength is in her femininity and only that. . . . But the part women have played in social life, military exploits, art, now, that's a question that has not been sufficiently studied. . . . What about the role of women in the appearance in the world of Dante's *Divine Comedy* or *The Sistine Madonna*, *War and Peace*, Beethoven's 'Moonlight Sonata' and the Sixth Symphony? No research has been done and no discoveries have been made in that area. Countess Walewska did not have to be a politician to get Napoleon to create the Grand Duchy of Warsaw, she simply had to be Countess Walewska. And now they've arrived at total equality. And what happens? Our houses are no longer homes and there are more divorces than marriages.[16]

The worrying theme of divorce and the fate of the children of one-parent families, surfaces again and again in the writings of the *derevenshchiki*. Belov depicts a heart-rending scene of a divorced father who is in league with his former mother-in-law, in order to enable him to meet his daughter on a regular basis. The granny takes care of the little girl while the former wife goes out to work, often cursing the child as she goes for causing some kind of delay. Zorin, the father, describes the scene from his strategically placed telephone-box and comments acidly on his former wife's 'thick make-up, pasted on as usual'. The little girl is united briefly with her father in a scene which contains all the sentimentality of Dostoevsky's stories of neglected children. ' "Daddy, you won't go away any more, will you?" she said, slowly quietening. And again he pressed closely that one faithful, helpless, dear bundle of life.'[17]

It may be detected in the writings of the *derevenshchiki* that their hostility to women's liberation contains at least two different points of view. The emotive and primitive reactions of Russia's challenged menfolk is predominant, with especially serious reservations and vituperation reserved for the subject of abortion.[18] However, Soloukhin's criticisms are also marked by a Christian spirit of forgiveness and charity towards women, while the writings of Rasputin generally avoid the polemics of Belov and Astaf'ev. In general, Valentin Rasputin's life and work form a very good base from which to study the ideology of the *derevenshchiki*, especially in his mature work published after 1970.

Valentin Rasputin was born in 1937 in the Siberian village of Ust-Uda on the river Angara, between the cities of Bratsk and Irkutsk. He studied at the University of Irkutsk, where he has lived in recent years. His stories include *Money for Maria* (1967), *Borrowed Time* (1970), *Downstream, Upstream* (1972), *Live and Remember* (1974), *Farewell to Matyora* (1976) and *Fire* (1985). Rasputin's favourite authors are apparently Dostoevsky and Ivan Bunin,[19] showing an abiding concern for the Russian and Siberian countryside, while at the same time developing psychological depth and strongly apocalyptic undertones in recent years. When questioned about the anti-industrialisation themes of *Farewell to Matyora*, Rasputin responded by saying, 'an artist is an artist only because he sees things not as he wishes to seem them but as they are.'[20] He is a man who stands for continuity with nineteenth-century Russian literary traditions, concerning himself with 'eternal' questions. From Dostoevsky, Rasputin inherits an understanding of 'underground man' and an apocalyptic feeling for Russia's purpose in an apparently morally degenerate world. However, unlike Dostoevsky, Rasputin seems to be almost wholly pessimistic about possible regeneration: a feeling of imminent catastrophe permeates much of Rasputin's work.

Rasputin equates truly Russian moral values with those of the village and possibly the Orthodox Church, although his work also contains elements of a kind of pre-Christian Russian naturalism. The village, however, is dying and the process of assimilation of adaptation to urban life is a painful one for the villagers. In the story *Money for Maria*, the hero Kuz'ma sets off for the town, where he hopes to get financial help from his brother, as if he were going to a foreign land. In *Borrowed Time*, the family of Anna Stepanovna, the 80-year-old grandmother who is on her deathbed, is already permeated with 'urbanism'. There are five children in this family. Anna lives with her son Mikhail and his wife Nadezhda, but Mikhail has forsaken agriculture for the local sawmill where he can earn higher wages than before. He drinks habitually and spends much of the time during the four-day action of the novel in a drinking bout. The older sister Varvara is a 'rural' character with a large family. She is provincial, poor, stupid, gullible but with the redeeming feature of being fecund. The second brother, Il'ya is neither a peasant nor a convincing 'urbanite'. He is a lorry driver who has been involved in military training in the north of Russia and a weak, vacillating character, lacking convictions or opinions of his own. Il'ya is depicted in Gogolian terms as a person who 'seems to have lost his face at cards'. The youngest sister and the darling of her mother is Tanya. She is a true 'urbanite' who never arrives at her mother's deathbed and her perpetual absence combined with the reiterated maternal expectation of her arrival is a masterstroke by Rasputin. As Gillespie puts it, 'Tanya's absence is never explained, but requires no comment.'[21] The most sophisticated of the sisters is Lyusya, whose speech is grammatically perfect as is her fashionable black dress and her high moral tone, especially when berating the others for their failings in dealing with the old lady. However, she does not herself have to look after the terminally ill mother; nor does she have any children of her own and being without issue she is, Rasputin implies, without purpose.

Rasputin's story depicts the tensions within this fissiparous Russian family, focusing particularly on Lyusya, with whom Rasputin clearly has some kind of emotional involvement. He analyses her thoughts and movements closely and observes that 'With family, close family, one should behave somewhat differently than with others, but she [Lyusya] did not feel any such particular and intimate kinship with them, which made her annoyed with herself.'[22] There is some hope for Lyusya, Rasputin seems to be saying, but in the end she fails to grasp that essential link between her rural past, her family, her nation and that which will alone make sense of her life and its moral and eschatalogical purpose. Lyusya wanders off during one of those interminable days when the family is waiting for their mother to die. Lyusya sees her old haunts, the scenes of her childhood, notes the neglect of many formerly cultivated fields and senses a kind of paradise lost: 'It seemed that the clock had been turned back because she, Lyusya, had forgotten something very precious and necessary, without which life cannot be lived.'[23]

However, Lyusya cannot grasp what is essential. Her mind and her reason finally gain the upper hand and as the old lady seems to recover, Lyusya and the others leave the family house. The old lady dies the following night, alone. Anna's death is also the death of the Russian village and with it, Rasputin suggests, the death of all real values and meaning for mankind. This, surely is the significance of the Russian-language title, which has the apocalyptic feeling of the 'last time' (*Poslednyi Srok*).

While they are waiting for the old lady to die, the men of the household are getting drunk in a bath house on vodka which had been purchased for the 'wake'. A drunken conversation between

Stepan Kharchevnikov (a villager) and the brothers helps to clarify Rasputin's views on many subjects. Countryfolk, the moujik, the traditional *babushka*, are the salt of the earth and no Russian should be ashamed of these appelations. Russian peasants, particularly the women of the village, embodied many of the finest values of Russian culture and possessed a life-force and a coherent world outlook which was spiritually valuable. They served heroically on the home front during the Second World War, saving the Motherland for her eventual victory. The greatness of Russian women lay in their capacity for work, sacrifice and childbearing. Kharchevnikov articulates a view of contemporary women which would indeed be offensive to modern feminists: he says that today's women, in contrast to the older generation are too selfish, ambitious and skinny.[24] 'These young city women, well, they're all like wind-up dolls, they're all so much alike you can't tell one from the other. They weren't born, they were made in a factory.'

Before the children leave, Anna tries to warn them about the bleak future which she believes awaits them:

I will die, but you have your whole lives still ahead of you. So keep in touch, go and visit each other. You're not strangers, you know, you have the same mother and father. . . . And come back here too once in a while, this is where your roots lie.[25]

Anna's death is depicted as natural, and in some sense blessed, in comparison with what (we infer) may await modern Russians and the human race as a whole. Rasputin seems to be pessimistic about the future and this fact imparts a sense of desperation in his search for the past as a means of making sense of the present.

The title of Rasputin's next story, *Downstream, Upstream (Vniz i vverkh po techeniyu)* seems once again to reflect the desperation of man's frustrated, perhaps ultimately fruitless, searchings. In this short novel, Viktor (the hero) goes back to his former village in Siberia which has been drowned in the development of a vast new hydroelectric scheme. The trees, we are told, seem to groan with pain under the water, while Russian stoves, too heavy to transport, lie about on the shore. Their abandoned hulks represent the loss of that family warmth which the stoves originally symbolised. Viktor remembers his childhood and the sound of the river Angara cracking up as its ice melted in the spring, a sound which somehow summarised and personified the majesty of a reawakened nature. Today, in contrast, the vast new artificial lake seems to push back the shores of his home country, the land which is surely a symbol of human life. Viktor is gloomy, pessimistic about man's conquest of nature and no longer immediately recognises his parental home. He is not at all at ease in the resettled village and the surrounding countryside, where he is regarded as an outcast, a failure whom the villagers suspect of coming back only 'to lick his wounds', and because, in all probability, he has nowhere else to go. The hero, a writer, is under pressure from the authorities because his characters are too introspective and fail the test of socialist realism and the cult of the positive builder of Communism. However, Viktor is certain that art and literature cannot lie: 'Nature and art,' he says, 'are perhaps the only things capable of resisting today's pace of life and happily, just like a hundred or two hundred years ago, can instil purely human, and not just professional, emotions and qualities.'[26]

A very similar view of man's attempts to conquer and use nature is to be found in *Farewell to Matyora* (1976). Three generations of one family, the Pinigins, live on the island of Matyora which is about to be flooded as a result of a gigantic hydroelectric scheme. The grandmother, Darya, is sceptical of change, but her son Pavel and grandson Andrey seem to believe in Communist construction. Pavel, it is true, entertains some doubts about the wisdom of the authorities but his son is an uncritical believer in progress:

You shouldn't give in to fate, you should hold it in your hands. . . . Man can do so much now that there aren't words to describe it. He has so much power at his disposal it fair takes your breath away. He can do just what he wants.[27]

In answer to such claims, Darya replies:

You want to jump out of your human skin. It's never been done, lad. You'll only tear yourself to bits and wear yourself out for nothing. And you won't manage what you set out to do. While you're huffing and puffing yourself up to make your great leap, death will creep up and won't let you out of its grip. People have forgotten their place under God, that's what I am saying. We're no better than those who went before us.[28]

However, the project goes ahead, with the authorities firmly in command. They insist on the 'decanting' of the inhabitants to an 'agro-urban' complex in the neighbourhood which is of modern, shoddy construction. Despite encountering various degrees of resistance from the inhabitants the authorities destroy the village cemetery and try to cut down the great tree which dominates the island. One villager, Petrukha, burns down his own house, which is a kind of 'listed' building, in order to claim his insurance. Petrukha, Pavel and the local Party official Vorontsov, all support the scheme which they regard as progressive. But Darya, Sima and an elderly man called Bogodul, all refuse to move. Darya visits the cemetery on the eve of its destruction and hears the voices of her ancestors calling her. In her turn, she comes to an important conclusion, namely, 'Truth is in remembering. He who has no memory has no life.'

A few hours before the flooding is due to commence, Vorontsov, Pavel and Petrukha set off in a motor boat to pick up those still left on the island, such as Darya, Nastasya, Bogodul, Sima and Katerina. However, the boat is defective, losing its power and rudder and drifts helplessly in the fog, surrounded by darkness and the misty, formless waters. The last survivors await their inevitable end, accompanied by a mysterious spirit, the *Khozyain* of the island. Is there a trace of animism and anthropomorphism in Rasputin's work? As Gillespie summarises, the typically ambiguous ending of Rasputin's story symbolises a world which is left hanging in the balance, caught between stability and catastrophe.[29]

Thus we can see that the optimism, the concept of the 'radiant future' of Communism, is markedly absent from Rasputin's work. Rasputin's pessimism may reflect a peculiarly Soviet experience of modernisation, in which huge administrative investments were put into place very rapidly in order to carry out technically ambitious schemes. It was the Stalinist tradition of the First 5-Year Plan, the belief that there were 'no fortresses which Bolsheviks could not storm', which provided the background to much Soviet industry and development. One cannot deny the great achievements, but they were nevertheless marred by falsification of statistics, misinformation and propaganda, within a political system which had little or no democratic content or even adequate technical support. The Soviet system is trying desperately to unravel its chaotic and arbitrary past, to come to terms with what happened and to try to ensure its survival in our dynamic world. One possible response to the rediscovery of the Stalinist past had been to question its validity in its entirety and to demand the recovery of a (probably idealised) and largely agrarian past.

The countryside writers have been criticised in the Soviet press for their tendency to write about old women, and they are prone to clichés such as 'eternal, national values', 'the truly Russian spirit' and so on. As Fyodor Abramov said in a speech to the Sixth Writers Conference mentioned above:

We have talked a lot lately about the conservation of our natural environment and . . . our material culture. Is it not time we showed the same energy and determination in the matter of preserving the eternal treasures of our spiritual culture?[30]

However, the attempt to found all morality on 'the eternal treasures of our spiritual culture' (that is, the culture of the Russian village and

Orthodoxy), must tend to lead to pessimistic conclusions in an age of urban dwelling. This incipient pessimism may be found in two other works of Rasputin, *Live and Remember* and *Fire*. Both stories deal in particular with the relationship of the individual to his or her society and echo the concern shown by nineteenth-century Slavophiles about the preservation of *sobornost*, the organic community of the Russian village.

In *Live and Remember* the deserter Andrei Gus'kov returns illegally to his native area, after demonstrating his inherent irresponsibility en route by an apparently adulterous relationship with a handicapped woman. He relies on his legal wife Nastyona to supply him with food and even weapons, thus involving her in systematic deception and theft. Andrei represents the masculine principle, assaulting nature and sometimes killing without cause. Like Anna's children in *Borrowed Time*, Andrei denies his heritage and dissociates himself from the coming victory of his country. He turns his back on the concept of motherhood, causing the suicide of his pregnant wife. The innocent Nastyona, representing nature, or the feminine principle, is therefore under threat and is ultimately destroyed. While not idealising the character of the villagers, Rasputin portrays the dangers of isolating oneself from truth, family, community and nation. Andrei is an outcast (*izgoi*) of traditional Slavophile ideology. Although he escapes retribution for his desertion in a legal sense, he is spiritually dead, being forced to hide in a cave on Kamenny (Stone) Island. He returns symbolically and literally to the Stone Age, where he has no remaining past, present, nor (we assume) any future. As Gillespie summarises:

The story's title could serve as a central motif for all of Rasputin's writing; it is a warning to society that the past, the community's roots and the sources of its identity and the lessons the individual learns in childhood, are only to be forsaken at the peril of man losing his humanity, his soul.[31]

Rasputin's latest story *Fire* seems to suggest that the village community, already incipiently criticised in *Live and Remember*, may be dying. The story, published in *Nash Sovremennik* in 1985, tells of a timber-settlement named Sosnovka, which has taken the place of another submerged village in Siberia with the more 'natural' name of Yegorovka. It is the story of a kind of bastard neo-village and analyses the strange characters who are attracted to such a place. These characters included the ruffian Savely, who has lost a hand in an industrial accident, and the villainous Sashka Devyatyi. These are tough, hard men somehow deformed and ready to loot and feather their own nests if the occasion presents itself. Rasputin comments that one 'could not diagnose at all' (*ne raspoznat'*) either what went on in such men's souls, or even to whom these souls belonged.[32]

The hero of the story is the law-abiding Ivan Petrovich, the man who tries to save the supply barns of the settlement when they catch fire in the early spring. He describes the pathetic attempts of the foreman to take remedial action while the local inhabitants loot, get drunk and murder an older man, Misha Khampo, who catches them in the act of looting the burning buildings. At the end of this marvellously constructed story, Ivan Petrovich leaves his family and the settlement. He is depicted totally alone, walking away from it all, and in Rasputin's words, also from himself. He is last seen as it were from a distance, despairing of finding his home. No land is homeless, says Rasputin, but the surrounding Siberian landscape remained silent, neither meeting that lonely figure, nor accompanying him. In this latest story from Rasputin we see the stark despair of a man who is still searching for his homeland, the 'real' Russia.

Fire may reflect in particular the pervasive corruption of the 'years of stagnation' under Brezhnev, which were especially disfigured in the early 1980s by economic crimes on a grand scale. However, like all Rasputin's themes, this one has universal significance, reflecting the loss of the sense of community and the rise of possessive individualism in communities of both East and West. Rasputin's didactic writing, sombre and serious, is the work of a man who believes in the role of literature as an educator of the emotions, among which he believes the capacity for repentance to be particularly important. Rasputin stands very much in the tradition of Russian Orthodox Christianity, but there are at the same time traces of animism in his writings which perhaps stem from an earlier tradition of Russian folk-culture. He always leaves a great deal unsaid and thus he emphasises the irrational and unpredictable element in human life. Rasputin prefers the short story (*povest'*) to the larger novel and the ambiguous ending to the moralistic epigram. Finally, there is an apocalyptic, even macropolitical, dimension to Rasputin's works, as there is in Dostoevsky and one hopes that Rasputin the artist will not be superseded at any stage by Rasputin the political commentator. In this context, the support of Rasputin for the extreme Russian nationalism of the Pamyat' Society has been something of a shock and a disappointment to his many admirers.[33] The heartfelt and profoundly comprehensible nationalism of the countryside school of writers should not obscure for readers their occasionally excessive fear of the modern world, their tendency to idealise the often brutal past, or their incipient chauvinism, all of which are much more evident when these writers articulate their political views and stray from their literary vocations.

Apart from a few stylised and unconvincing examples, a genuine literature of the Soviet industrial working class does not, as yet, exist.

The *derevenshchiki* represent a very significant development in Soviet and Russian literature, since they are focusing on their own society as it is and was, while clearly abandoning the compulsory optimism and artificial enthusiasms of socialist realism. The Motherland is their focus and they have seemingly turned their backs on the Communist millennium and foreign 'wars of national liberation'. They are searching for their real roots in the native soil (*pochva*) and their national and cultural heritage. They are truthful in their nostalgia and nostalgic in their ideology. They are wholly comprehensible in their concerns, since they deal with the cataclysmic effects of a radical rural and social transformation and the rediscovery of a falsified national history. Particularly in the work of Valentin Rasputin we sometimes see literature of universal relevance and international stature. The literature of the *derevenshchiki* is often the literature of truth, but it is only the literature of new beginnings, expressing a deeply felt nationalist ideology which is at the same time genuine in a sense in which official ideology no longer is, nor ever again can be.

NOTES

1. A. Solzhenitsyn, *The First Circle* in *Sobranie Sochinenii* (Vol. 4, Frankfurt, Possev, 1970), p. 503.
2. M. Sholokhov, *Virgin Soil Upturned*, 2 vols (Moscow, Progress, 1979).
3. P. Carden and G. Zakulin, Papers, in R. Freeborn, R. Milner-Gulland and C. Ward (eds), *Russian and Soviet Literature* (Cambridge, Mass., Columbus Slavic Publishers, 1976).
4. A. Solzhenitsyn, *Stories and Prose Poems* (London, The Bodley Head, 1971), p. 54.
5. V. Soloukhin, *A Walk in Rural Russia* (London, Hodder & Stoughton, 1966), p. 34.
6. G. Hosking, *Beyond Socialist Realism* (London, Granada, Elek, 1980).
7. D. C. Gillespie, *Valentin Rasputin and Soviet Russian Village Prose* (London, Modern Humanities Research Association, 1986), p. 10.
8. F. Abramov, *Brat'ya i Sestry* (Moscow, Sovietskaya Rossiya, 1987).
9. Quoted in D. C. Gillespie, op.cit., p. 11.
10. F. Abramov, *The New Life: A day on a collective farm* (New York, Grove, 1963).
11. Quoted in G. Hosking, *Beyond Socialist Realism*, op.cit., p. 52.
12. V. Belov, *Morning Rendezvous* (Moscow, Raduga, 1983), p. 208.
13. V. Shukshin, *Articles* (Moscow, Raduga, 1986), p. 218.
14. Ibid., pp. 219–20.
15. V. Soloukhin, *Scenes from Russian Life* (London, Peter Owen, 1988), p. 150.
16. Ibid., p. 159.
17. V. Belov, *Morning Rendezvous*, op.cit., p. 280.
18. V. Soloukhin, *Scenes from Russian Life*, op.cit., p. 169.
19. *Voprosy Literatury*, 9 (1976), p. 145.

8 The road to Pamyat'

It has already been noticed that nationalism is a complex, Janus-like phenomenon. In the early nineteenth century, a cultural-philosophical Slavophilism with strongly religious (Orthodox) overtones merged into a more aggressive ethno-cultural Panslavism where Orthodoxy was seen as an attribute of nationality. In the early twentieth century, the parties of the Russian Dumas indicated at least a four-way split between neo-Slavophile Octobrists, nationalists, rightists (*Pravye*) and the Union of the Russian People. In terms of the typology suggested by A. D. Smith,[1] there was a preservation nationalism in certain sections of the Petersburg bureaucracy, while that of Stolypin and the Octobrists may be seen as a renewal nationalism. To the right of them one sees the prestige nationalism of the Union of the Russian People, with its paramilitary Black Hundreds and the lunatic theories of the *Protocols of the Elders of Zion*.

The Russian nationalism of today is no less complex and may be discerned in literary movements and 'cultural politics' as well as the samizdat journals of the 1970s and 1980s and the embryonic political associations of the era of Gorbachev. In 1989 no really clear political groupings, still less parties, have emerged within the newly elected Congress of People's Deputies, although in the nature of things such groupings may be expected in the course of time. Nevertheless, a chronological survey of events in the intellectual history of nationalism from the early 1970s does help to establish currents of thought and directions of development.

By the early 1970s, the liberal, religious nationalism of Solzhenitsyn was clearly a dissident variety. 'Young Guardism', or 'Chalmaevism' had an ambiguous status and may have had some kind of following in the Soviet establishment. While attacks on 'Zionism' were officially approved, the anti-Semitic extremism of Fetisov and others seemed in the West to be a lunatic fringe, scarcely worthy of attention by serious scholars. However, over twenty years (1970–90), the stream of Russian nationalism swelled into a flood and the neo-fascist and aggressively anti-Semitic variety of nationalism became more voluble. Russian nationalism entered the Soviet political scene and took up an important position on the stage. I hope to indicate (in Chapter 10) the way in which the varieties of Russian nationalism relate to the politics of the Gorbachev era and to explain why the observer and student of Soviet politics in the 1990s will need to understand this important subject.

A useful starting point from which to proceed is the Veche group of 1971–4 which formed around the editor Vladimir Osipov. The samizdat journal *Veche*, named after the supposedly democratic assembly of the medieval city-state of Novgorod, was a voluminous publication which emerged regularly for nearly four years (ten editions) between 1971 and 1974. It bore the editor's name and address on the title page and represents one of the triumphs of samizdat publication, although presumably its contributors were under KGB observation for some years. Osipov's biography and beliefs are well summarised in an article by Darrell P. Hammer[2] and indicate a significant political evolution.

Vladimir Osipov was born in 1938 in Pskov oblast' and entered the history faculty of Moscow State University in the late 1950s. He was at that time an enthusiastic Leninist and had participated as a member of the Komsomol in the Virgin Lands campaign, for which he received two decorations. Like many of his generation, he was deeply disturbed by Khrushchev's revelations about Stalin's crimes at the xxth Party Congress. Many of his contemporaries began at this time to take an interest in the early years of the Soviet regime, and in the ideas of the 'Workers Opposition', as well as alternative models for socialist development, such as that of Yugoslavia. There is no evidence at this stage that Osipov joined a political group, although in 1958 he became friendly with a certain A. M. Ivanov (Skuratov).

In February 1959 Osipov was expelled from the University and the Komsomol for protesting about the expulsion of a fellow student. At this stage he was a sceptic in respect of the regime, but still a Marxist. Osipov was married by this time and managed finally to qualify as a history teacher, although he was expelled from the Moscow Pedagogical Institute when his political record became known and had to complete his studies extramurally. On becoming involved in the dissident poetry readings in Mayakovsky Square, Osipov was arrested in October 1961 and was sentenced to seven years in a labour camp in February 1962. It was during this first sentence that Osipov's views radically changed, as he summarised in his own words:

It is not for nothing that the . . . camp is called a 'corrective-labour camp'. People go in as atheists and leave as Christians. . . . I was certainly reformed by the corrective-labour camp. In the past I had been a materialist, socialist and atheist. The camp made me a believer in God and a believer in Russia.[3]

It is difficult to know precisely how Osipov made the transition to that of a believing Russian nationalist. One theory is that he resented the ridicule Russians experienced at the hands of other nationalities such as the Ukrainians and the Finns.

On his release, Osipov, now divorced, was compelled to start a new life, facing the usual difficulties of ex-convicts with respect to housing and employment. He eventually obtained a job as a fireman in the vicinity of Vladimir oblast', where he became acquainted with Orthodox believers such as Anatolii Levitin and Father Dmitry Dudko. In his own words, he 'ceased to be a democrat and became a Russian nationalist'.[4]

As editor of the journal *Veche*, Osipov developed Russophile themes, which drew attention to declining moral standards among Russians, and attacked drunkenness, theft, the break-up of the family, and so on. He attributed much of this to 'modernism': 'The 20th century, a century of progress in science and technology, is at the same time a century of unprecedented growth in self-interest and crime.'[5] In *Veche* No. 2 an unidentified Orthodox priest wrote an article which advocated the voluntary teaching of Orthodoxy in Russian schools. 'In ten years,' he wrote, 'we won't recognise ourselves.' Not only Orthodoxy but also the teaching of respect for the customs and traditions of the Russian people was suggested. Osipov attacked the concepts of 'Soviet', proletarian and socialist culture: Sovietisation, he said, was dangerous to the survival of Russian culture. However, Osipov was not in favour of 'Russification', since he specifically applied his teachings to the respect for cultures and religions of non-Russians.

In *Veche* No. 7, Osipov wrote an article in response to Yakovlev's famous 'Anti-historicism' published in *Literaturnaya Gazeta* in November 1972. Osipov distinguished between a 'multinational state' and a non-national 'cosmopolitan state'. The second kind of state, he said, was implied in the strictures of Yakovlev and would require the repression of national cultures, which in turn would lead to an intensification of national feelings and the development of what he termed (following Solov'ev) 'zoological nationalism'. Instead, Osipov advocated a multinational state, a state within which national cultures could be preserved, including Russian national culture which was the particular interest of his publication. This places Osipov in the ranks of the liberal-nationalist school of thought.

The theme of Osipov's last essays before his arrest was that of Russia as a crucified nation and he clearly believed that the very survival of Russian national culture was at stake: 'Russia is hated, Russia is accused, ruin is predicted for Russia. . . . But the main thing is that Russia is not understood . . . Russia is a great sufferer, slandered and crucified. Russia will rise again in spite of it all.'⁶ Like Solzhenitsyn, Osipov is a patriot and taking into consideration the political history of Russia, he concluded that democratic reforms might not be appropriate for the new Russia. Instead, he advocated an authoritarian regime with legality (*zakonnost'*) and *openness (glasnost')* but without Marxism, within the framework of the existing constitution. In this respect, as in the case of Solzhenitsyn's *Letter to Soviet Leaders*, a cultural Russian nationalism coincides with a neo-Slavophile lack of definition about politics. Both Osipov and Solzhenitsyn have expressed their fears about the consequences of rapid democratisation in Russia and the USSR. They conclude that it might lead to a kind of mob-rule and social anarchy, as it did in the chaotic period between February and October 1917.

Osipov exercised very little editorial control over the contributors to *Veche* and some of his collaborators were people of authoritarian or even anti-Semitic views. One of the most active writers in the *Veche* collection was Anatolii M. Ivanov (Skuratov) who was apparently the author of the racist manifesto 'Word of the Nation' ('Slovo natsii') which appeared in 1970. In *Veche* No. 3 Osipov published a manifesto entitled 'The Letter of the Three' which attacked Zionism and equated it with Satanism. A letter to the editor signed 'N. V.' attacked mixed marriages and 'random hybridisation' between Russians and other races or peoples, in the name of racial purity. It may be said in Osipov's favour that he also published editorial rebuttals of such articles as 'The Letter of the Three' and letters attacking the views of 'N. V.'. Articles by the Jewish activist Mikhail Agursky, which argued that Zionism and Russian nationalism were compatible, also appeared in *Veche*. However, it became clear that *Veche* was a journal with many faces and extremely heterogeneous views. Osipov announced in March 1974 that the ninth edition was to be the last and the journal passed for one brief final edition into the hands of more militant nationalists.

Between March and November 1974, when Osipov was again arrested and sentenced, he managed to publish a new and much more Christian samizdat journal called *Zemlya*, which carried material by Levitin and some of Father Dudko's sermons. The manifesto of *Zemlya* contained the proposition that any form of nationalism in Russia which was not based on Christianity would be 'the work of the devil'. It also stated that the main task of nationalists today must be the rebirth of national morality and culture and that the lack of open procedures and constitutional guarantees in Soviet life were obstacles to the achievement of these national tasks. This last point, which allied Osipov and *Zemlya* with the human rights activists, distinguished him from Gennady Shimanov, with whom Osipov corresponded in 1973, Shimanov, the prophet of collaboration between the Party and Orthodox nationalism, hated the human rights movement and considered its activities disloyal to the state. To this, Osipov replied that such 'loyalty' was *sverkhposlushanie* ('over-obedience'), the prostration of the slave. However, Osipov was sentenced, and his work continued only through the religious-philosphical seminars of Father Dudko and his younger disciples, Alexander Ogorodnikov and V. Poresh, themselves arrested and tried in 1979–80. It was Gennady Shimanov who survived and continued to write in freedom and it is to his very different brand of nationalism that I now turn.

Shimanov was already well known in Moscow by the early 1970s. He had chosen to work as an elevator operator, living on very meagre wages, and adopted the ascetic and self-disciplined life-style of the Russian thinkers and revolutionaries of pre-revolutionary times. In this role, he was virtually immune to political pressure. Leonid Borodin, an articulate and deeply religious Russian patriot, famous as a founder member of VSKhSON and a contributor to *Veche*, published Shimanov's works in the collection *Moskovskii Sbornik* in the mid-1970s. To many members of VOOPIK (The All-Russian Society for the Preservation of Historical and Cultural Monuments), Shimanov was an 'ultra', an extremist. He wrote with a sense of urgency, an apocalyptic tone which captured the pathos of a Russian nationalist at a time of national failure. His samizdat writings, many of which are to be found in the archives of Keston College, England, are voluminous.[7]

Shimanov believes that the Communist utopia has irredeemably collapsed, but that Russia is still faced with merciless and implacable enemies, while suffering from a serious internal, moral crisis. The Western world, he believes, cannot provide a model for the future regeneration of Russia. Western Europe is weak, while the Anglo-Saxon world of England and the United States has sunk into a kind of 'liberal slime' and a shopkeeper's mentality, controlled by sinister Zionist interests.

Paradoxically, it has been the Bolshevik Party which, for all its faults, has protected Russia from the blight of Westernism and commercialism. But Russian civilisation is not dependent on the outmoded doctrines of Marxist-Leninism; it is based on Orthodoxy, the highest form of Christianity, and which must now be reborn in Russia in order, ultimately, to save the world. The terrible sufferings of the Soviet period, such as civil war, collectivisation, the purges, the World War and Stalinism have been actually positive for the Russian people, for these experiences have strengthened the spirituality of the nation and demonstrated its resilience. Shimanov thus advocates a fusion of the Party with the Russian Orthodox masses.

In an interview with David Shipler,[8] Shimanov recommended a system of 'national republics' for the Soviet Union and the rejection by Russians of all foreign influences. Shimanov's son is apparently both a church-goer and a member of a Communist youth movement. He believes that Leninism and Orthodoxy are compatible:

Today the Soviet system can no longer strive toward the spectre of Communism – but at the same time it cannot yet abandon the grandeur of its tasks, for otherwise it would have to answer for fruitless sacrifices which are truly innumerable. But in what then can the Soviet system find its justification? Only in the consciousness that it was unconsciously in the past, as it is now quite consciously, God's instrument for constructing a new Christian world. . . . Only the Soviet system, having adopted Russian Orthodoxy, is capable of beginning THE GREAT TRANSFORMATION OF THE WORLD.[9]

On the one hand, the self-disciplined ascetic Shimanov, depicted with sympathy and some curiosity by the ever-observant Shipler, is a harmless crank who advocates the exclusive consumption of Russian products, a patriarchal idyll of pastoral family life dedicated to hard work and childbearing for the Fatherland.[10] On the other hand, as Yanov points out,[11] Shimanov is a man who bridges the gap between the Russian nationalist intellectual and the masses. He eschews the militant anti-Communism of VSKhSON and Solzhenitsyn's naïve appeal to the Soviet leaders to abandon their ideology. He does not flirt with human rights activists like Osipov and *Veche*. On the contrary, he declares the war against Marxism-Leninism to be over, as the official ideology is already obsolete. However, he proclaims the whole Soviet period to have been positive in its effects; he declares the Party to have been basically correct, if flawed, in its rejection of bourgeois capitalism and Zionism; he says that Russia is threatened by powerful and contemptuous enemies and that the people must mobilise themselves for a struggle to survive; he castigates contemporary morals and corruption, but also declares his faith in the Russian people and Orthodoxy, which he claims is superior to all other forms of faith. Finally, he is a great-power chauvinist, demanding the retention of the Soviet Empire and asserting Russia's world-wide mission:

The Soviet Union is not a mechanical conglomeration of nations of different kinds . . . but a MYSTICAL ORGANISM, composed of nations mutually complementing each other and making up, under the leadership of the Russian people, a LITTLE MANKIND – a spiritual trigger for the explosion of the great mankind.[12]

Shimanov thus offers to the Russian masses a way forward with a sense of urgency and purpose. He retains the millennial expectations so beloved of Russians and their sense of still being a great power, which is today made all the more poignant by the rapidly growing inferiority complex induced by Gorbachev's revelations of national failures. Instead of 'democratisation' and internal disputes, Shimanov demands unity and internal discipline. Instead of economic reforms, the market and incipient capitalism, Shimanov extols the old order, austerity, hard work and a return to the soil. He castigates the liberal intelligentsia and their worship of the Western world, using the language of the extreme Right, as 'kike-freemasonry'. He says that it is the duty of Russian Orthodox Christians to unite with the Leninist Party, which, for all its faults and past blasphemies, is in fact the unwitting agent of the Almighty. This is indeed a 'breakthrough' for Russian nationalism, which in the hands of the liberal Slavophiles had offered only Orthodox monarchy, agrarianism and the self-sacrificing settlement and development of the Siberian North.

I have no information about the direct influence of Shimanov's writings on the emergence of the Pamyat' 'Memory' Society, but it may be that Shimanov was known to members of the VOOPIK such as Vladimir Yemelyanov, described as an Arabic translator and head of an Arabic Department at a Moscow language institute. A fanatical supporter of the Palestinian cause, Yemelyanov seems to have been among those who disseminated and popularised the *Protocols of the Elders of Zion* and some wildly anti-Semitic samizdat writings, which among other things accused Brezhnev and several Central Committee members of being secret Zionists. Dismissed from the Party and his teaching post in 1980, Yemelyanov subsequently killed his wife in an ensuing domestic row and was incarcerated in a mental hospital from which he has been discharged in 1989. Yemelyanov and his friends have indeed sown dragon's teeth in the contemporary atmosphere of social questioning and continuing economic failure. The intricate conspiracy theories of the *Protocols*, which are impervious to proof or disproof, have fallen on fertile ground in the current state of confusion and rapid but often ill-considered political reform. The search for scapegoats and Zionist conspirators has begun. The major instigator of this witch-hunt in the 1980s has been the Pamyat' Society.

Initially proceeding from clubs with such innocent names as Rodina in Moscow and Rossiya in Leningrad, Pamyat' was formed in 1979 or 1980 and was originally a literary and historical society attached to the Ministry of Aviation Industry of the USSR. Its original concern for the restoration of national monuments won the society thousands of supporters, but its leadership after about 1985 seems to have fallen into the hands of extreme nationalists and anti-Semites. By the end of 1985, the Society's leaders were blaming the destruction of architectural landmarks in Moscow on Jews employed by the Main Administration for Architecture and Planning.

In December 1985 Pamyat' held a meeting which took as its slogan a quotation from Pushkin's *Yevgeny Onegin*: 'Moscow! How much this word tells a Russian Soul!' A Pamyat' leader, Dmitry Vasil'ev, read aloud extracts from the anti-Semitic forgery *The Protocols of the Elders of Zion*, claiming that there was a Zionist plot to take over the world by the year 2000. Vasil'ev, a former photographer and actor, is a stirring orator whose speciality is the 'big lie' and the (often unattributable) smear. To give one example of Vasil'ev's strange mental world, he has claimed that Adolf Eichmann was in fact a Jew and that his mass murders were part of an intricate plot in accordance with *The Protocols of the Elders of Zion*. Cassette recordings of the meeting circulated widely in the USSR and copies reached the West.[13] As a result of this meeting, Pamyat' was refused application for its official status to be recognised. The so-called Patriotic Union then began to look for new venues for its meetings, holding one at the House of Culture attached to the Dinamo Works in Moscow. The chairman of Pamyat', Kim Andreev, was there proposed as a candidate for the local soviet.

Pamyat' has held its meetings in Party Committee buildings, such as the Leninsky Raion Committee building in Moscow, suggesting that the Patriotic Union has protection in high Party circles. A typical Pamyat' meeting will show films about the destruction of historical monuments, which are then followed by discussions on the theme of the Zionist threat. It has been alleged by a member of Pamyat' that designs for the projected victory monument on Poklonnaya Hill in Moscow include masonic symbols.[14] In April 1987 Pamyat' seized control of the All-Russian Society for the Preservation of Historical and Cultural Monuments (VOOPIK). On 6 May 1987, the Society held a meeting with the First Secretary of the Moscow Party, Boris Yel'tsin, where they discussed the subject of Poklonnaya Hill, the opposition to Gorbachev's *perestroika* (which, oddly, they claim to support) and official recognition of the Society. Later that month, apparently because they were dissatisfied with Yel'tsin's response, they demonstrated again at Poklonnaya Hill and at a Temperance Meeting, demanding total prohibition and carrying placards of handicapped children, claiming that Jews and Freemasons were responsible for the drinking habits of the Russian people.

It would be misleading to claim that Pamyat' is unopposed by other preservation groups, or that the Society has a monopoly of influence over contemporary Russian nationalist movements. Nevertheless, there is strong evidence of a mass following for the Society. They have another active group in Leningrad and often try to recruit disaffected returnees from Afghanistan. A reader of the newspaper *Sovietskaya Kul'tura*, S. Filatov, claimed that Vasil'ev had used a public rostrum to provoke anti-Semitic activities. Those who tried to argue with Vasil'ev were ejected from the hall, he said.[15] In Novosibirsk, Pamyat' has made use of the House of Culture of the USSR Siberian Academy of Sciences for its meetings and has a large membership. One of its members, Alexander Kazantsev, was recently expelled from the City Party Committee by the CPSU for slandering 'top Party and State Officials and leading scholars'.[16] In Sverdlovsk, members of a 'sister society' named 'Otechestvo' ('Fatherland') recently criticised a production of Pushkin's *Tale of Tsar Saltan* because the Sverdlovsk Opera Theatre had used, they claimed, hidden Zionist, Nazi, Masonic and anti-Russian symbols. The Societies are also strongly opposed to Western music and in particular to rock music.

The ideology of Pamyat' is extremely odd, for it clearly eulogises late tsarist society and the person of Nicholas II, while at the same time usually deifying Lenin. Members of Pamyat' say, however, that Lenin was surrounded by Jewish and Masonic cadres and they exhibit particular hostility towards Trotsky. They believe that many prominent Soviet scholars, artists and politicians are involved in plots of Jews and Freemasons. In this number they include Dmitry Likhachev, chairman of the USSR Cultural Foundation, Oleg Efremov, director of the Moscow Arts Theatre, Alla Pugacheva, the pop-singer and Andrei Voznesensky the poet. They object to the Jewish origins of Georgy Arbatov, one of Gorbachev's top advisers and oppose the publication of books by Nabokov.[17] The Society is similarly ambiguous about religion: while many of its members are church-goers, there exists an anti-Christian element who regard the Christianisation of Kievan Rus' as a Zionist plot designed to undermine the warrior-like qualities of the Slavs and they have supported the artist Konstantin Vasil'ev who painted a canvas of Il'ya of Murom victorious over the 'Christian plague'.[18]

Pamyat' and Otechestvo apparently have influential supporters, including a Soviet Army General; writers Vadim Kozhinov, Yuri Bondarev, Petr Proskurin and even Valentin Rasputin; film director Nikolai Burlaev and (at one time) the artist Il'ya Glazunov. Official Soviet anti-Zionists such as Vladimir Begun, Yevgeny Yevseev and Alexander Romanenko, are also strong supporters of the Society, and may have contributed in their writings to the formation of the Society's ideology. The journals *Molodaya Gvardiya*, *Moskva* and *Nash Sovermennik* generally support the Pamyat' line.[19]

At the same time, Pamyat' has a lot of enemies, including of course Alexander Yakovlev, a member of the Politburo; Fyodor Burlatsky, a leading adviser to Gorbachev, Vitaly Korotich, editor of *Ogonyok* and Gorbachev's leading economists. Some letters to the Soviet Press have called for the prosecution of Pamyat' under Article 74 of the RSFSR Criminal Code, which now imposes up to 10 years' imprisonment for 'violation of the equality of rights of nationalities and races'. In 1988 the KGB apparently warned Vasil'ev that the Society might face prosecution under this law, but so far (1989) no formal charges have been made. Any major public trial of Pamyat' (which has amply demonstrated contempt for the law), would be extremely interesting and would have to be handled carefully by the authorities if they want to avoid making martyrs of these fanatics. There is no doubt about the strength of feeling which Pamyat' arouses and they have been accused of fomenting the appearance of National Socialist or neo-Nazi groups of youths sporting paramilitary uniforms and wearing swastikas in a number of Soviet cities in the late 1980s.[20]

How large is the membership of Pamyat' today? Identifiable leaders who have gained prominence in the Press number about thirty-two,[21] and in late 1988 Pamyat' claimed 5,000 members in Leningrad and 10,000 letters of support. More recently, a membership of 20,000 in Moscow has been claimed, with chapters of the Society existing in thirty Russian cities and towns. It is clear that we have to take the strange and twisted world of these latter-day anti-Semites seriously, despite their apparently insane and convoluted conspiracy theories and their oddly articulated ideology which is outlined below. There are many reasons for this.

First, the Pamyat' Society has already received a kind of 'All-Union' recognition, if only because references to it in the Soviet Press are now so numerous. Articles have appeared in such newspapers as *Izvestiya*,[22] *Komsomolskaya Pravda*[23] and *Moscow News*[24] among many others. The Society is being taken seriously enough by the authorities to merit refutation and ideological struggle.

Second, the Society is well organised. Its samizdat publications are well produced and annotated, with the famous symbol of the Society – a tocsin or alarm bell crossed with the word Pamyat' in Cyrillic script. It is a kind of secret society, potent for its adherents, like the secret symbols of masonry, whose dastardly works Pamyat' purports to expose. In the Soviet context, where informal groups are a relatively new phenomenon and their status even today may still prove tenuous, membership of a secret society has a kind of weird security and status.

Third, despite the apparent absurdity of the Society's ideological position, open discussion of political views, a facet of *glasnost'*, is recent in the USSR and extremism tends to be more prevalent than tolerant, moderate and considered positions. Only the continued, consistent development of *glasnost'* can expose Pamyat' for what it is and clarify its atavistic, pre-revolutionary origins in the forgeries of proto-fascists and the tsarist secret police. And here too lies a problem. The dark paranoid world of hidden plots, by Jews and the intangible international Zionists or secretly powerful Freemasons, is logically impossible to refute or to prove. In any case, political convictions are not primarily a matter of empirical proof or disproof, especially when based on the 'gut-reactions' of a population unschooled in political discourse and which is now looking back on its past (pre-revolutionary) history for guidance and new principles after the failure of seventy years of Communist rule.

Fourth, as John Dunlop points out: 'Marxist materialism can easily generate right-wing extremism. The Jewish–Masonic–Plutocratic conspiracy, to take one example, feeds on the Marxist legacy of class suspicions, dark paranoias, and conspiracy theories.'[25] The ideological world of Pamyat' was to some extent clarified early in 1988 by a samizdat document entitled 'Appeal to the Russian People, to Patriots of all Countries and Nations'. It deserves quotation *in extenso* as it serves as a primary source of the political ideas of Pamyat' and at the same time represents their reply to many charges made against them in the official Soviet Press. In quoting this manifesto, I have not included every upper-case typesetting, every italicised passage, as I wish to concentrate on content rather than emphasis:

Fellow Countrymen!
Brothers and Sisters!
Friends!
SOME YEARS AGO THE WORLD looked again with hope upon RUSSIA. In her, forces of good had revived. A ray of reason had shone forth and illumined dark corners. Shone forth – and expired?
In the country itself, the mass media grew sated with empty words, as though deranged, and failed to uncover the heart of the problems.
What in fact has happened in our country?
The true situation may be clarified by a single sentence:
'WE HAVE DEMOCRATISED A LITTLE AND THAT IS ENOUGH!'
The intelligent and healthy forces in our country have not yet revived, and again seem to have fallen in the dirt. This tinkering with *perestroika* cannot continue any longer. The world should know THE WHOLE TRUTH. The activity of the ENEMIES has become still more evident recently in our country, enemies who accumulate in every branch of the Party – leaders of Soviet power. In practice, dark elements in the Party, speculating with Party slogans and phraseology, carry on warfare with the indigenous peoples of the country, and annihilate the national character of the peoples. They reactivate Trotskyism, in order to discredit socialism, in order to sow chaos in the state, in order to open the floodgates to Western capital and Western technology. . . .
These characters now instil into the people that there are no dark forces in

the state, that there in no conspiracy. NO?! THEN LET THEM ANSWER
THIS FULLY: Who, for the last 70 years has unleashed political terror on
the country?
Who annihilates and eliminates any dissent?
Who flagrantly violates the Constitution and the Law?
Who defiled our history and our culture?
Who destroyed a huge quantity of monuments of world-wide fame which
belonged to the Russian people and other peoples?
Who reduced to a state of extreme desolation, annihilation, our sacred
places, temples, churches, monasteries, country churchyards, and tombs of
the national heroes of our Fatherland?
Who perpetually mismanages our economy and agriculture?
Who reduced the ecology of the country to castrastrophe?
Who allowed the Chernobyl disaster to happen, and took a vast region out
of cultivation?
Who exhausts our resources and sells them abroad for a pittance?
Who is destroying the nation with ideological and alcoholic narcotics?
Who, like some watchdog, barks the charge of chauvinism and nationalism
at us at the sound of the word 'Russian'?
Who tries to transmute the word 'Russian' into the meaning 'enemy'?
In whose hands are the mass media?
We are told that the Party press must be believed. But how can one believe it
. . . if it lies? Yet hundreds of thousands do believe it when they read articles
about the Patriotic Union Pamyat'. They try to accuse us of being a political
opposition. We categorically reject this formulation. BUT WE OPENLY
ADMIT TODAY THAT WE ARE A POLITICAL OPPOSITION TO
EVERY DARK FORCE IN THE PARTY AND STATE! . . . THE
PEOPLES ARE IN DANGER! TODAY, NOW, IN THESE VERY
MOMENTS, THE ETERNAL QUESTION IS BEING DECIDED FOR
THE PEOPLES: 'TO BE OR NOT TO BE?' AND IT IS NOT ONLY
THERMONUCLEAR WAR WHICH WILL BRING CATASTROPHE
TO THEM.
We demand the convocation of a Peoples' Tribunal for the investigation of
the activities of all usurpers of power . . .. Enough about 'mistakes'! Their
result was the loss of millions of human lives, seas and rivers of blood! . . .
Four decades have passed since the Nuremburg trials, but even today,
former Nazi criminals are hunted down and given their just retribution.
Why, then, for political 'mistakes' . . . are those responsible for crimes not
indicted on a capital charge, but instead merely retired on a pension?
We have had enough of hypocrisy and deceit! . . . We can see that many
people still dwell in darkness . . . or in complete despair, who do not
understand the real causes, who do not see the real enemy, who are not
prepared for the struggle with him. The Battle of Kulikovo, the Battle of
Borodino, already stare them in the face. International Zionism and
Freemasonry have shown their faces and go over to the open attack against
the last remaining islets of spirtuality, of national consciousness. Three
years ago, Pamyat' began to sound the tocsin of alarm! THE TOSCIN
SOUNDS LOUDER STILL! SOCIAL FORCES ARE AWAKENING
WHICH ARE CAPABLE OF RESOLVING ALL PROBLEMS OF

THE ROAD TO PAMYAT' 115

PERESTROIKA BUT THEY ARE WILFULLY EXCLUDED FROM THE TASK IN HAND. Pamyat' is evidence of this.[26]

The manifesto goes on to complain that its many long telegrams to the central organs of the Party and state with recommendations for the creation of national parks and the revitalisation of village life and so on have remained unanswered. The Manifesto demands official recognition of the Patriotic Union and a newspaper. Failure to grant these demands and to answer telegrams, says Pamyat', is evidence of the existence of enemies of the people in high places and names in particular Alexander Yakovlev. Enemies of the people control the Press, radio, television, which all proclaim cosmopolitanism, idolatry before the West and which exclude the 'fundamentals of national and popular life'.

A series of demands is made in the name of the majority of the people, including television time for Pamyat' spokesmen, official recognition and the broadcasting of letters received by the Press in support of Pamyat'. It makes a particular plea to officers of the KGB, MVD and the armed forces, who may one day be ordered to arrest members of Pamyat' for such 'crimes' as chauvinism, anti-Semitism, anti-Sovietism and 'Blackhundredism'. The manifesto hints darkly that the 'events' in Czechoslovakia in 1968 and in Poland in 1980 were the work of Zionist elements in the apparently Communist leadership of those countries. The slogan adopted by the manifesto is 'Stop the cosmopolitans!'[27]

The document then goes on to defend the 'pure' Russian speech against foreign imports, technical words and 'double dutch' and advocates the study of folklore and popular tradition. It calls for the setting up of patriotic Pamyat' societies in the republics, oblasts, okrugs, cities and villages. It demands accountability of local officials to 'the people', a national debate on housing and agriculture and seems to favour home-ownership and landownership by the workers. It is against urban dwelling and the 'permissive society', rock music and other Western imports.

The manifesto claims that the Press is an organ of disinformation, as in the days of repression and the 'cult of personality'. When Pamyat' is attacked in the Press, it says, especially since May 1987, 'the whole Russian people is being defamed and degraded.'[28] In this connection attacks are launched against *Moscow News*, *Komsomolskaya Pravda, Izvestiya, Sovietskaya Kul'tura, Ogonyok* and, more surprisingly, *The New York Times, The Washington Post, Le Monde,* and *The Christian Science Monitor.* Radio stations such as the BBC, Voice of America, Voice of Israel, Radio Free Europe, Deutsche Welle and Radio Liberty all echo the Press and broadcast second-hand opinions back into the USSR. Therefore, concludes the manifesto: 'THERE IS AN INTERNATIONAL CENTRE OF PRESS CONTROL WHICH DEFENDS THE INTERESTS OF ZIONISM.'[29] In time, says the manifesto, Pamyat' will publish a full record of the dastardly deeds of these 'gangsters of the pen', but it notes in parenthesis that some Arab newspapers are honourable exceptions to its general rule.

Pamyat' goes on to demand reinstatement to the Party of those who were expelled on account of their membership of the Patriotic Union. It demands that it should be allowed to unite with what it defines as 'healthy forces within the Party'. The document also makes demands for religious freedom and proposes that atheistic propaganda, like the church, should be separated from the state. It proposes that the Uspensky Cathedral within the Kremlin should be open for worship, since this, it argues, would provide proof of a real change of policy in the USSR and would aid the development of religious belief and morality. The manifesto also demands a military tribunal for those responsible for the war in Afghanistan. Any attacks against Pamyat' are themselves examples of 'Russophobic extremism'[30] and those who are guilty of such attacks are the real enemies of the people, it says. Those who concentrate solely on post-revolutionary history to the exclusion of 'the historical experience of our peoples' are also enemies, as are those who consider the problems of Zionism and Freemasonry to be an idle illusion. Various slogans terminate the manifesto, which is signed by Kim Andreev and members of the 'council', Alexey Gladkov, Dmitry Vasil'ev (Secretary), Yevgeny Rusanov, Alexander Barshakov, Alexander Linev and Nikolai Detkov.

This manifesto is perhaps only partially explicit about the full aims and tactics of Pamyat'. The supporters of the Society include professional anti-Zionists such as Vladimir Begun, whose works are thought to be a direct plagiarism of Hitler's *Mein Kampf*. It would be surprising if this society, based on authoritarian principles, did not have secret organisational instructions and even insurrectionary plans. Its behaviour during 1988 and 1989 has been scandalous, including noisy demonstrations in the Rumyantsev Gardens in Leningrad, court cases against major Soviet newspapers such as *Sovietskaya Kultura*, and a campaign of threats and intimidation against liberal journals such as *Znamya*.[31] At the same time, the organisation which is now called The Russian Popular Front Pamyat', presumably in response to the popular fronts emerging in non-Russian republics, has shown signs of amateurism and splits. At the end of 1987 Yemelyanov broke away from the main organisation and formed his own group called 'Rus' ('Russia'), while a second Pamyat' made its appearance in 1988.

At the moment it is clear that Pamyat' has many friends in high places. It has not yet been prosecuted and the police seem unwilling to intervene when it holds demonstrations. On one occasion a worker carrying a banner inscribed with the Communist slogan 'Workers of all lands, unite!' was attacked and his banner torn up by Pamyat' thugs. The police did nothing.[32] Although the reaction of the Soviet press has been vociferous, in particular by such courageous journalists as Elena Losoto, Pavel Gutiontov and Nina Katerli, their tone has been increasingly desperate in view of the ever-expanding growth of Pamyat'.[33] In a recent exchange of letters between the historian Natan Eidelman and the famous writer Viktor Astaf'ev, the latter demonstrated the depths to which Russian anti-Semitism can go. Astaf'ev (whose novel *The Sad Detective* was published and sold about 3 million copies in recent years) wrote a short story in *Nash Sovremennik* entitled 'Catching Gudgeons in Georgia', which was thought by some to be anti-Georgian. Other passages were interpreted by Eidelman as being critical of Kazakhs, Buryats, Kalmyks and Crimean Tartars and showed signs of Great Russian chauvinism. Astaf'ev replied that Eidelman's letter was

not simply overflowing with malevolence but boiling over with the puss of Jewish high-intellectual arrogance. . . . As you see, we Russians have not yet lost our memory and we are still a Great People. Killing us amounts to little. And we have yet to be overthrown.[34]

Russian anti-Semitism and the Pamyat' phenomenon have become prominent in the 1980s and cannot now be overlooked, although conceivably the name of the Society may change and its leaders may be arrested. Pamyat' is a surprising development in Soviet politics in the late twentieth century, but it does have a long and notorious pedigree in Russian history, and its direct ancestor, the Union of the Russian People, also emerged at a time of crisis for a former autocratic regime. History does not repeat itself exactly, and while some analogies and parallels may be drawn with advantage to the political scientist, all that one can say with certainty at present is that the Pamyat' Society will not go away. Its evolution, both as an organisation and an ideology, merit our close attention and serious research between now and the end of the century. In the next chapter I shall attempt to place Pamyat' in context and to relate it both to the spectrum of Russian nationalist thought as a whole and to the present conflicts within Soviet politics as they developed at the end of the 1980s.

NOTES

1. Anthony D. Smith, *Theories of Nationalism* (London, Duckworth, 1983) p. 200.

2. Darrell P. Hammer, 'Vladimir Osipov and the Veche Group (1971–74: a page from the history of political dissent', *The Russian Review*, No. 43 (1984), pp. 355–75).
3. Ibid., p. 361.
4. Ibid., p. 362.
5. 'Tri otnosheniia k rodine', *The Russian Review*, op. cit., p. 367.
6. Ibid., p. 369.
7. Important titles of Shimanov's works include *Protiv techeniia* (*Against the Current*), *Ideal'noe gosudarstvo* (*The Ideal State*) and *Kak ponimat' nashy istoriyu* (*How our history may be understood*).
8. David K. Shipler, *Russia: Broken Idols, Solemn Dreams* (London, Macdonald, 1983), p. 342.
9. Quoted in A. Yanov, *The Russian Challenge* (New York, Basil Blackwell, 1987), p. 236.
10. David K. Shipler, op. cit., pp. 341–2.
11. A. Yanov, op. cit., Chapter 18.
12. A. Yanov, op. cit., p. 241.
13. The text of this speech had also been published in *Jews and Jewish Topics and Soviet and East European Publications*, No. 4 (Winter 1986–7), pp. 46–53.
14. *Russkaya Mysl*, 27 March 1987.
15. *Sovietskaya Kul'tura*, 23 July 1987.
16. *Sovietskaya Kul'tura*, 28 June 1987.
17. *Russkaya Mysl*, 31 July 1987, pp. 6–7.
18. Ibid.
19. For example, see *Molodaya Gvardiya*, No. 3, pp. 250–77.
20. See, for example, V. Konovalov, 'Neo-Nazis in the USSR: more "mindless childish games"' in *Radio Liberty Report* RL 394/88.
21. Julia Wishnevsky, *Radio Liberty Report* RL342/87, p. 17.
22. P. Gutiontov, *Izvestiya*, 27 February 1988.
23. E. Losoto, *Komsomolskaya Pravda*, 22 May 1987 and 19 December 1987.
24. V. Voskoboinikov, *Moscow News* (English language edition), August 1988.
25. J. Dunlop, *The New Russian Nationalism* (New York, Praeger, 1985), p. 86.
26. *Archiv Samizdata*, No. 6138, 1 February 1988, pp. 1–4.
27. Ibid., p. 7.
28. Ibid., p. 9.
29. Ibid.
30. Ibid., p. 14.
31. *Radio Liberty Research Bulletin* RL 454/88. The editor, G. Baklanov, published this threatening letter in *Znamya*, No. 10 (1988).
32. *Moscow News*, No. 32 (1988) p. 2.
33. See Chapter 9.
34. V. P. Astaf'ev to N. Ya. Eidelman, Ovsyanko Village, 14 September 1986; published in *Détente* (Winter 1987), p. 7.

9 Theories of Russian nationalism

The emergence of Russian nationalism as an important factor in Soviet politics in the late twentieth century has caught many people by surprise. Political scientists have had difficulty in relating the spectrum of nationalist thought to their traditional models and Soviet Marxists have had no less difficulty in adapting to this relatively new phenomenon. Above all, the emergence of Pamyat' in its anti-Semitic and neo-Nazi guise has proved to be a shocking experience for the Soviet establishment. In this chapter I shall deal first with a few of the typical reactions of Soviet journalists to Pamyat' and then go on to investigate the role of Russian nationalism as discussed at a recent international conference in Honolulu.[1]

Among the most important articles in the Soviet press which have attacked Pamyat' are those by Elena Losoto in *Komsomolskaya Pravda* (22 May 1987 and 19 December 1987), Pavel Gutiontov in *Izvestiya* (27 February 1988) and Nina Katerli in *Leningradskaya Pravda* (9 October 1988). Losoto's first article describes and analyses the Pamyat' meeting which took place at the Leninsky Raion Committee Building in Moscow. Losoto is a Marxist with predictable views. She distinguishes between Leninist patriotism (socialism is our fatherland), patriarchal patriotism, which she describes as belief in tsarism, Orthodoxy and Mother Russia and 'petty-bourgeois patriotism', which always degenerates into nationalism. Losoto argues therefore that Pamyat' is a form of 'petty-bourgeois' nationalism, with the added 'fiery torch' of anti-Semitism. She also distinguishes between 'progressive' and 'reactionary' culture, and while exonerating those who study the past in order to understand the present, she says that the tone of the leadership of Pamyat' today is reactionary. It now seeks to revive the past and it admires the ideology of past political movements, such as the Black Hundreds.

Losoto goes further when she charges Pamyat' with lack of real historical and political knowledge. The title of Losoto's article reflected this central theme, for it was entitled 'What Pamyat' (Memory) has forgotten'. She reminded her readers that Lenin was very opposed to Orthodoxy, clericalism, mysticism and national chauvinism. She also claimed that some senior Soviet journalists, such a V. Kozhinov in the journal *Moskva* persistently misinterpret Lenin.[2]

Losoto described the extraordinary elation which attached itself to the meeting held at the Leninsky Raion, the proposal that Kim Andreev should stand as a member of the local soviet, and the threatening tone adopted by the platform and audience towards the Jews. She gave a full report of the proceedings, their attacks on bureaucracy, their conspiracy theories, which included the idea that babies' clothing on sale with the sign of the Moon on them was a Masonic plot. She attacked the theories of an automatic racial and national unity among Russians and ascribed the nationalism of Pamyat' to an inadequate sociological analysis, namely that of 'petty-bourgeois' ideology. Only a genuine Leninist proletarian internationalism could combat this, she said. Commenting later on the insidious and widespread nature of Pamyat' theories about Masonic conspiracies, Losoto mentioned that a close friend of hers had even ascribed the double line bordering her article to a secret Masonic obituary symbol.[3]

Losoto's article of 19 December 1987 analysed the post-bag of *Komsomolskaya Pravda* since the original article in May. It contained some surprising letters. Many of these were short and insulting, usually unsigned, such as this one:

Dear Editor,
Why do you publish Losoto, an insolent Zionist? Her articles reek of Stalinism. She has pretensions towards topicality, but it is time to 'reconstruct' Komsomolka from demagogy to fact.[4]

Another letter attacked Lenin, a trend which is now growing stronger:

Hello fellow workers from 'Komsomolka' (apart from Jews and Nazis). We are in complete support of Pamyat' . . .. V. I. Ul'yanov [Lenin] wrote: 'Shame on this accursed Tsarism', which is why he himself was [expletive deleted].

The letter was signed, 'We are from Peter' (Petersburg–Leningrad). Some of the letters received by *Komsomolskaya Pravda* in favour of Pamyat' were signed with name and full addresses. One letter from Yu Fedin, aged 27, from a Moscow address explained:

Lenin hated Russia, but why should I share his views? The Tsar's family was slaughtered, the aristocracy annihilated, the bourgeoisie were dispossessed, the churches were destroyed. What in fact remained? Surely not all our monuments were ruined? . . . If the land taken from the peasant at the time of collectivisation were to be returned to him, and he were able to bequeath it to his heirs, he would have children, which he does not want to do now: Why beget slaves for the State? This is why the enemies of the Russian people do not want to hear the name of Stolypin!

The majority of letters received, said Losoto, were in favour of Pamyat', but some had criticised the Patriotic Union, including a certain Sergei Obraztsov, and Losoto reports that he had received a threatening anonymous note, which bore the sign of the swastika. Losoto was also roundly abused in an article in *Moskva* by the critic, Kozhinov, who charged her with being a Trotskyite.[5]

In her December article, Losoto went much further than she had done in May. Now she drew a direct parallel between the anti-Semitism of Pamyat' and German fascism.[6] She also likened the ideas of Pamyat' to those of A. S. Shmakov, whose book about the secret 'government' of international Zionism and Freemasons was published in 1912.[7] Shmakov was a member of the Union of the Russian People. The article's ominous title was 'Too Similar!' and it amounted to a declaration of war on Pamyat'. However, one wonders if *Komsomolskaya Pravda* can sustain this line of attack for long. How effective is it really to charge people like the ascetic Shimanov or the fanatic Vasil'ev with petty-bourgeois nationalism? They might also gleefully accept the appellation 'Blackhundredist' and be proud of it. In 1988 the official line became sophisticated and more cautious than it had been in 1987.

Following a sensational civil action against the newspaper *Sovietskaya Kul'tura*, *Izvestiya* took up more substantial cudgels against Pamyat' in the form of a lengthy article by Pavel Gutiontov at the end of February 1988. The article is entitled 'Podmena',[8] which implies the subject is the substitution of something false for something real. The subject is specifically the samizdat 'manifesto' summarised in the last chapter, but with a more general survey of the activities of Pamyat', including their direct appeal to military personnel and the proposal to set up 'Peoples' Tribunals' which Gutiontov says has the ring of German fascism. Pamyat' members apparently wear black shirts with the symbol of the tocsin or alarm bell on them – the symbolism is obvious. Clearly the aims of Pamyat' are now more ambitious than merely preserving ancient monuments. At a meeting of the Patriotic Union with auto-workers at the ZIL Palace of Culture on 26 January 1988, Pamyat' leaders claimed that their mission was 'to save Russia as a whole'. They proclaimed Russian supremacy over other nations and asserted that a whole series of plots, orchestrated by Jews and Freemasons had been directed towards causing the Russian nation to rot from within. Gutiontov condemns such national chauvinism and denies the society its claim to the title 'patriotic'.

Gutiontov analyses the civil action taken against the newspaper *Sovietskaya Kul'tura* by theorists of the society, Y. Yevseev, V. Begun and A. Romanenko. Apparently there had been a series of scandalous scenes at the Sverdlovsk Raion Courthouse in Moscow, where one of the plaintiffs, Romanenko, had charged the newspaper with giving 'aid to the Zionists . . . in their political struggle against the USSR'. At the start of the trial, Romanenko demanded to know the nationality of the judges and having been refused this information, he left the court ostentatiously before proceedings began. When they started, supporters of the plaintiffs persistently interrupted, taped the hearings, took photographs and cheered their leaders wildly. The newspaper had taken Begun's writings to the Institute for the Study of the USA and Canada, and the Institute for Oriental Studies (Academy of Sciences of the USSR). Their researchers had found clear literal parallels between Begun's work and Hitler's *Mein Kampf,* and had listed several knowingly misquoted passages which were designed to mislead, and so on. When questioned about this by the chairman of the tribunal, Begun apparently replied that he found the charges laughable. '*Izvestiya*,' said Gutiontov, 'is not amused.'

Despite the overwhelming evidence of the fascist connections of Pamyat', many highly placed writers and critics such as Vladimir Bondarenko in the journal *Moskva* and Valentin Rasputin in the journal *Nash Sovremennik*[9] were sympathetic towards Pamyat'. This is most regrettable, says Gutiontov, but the tone of his article is very sober and thoughtful, in comparison with the tone of Losoto. Gutiontov admitted that the complacent conclusions of Soviet nationalities policy, with its claims about the inherent 'internationalism' of the Soviet people, would have to be very drastically reviewed, particularly after the events in Kazakhstan in 1986 and many other places since.[10] Gutiontov went on to admit:

Unfortunately, Pamyat' is not just a group of lunatics, although it would be comforting if that could be believed. In all honesty, it is better to admit that serious causes, social and economic, have given rise to Pamyat', and that it expresses the mentality of a definite (although, to be sure, not a large) section of the population, that part of it which did not adapt easily to the recent re-evaluation of formerly unshakeable truths, and which reacted with confusion and even panic. And this is why the voluntarists of Pamyat' seize with such readiness on the easy little idea about the 'intrigues of our enemies'. How easy it is to ascribe everything to them, from the 'uneconomic economy' to drunkenness.[11]

However, the hypothesis about the existence of secret 'intrigue' by shadowy enemies is a dangerous one, says Gutiontov, and reminded him of the period of repression from 1937–8, when everything was blamed on saboteurs, spies, wreckers and enemies of the people. Such a mentality could conceivably lead to similar consequences.

This recent assessment of Pamyat' and the general tone of critical articles in 1988 showed the seriousness with which Soviet authority has begun to view the Pamyat' phenomenon and its apparently potential mass support. The trouble with Pamyat', says Gutiontov, is that it is taking advantage of *glasnost'* and the freedoms which go with it for quite anti-democratic purposes. The problem with Pamyat' is that it puts forward 'lies' as its point of view, and 'wilful slander' as its opinion. And this, concludes Gutiontov, is an impossible substitution of something false for something real. The anti-democratic aims of Pamyat' disqualify it from participation in the democratic process.

Nina Katerli, writing in *Leningradskaya Pravda* in October 1988 after a series of Pamyat' demonstrations in Leningrad that summer, painted a sombre picture and sounded a serious warning to her readers. Claiming that the relative impunity with which Pamyat' had demonstrated at the Rumyantsev Gardens must be due to protection from sections of the Leningrad party, Katerli launched an impassioned protest. She stated unequivocally that Pamyat' was a Nazi organisation and that far from protecting national memorials, it would create new ones, like those she had recently seen in Belorussia: monuments to the Jewish dead, killed by the German Gestapo in 1943 when several hundred Belorussian Jews were burnt alive.[12] Katerli mentions that Pamyat' has branches in over thirty Soviet cities and towns. The chorus of concern among liberal Soviet journalists, such as Korotych of *Ogenok* and Rogov and Nosenko in *Sovietskaya Kul'tura* has, if anything, grown in volume in 1989, with the journals *Nash Sovremennik* and *Molodaya Gvardiya* taking up a protective and defensive line against the opponents of Pamyat'.[13]

The Pamyat' Society and Russian nationalism seem to exercise the minds and pens of an increasingly large part of the Soviet press. In the West, too, there has been growing interest in the subject, and it was discussed at a recent conference of Slavists. The conference of the American Association for the Advancement of Slavic Studies (AAASS) was held in Honolulu in November 1988. There were about 1,500 specialists on Soviet and East European Studies from all over the world and 238 panels on a very wide range of topics, but one of the most popular sessions was one on Russian nationalism. Papers edited by Elizabeth Teague were subsequently published as a special collection by Radio Liberty.[14]

The major contributors were: John B. Dunlop, Senior Fellow at the Hoover Institution in Stanford; Darrell P. Hammer, Professor of Political Science at Indiana University; Andrei Sinyavsky, the Russian writer who teaches at the Sorbonne; Ronald Suny, Professor of Armenian History at the University of Michigan; and Alexander Yanov, Professor of Political Science at the City University of New York.

John Dunlop concentrated on the spectrum of Russian nationalist thought and related this spectrum of activity to the central political struggle which he defines as being between 'an amalgam of radical reformers, led by Mikhail Gorbachev and Alexander Yakovlev and an alliance of conservatives, led by Egor Ligachev and Viktor Chebrikov'. Dunlop related the clarification or sundering of the different 'strands' of Russian nationalist thought to the period 1986-7. He saw this clarification as being the result of an all-out attempt by Gorbachev and Yakovlev to take over as much as possible of the Soviet media and creative intelligentsia, including the Union of Soviet Cinematographers and the Union of Soviet Writers. As a result, the conservatives tried to gain support among important figures in the RSFSR Writers Union and the USSR Writers Union in 1987. Dunlop interpreted Gorbachev's appeal to certain sections of the more 'enlightened' Russian nationalist writers as an attempt to 'broaden his base' beyond that of his natural constituency among reform-minded Marxists and Western-style social democrats, and to prevent the formation of a united Russian nationalist opposition. For example, in 1986 the eminent scholar of Russian national culture, Academician Dmitry Likhachev, was made head of the Soviet Cultural Foundation; the 'countryside writer' Sergei Zalygin was made editor of *Novy Mir*; and film-maker Elem Klimov was made first secretary of the Cinematographers' Union. Gorbachev also stressed his support for the Russian Orthodox Church during the Millennium Celebrations in 1988, meeting Patriarch Pimen and members of the Synod at the end of April. This was the first official meeting between a party leader and the patriarchate since the War. Religious relics were transferred from the Kremlin museums to the church, and *Izvestiya* carried a full-page interview with Patriarch Pimen. Even the anti-religious monthly *Nauka i Religiya* carried an article praising the work ethic of Orthodox religious communities.[15] A full day of festivities to honour the millennium was held on 10 June at the Bolshoi Theatre and was attended by Raisa Gorbachev.

The liberal-nationalists thus co-opted by Gorbachev include the scholars Dmitry Likhachev and Sergei Averintsev. Both are practising Orthodox believers with impeccable patriotic and preservationist credentials. Likhachev has stressed the international character or Orthodoxy and declares it to be incompatible with chauvinism. He castigates people such as Academician Boris Rybakov, who promotes indigenous Russian paganism, and he regards anti-Semitism as the preserve of the 'semi-intelligentsia'.[16] Likhachev has concentrated much of his energies of late in combating the extremism of other Russian nationalists. Averintsev has also attacked nationalist extremism, but he also regards many of the Communist 'Saints' such as Bukharin and Lunacharsky, recently rehabilitated by Gorbachev, as 'national nihilists'.[17]

The writer and editor Sergei Zalygin can be regarded as the major liberal-nationalist organiser, working through the journal *Novy Mir*. A recent initiative by the liberal-nationalists has been the attempt to rehabilitate Alexander Solzhenitsyn and publish all his works, including *The Gulag Archipelago*. Clearly the rehabilitation, publication and above all the return of Solzhenitsyn to the USSR would be a major gain for the liberal-nationalists. At the same time, one wonders what Solzhenitsyn and the Gorbachevites would really have in common. Gorbachev's political and ideological 'base' is quite narrow and this is perhaps indicated by the print-runs for popular novels: a 'Gorbachevite' novel, Anatoly Rybakov's *Children of the Arbat* was published with an initial print-run of 1.2 million while anti-Western works such as Vasily Belov's *Everything is still to come* had a run of 2.7 million and Viktor Astaf'ev's *The Sad Detective* came out in 2.7 million copies. Novels by Valentin Pikul' and Chingiz Aitmatov probably have even wider readership.

The next group of nationalists indentified by Dunlop are the 'centrists', whose politics are opposed to the 'hard' Marxism-Leninism of the Stalinists, but who cannot do a deal with the Gorbachevites because these writers are equally hostile to Western values. The centrists are rather suspicious of the 'non-Russianness' of the Gorbachev circle, such as Mikhail Shatrov, Anatoly Rybakov, Grigory Baklanov, Abel Aganbegyan and Otto Latsis. The centrists do not generally have official positions and include such people as Viktor Astaf'ev, Vasily Belov, Valentin Rasputin, Vladimir Soloukhin, Vadim Kozhinov and Ilya Glazounov. Dunlop suggested that this group, which has many people of enormous charismatic influence, is subject to conflicting pressures from Gorbachevites and neo-Stalinists. There are signs that Glazounov may be moving in the direction of the liberals, as he dissociated himself from Pamyat' in 1989.

Dunlop associated the 'centrist' group with Pamyat', but admitted that the Patriotic Union should be treated separately owing to its penchant for action and its noisy 'street' presence. Its militant anti-Semitism, Dunlop suggested, might lead to prosecution under Article 74 of the RSFSR Criminal Code.

Dunlop next turned his attention to the 'National Bolsheviks', who while being relatively indifferent to Communism, are ready to use the language of Marxism-Leninism, and have close links with the Soviet military. Many of these people hold influential positions in Soviet society and include Yuri Bondarev, Petr Proskurin, Mikhail

Alekseev (editor of *Moskva*) and Anatoly Ivanov (editor of *Molodaya Gvardiya*). In general, the National Bolsheviks have unambiguously allied themselves with the neo-Stalinists. For example, at the xixth Party Conference in 1988, Bondarev compared the process of *perestroika* with a 'plane that had taken off without any idea of where it was going to land'.[18] Bondarev is identified by Dunlop as the main recruiter for the conservatives or neo-Stalinists and has tried to attract support from Mikhail Alekseev, Anatoly Ivanov, film-maker Sergei Bondarchuk, and Ilya Glazounov. Recently these figures have also attempted to express their support for the Orthodox Church.[19]

Dunlop mentioned next the neo-Stalinists such as the editor of *Sovietskaya Rossiya*, Valentin Chikin, and the editor of *Sovietsky Soyuz*, Nikolai Gribachev, writer Ivan Shevtsov and lecturer Nina Andreeva. In her famous letter of 13 March 1988 to *Sovietskaya Rossiya*, universally regarded as a Ligachev-inspired 'anti-*perestroika* manifesto', Andreeva attacked not only the Gorbachevites but also the 'traditionalists' (i.e. the nationalists) who, while performing useful services against corruption, alcoholism, ecological damage and (Western) mass-culture, had failed to understand 'the historical significance of October for the fate of the Fatherland'.[20] Andreeva's major target was (of course) the cosmopolitan left-liberal Gorbachevites, and she invited support from the 'traditionalists' while making it fairly clear that the neo-Stalinists could make do without that support if necessary. Dunlop excluded the neo-Stalinists from the ranks of Russian nationalism, therefore believing that there are three major groupings of nationalists (he identifies the 'centrists' with Pamyat'). Dunlop argued that the nationalists are split and weakened by internal differences which amounts to a total lack of political definition. Nevertheless, Dunlop concluded by saying that the nationalists are key players in the Gorbachev–Ligachev conflict and he admitted that Russian nationalists could become an important 'third force' in the event of a military dictatorship. Recently, Ligachev has been wooing nationalists and it has been suggested that he may be about to renounce the anti-nationalist sentiments of Andreeva's letter of 1988.[21] It is known that Dunlop is a supporter of the liberal-nationalist school and in previous publications has compared the liberal nationalism of VSKhSON to a programme of 'New Russian Revolutionaries'.[22] However, Dunlop does not advocate Western support or action on behalf of Gorbachev, while at the same time acknowledging that neo-Stalinism and National Bolshevism are hostile to Western values. Dunlop's scholarly investigations afford us an understanding of the important place of the many shades of Russian nationalism within the Soviet political scene, but many would see his political conclusions and prescriptions for Western action as weak. Above all, his vitally important 'spectrum' is linear, as depicted in Figure 9.1. As it stands, this diagram is somewhat paradoxical, for both Gorbachev and the conservatives such as Ligachev are members of the same Party. A suggested solution to this problem is afforded in the next chapter.

Gorbachevites Lib.–Nationalists Centrists–Pamyat'   Nat.–Bolsheviks Neo-Stalinists Conservatives

Left   Right

Figure 9.1 Dunlop's 'spectrum'

Darrell P. Hammer sees three major political forces in modern Soviet politics: the left-liberal 'Westernising' Gorbachevites; the conservatives and neo-Stalinists led by Ligachev; and the Russian nationalists. However, Hammer stated that 'Russian nationalism is a complex phenomenon, a state of mind, and not an ideology with a well-defined line.'[23] Distinguishing between the official 'Russian' party (Rasputin, Glazounov, Astaf'ev, Likhachev and others) and dissident Russian nationalists such as Osipov, Borodin and Father Dudko, Hammer also posited a difference between Pan-Slav 'statist' National Bolshevism and neo-Slavophile Russophiles such as Solzhenitsyn. Oddly, Hammer sees Pamyat' as a sideline and a temporary aberration.[24] Hammer believes that Gorbachev's flirtation with the Orthodox Church and the regime's relative toleration of Osipov and Borodin are based on real policy considerations and not just political expediency. Certain prescriptions taken from writings in *Veche* in the early 1970s, such as *zakonnost*, have now become official policy, and Gorbachev clearly wants the church to exert its influence over such matters as alcoholism and corruption, where to some extent the official policies (such as the anti-alcoholism campaign from 1985) have failed. Hammer also stressed that real demographic imbalances have inclined the present regime towards child-benefit policies favouring the Slav populations of the USSR.

Hammer's analysis also deals with the economic policies of Russian nationalists, saying that they are incompatible with Gorbachev's 'Westernism' and the input of Western technology, which is seen by such as Antonov as 'capitulationism'. Moreover, Hammer pointed out that while many Russophiles hark back to NEP and co-operative enterprise, others, such as Vasil'ev and Pamyat' idealise Stolypin and small-scale agriculture. All the nationalists would seem to reject the central planning model of Stalinism.

The conclusions drawn by Hammer seem a little unclear. He regards the extent to which Gorbachev can co-operate with the

Russophiles and the Orthodox Church as limited. If carried too far, this alliance would tend to alienate non-Russian nationalities. However, an alliance between neo-Stalinists and National Bolsheviks or Pamyat' looks impossible, says Hammer, from the point of view of economic principle, Leninism and the role of religion. In the end, Hammer's scholarly analysis and accurate descriptions leave out both explanations and prescriptions.

Andrei Sinyavsky is a writer, not an academic, and accordingly adopts a methodology of his own. His profound, dialectical analysis is peppered with stimulating insights. Adopting an historical approach, he shows the roots of the messianism and anti-Semitism in the 'Russian Idea' and demonstrates the connection between Stalinism, imperialism and great power chauvinism. He believes that the failure of Marxism-Leninism and the destruction of national monuments has given birth to a widespread nationalism which is allied to 'tribal' feelings which in turn externalise the blame for past depredations. This tends to lead to the attractiveness of theories about an international Judeo-Masonic conspiracy. The hostility of Russians to inegalitarianism and conspicuous consumption is also directed, not so much against Communism, as against the West. Therefore, says Sinyavsky, Pamyat' is to be taken seriously. Basing his arguments on his interpretation of Russian national characteristics, and the marked messianism of Russian thought, Sinyavsky draws some fairly apocalyptic and prophetic conclusions about the aggressive aims of the new nationalists, who can easily disguise their real aims as a crusade against sinister international forces. The new Russian Right might conceivably come to power, he thinks, and if so it would prove to be centrifugal and not centripetal; 'in the full knowledge that "soulless" Westerners are second-class people, [and] would see Europe as the next piece of virgin land to be cultivated'.[25]

For Ronald Suny, the Russian nationalists are so complex and contradictory in their aims that one cannot see them in any way as a political movement. In a series of brilliant insights, Suny describes the genesis and explanations for a revival of Russian national consciousness alongside those of many non-Russian cultural nationalisms. However, he sees large areas of Russian nationalist thought, particularly in the areas of ecology, culture and even religious-moral concerns, as being compatible with Gorbachev's policies of *perestroika, glasnost'* and the renewed dialogue between state and society. Great-power chauvinism and neo-Stalinism, according to Suny, have been relatively discredited in the new era of revelations about Stalin's crimes. Accordingly, Suny believes that support for Gorbachev's policies can allow the West to be 'sanguine about the unlikely victory of the more aggressive forms of statist chauvinism over the Communist Party'.[26]

By far the most impassioned message was that of Alexander Yanov. He stressed the dynamic nature of Russian nationalism and the difficulties of precise definition, but considered that the New Right is in essence an ideology of counterreform'.[27] Yanov is very aware of the historical context of the Soviet regime and draws interesting parallels between today's re-emergent Russian nationalism and the powerful ideologies of the Russian Right in the late nineteenth and early twentieth centuries. It will already be clear to the reader that this writer also believes that Pamyat' and other varieties of Russian nationalism can be understood only in this context.

Yanov points out that the degeneration of the Russian Right in tsarist times and the emergence of the Union of the Russian People and the Black Hundreds coincided with the 'regime crisis', which again coincided with the emergence of a militantly anti-Semitic nationalism and the corresponding decline of moderate neo-Slavophile and cultural nationalism. He cites the split in *Veche* as a typical example of this process and claims that by the end of the 1970s Shimanov's 'ultras' dominated the debate, providing the main alternative to reform and 'Westernism'. As in the 1870s, the New Russian Right developed as the major ideology of counterreform. It is now the only force capable of providing an alternative if Gorbachev faces a 'systemic crisis' in the 1990s, says Yanov.[28]

Yanov justifies this claim by saying that Russian nationalism has already met some vital preconditions for its emergence as an opposition ideology. First, there is already a mass protofascist movement, namely the Pamyat' Society, which will gain adherents in its new incarnation as 'The Russian Popular Front Pamyat'. Second, there have recently been a series of increasingly open attacks on official newspapers and politicians by anti-Semites, as outlined briefly in Chapter 8. Third, there has been extensive and successful recruitment of major intellectual and literary-artistic figures to the movement, including Rasputin and Astaf'ev among others. Fourth, many influential journals now articulate an increasingly coherent counter-reform, anti-Western 'opposition' ideology. These journals include *Nash Sovremennik* and *Molodaya Gvardiya*, while mass-circulation novels such as Belov's *Everything is still to come* exercise a hold on the public's collective imagination.

Yanov distinguishes between patriotism, nationalism and chauvinism and he does not claim (as some nationalists do) that the reformers such as Gorbachev are Russophobes. Quite the contrary: Gorbachev is a Russian patriot, but he is saddled with the legacy of a tired and discredited Marxism. As a convinced Marxist, Gorbachev cannot easily introduce the major reforms of the economy which alone can save the system, namely marketisation and integration with the world economy. The USSR therefore faces a full-blown 'systemic crisis', which Yanov summarises as 'a dramatic transition into the unknown at the end of the second Christian millennium'.[29] Yanov believes that we should take the new Russian nationalism very seriously indeed, as it is a powerful force in Soviet politics despite its apparent absurdities, its irrationality and its totally discredited intellectual origins. The political inexperience and the intellectual infantilism of the Soviet intelligentsia and above all of the Soviet masses, are barriers to underestanding, as is the limited power of *glasnost'* which like *perestroika* itself may prove to be reversible. Yanov suggests that the success or failure of *perestroika* will be decided in the 1990s and if it fails, the collapse of the Soviet Union as a unified political system could only be forestalled by the Soviet military. Their ideology, he suggests, would have to be based on that of the new Russian Right disguised as anti-Westernism. Yanov's chilling message is therefore: 'the defeat of the current reform process is likely to result in a brutal counterreformist dictatorship. . . . But this time, unlike all previous cases, we are talking about a fascist nuclear dictatorship.'[30]

Yanov's clarity of exposition, honed by long years of argumentation and publication in the wilderness, marks out his paper as the outstanding contribution of the collection. Both Yanov and Sinyavsky are powerful in their pessimism; they are prophets rather than scholars, and their thought is paradoxically located in that very apocalyptic 'Russian' mould which they castigate among the nationalist ideologues. In contrast, Dunlop, Hammer and Suny are scholars in the tradition of Anglo-Saxon (and Armenian) empiricism; they studiously avoid futurology, but at the same time both Dunlop and Suny express tentative hypotheses about future trends. In order to test these trends, however, it will surely be necessary to locate the many varieties of Russian nationalism within the overall pattern of the political spectrum. In other words, a 'working model' is now required. The subject of model construction, defence of its methodology and exposition of its mode of operation form the content of the next chapter.

NOTES

1. See Elizabeth Teague, *Radio Liberty Research Bulletin*, RL556/88 (5 December 1988).
2. E. Losoto, *Komsomolskaya Pravda*, 22 May 1987.
3. Ibid.
4. E. Losoto, *Komsomolskaya Pravda*, 19 December 1987.
5. *Nash Sovremennik*, No. 10 (1987).
6. The title of Losoto's article was 'Slishkom pokozhe!' ('Too Similar!').

7. A. S. Shmakov, *Mezhdunarodnoe Tainoe Pravitel'stvo* (*The International Secret Government*) (Moscow, 1912).
8. P. Gutionov, *Izvestiya*, 27 February 1988.
9. *Nash Sovremennik*, No. 1 (1988), pp. 169–72.
10. *Izvestiya*, 27 February 1988, column 5.
11. Ibid.
12. N. Katerli, *Leningradskya Pravda*, 9 October 1988.
13. See Julia Wishnevsky, 'A Guide to Some Major Soviet Journals', RL Suplement 2/88 (20 July 1988), pp. 15, 18.
14. *Radio Liberty Research Bulletins*, Special Edition (19 December 1988).
15. *Nauka i Religiya*, No. 3 (1988) pp. 45–8.
16. *RL*, Special Edition, op. cit., p. 4.
17. *Druzhba Narodov*, No. 6 (1988) pp. 245–62.
18. *Pravda*, 1 July 1988, p. 3.
19. Press Release (*Moscow Patriarchate*), English Edition, 4 June 1988, p. 6.
20. *Sovietskaya Rossiya*, 13 March 1988, p. 3.
21. *RL*, Special Edition, op. cit., p. 9.
22. J. Dunlop, *The New Russian Revolutionaries* (Mass., Nordland, 1976).
23. *RL*, Special Edition, op. cit., p. 12.
24. Ibid., p. 11.
25. Ibid., p. 35.
26. Ibid., p. 42.
27. This was the title of Yanov's paper.
28. For a discussion of the difference between 'regime crisis' and 'systemic crisis', see A. Yanov, *The Russian Challenge and the Year 2000* (New York, Basil Blackwell, 1987), pp. 273–6.
29. *RL*, Special Edition, op. cit., p. 50.
30. Ibid., p. 52.

10 Gorbachev and the politics of Russian nationalism

This chapter is concerned with the politics of Russian nationalism and not with the Kremlinology of the Gorbachev era. However, there was a consensus among Western scholars at the end of the 1980s that, despite the demotion of Egor Ligachev and Victor Chebrikov at the Central Committee Plenum in September 1988 (and the latter's subsequent removal from the Politburo), Ligachev continues to form the centre of a conservative opposition to *perestroika* in 1989. This was still the central focus of all Soviet politics in 1989 and Russian nationalism must be seen in this context and not simply as a focus of attention to be studied independently. Russian nationalism is the 'third' force of Soviet politics, and will surely remain important in that context for the foreseeable future. The crucial question, then, is how nationalism relates to the rest of the political spectrum.

At the centenary of Dostoevsky's death in 1981, I was still studying for my doctorate, which was connected with Dostoevsky's political and social thought. I was amazed to read several adulatory articles in the Soviet press, commending Dostoevsky's Russophilism, which I had already concluded as being an apology for Russian imperialism and autocracy.[1] A decade earlier, leading Soviet journals such as *Nash Sovremennik* and particularly *Molodaya Gvardiya* had published several Russophile articles which were profoundly nationalist with a strongly anti-Western tone. Like most political scientists, I had believed that nationalism is generally associated with the right wing of the political spectrum. How then, could it prove attractive to Communists from the centre of the Soviet Party such as Brezhnev and Suslov? The apparent paradox of this 'linear spectrum' is illustrated in Figure 10.1. The solution to this paradox, I suggest, is to view the linear spectrum not as a straight progression from right to left, but as the circumference of a circle, or even of a sphere. This idea owes something to the influence of Andrei Amalrik, whose essay 'Ideologies in Soviet society' suggested something similar,[2] and to Professor H. J. Eysenck, whose suggestion of a vertical (Tough–Tender) axis in the political spectrum has been tested empirically.[3]

This circular or spherical spectrum helps to explain the relative proximity of right-wing communism and left-wing nationalism, but so far the model is extremely elementary. In the first place, it is static and cannot even describe political change, let alone explain it. Second, it does not adequately explain the political economy of the system. Third, if we are to see the system as analogous to a sphere floating in a medium whose surface lies along the horizontal axis, any movement of the sphere will create instability. Yet we know that both liberal-democratic systems of the Western European and North American type are relatively stable, and that Soviet-type one-party systems have been fairly stable in the post-war period until the present time. Fourth, the model does not allow for the varieties of Russian nationalism, the 'Dunlop Spectrum' if I may so describe it,[4] or for the political conflicts which we know to exist within the ranks of the CPSU. However, thanks to the work of Roy Medvedev[5] and others, it is possible to suggest that on the left wing of the Party today, we have 'democratisers' like Gorbachev and Yakovlev, while in the centre there are 'conservatives' such as Ligachev, and on the Right of the Party the neo-Stalinists such as Andreeva.

I believe it may be possible, as an heuristic device, to regard the political system as a 'rotating sphere'.[6] Carter's Rotating Sphere (CRS) is analogous to an orange floating in water: the empirical political scientist will note that such an orange floats with about three-quarters of its volume submerged. The exposed surface is the operative political spectrum of the country concerned, while the substantial mass beneath the surface provides stability. Political change from one part of the spectrum to another nearly adjacent part of the surface can occur without significant destabilisation.

The political discourse of the system concerned will be dominated by those parts of the spectrum which are above the surface. In the case of the Soviet system (see Figure 10.3) the dominant discourse will therefore take place between the extremes indicated by the range from left-wing 'democratisers' to the right of 'national bolshevism'. Any proximate area which is just below the 'surface' will contribute to the political debate of the country, but only in the guise of dissident politics. In the case of the Soviet system, this will be the area which I have called 'New Left' (including such figures as Yel'tsin and Kagarlitsky) on the Left and the area which I have called 'Pamyat'–Centrists',[7] including Vasil'ev, Astaf'ev and Rasputin on the Right. Areas of the spectrum which are deeply below the surface, such as capitalist Christian-Democracy would be regarded as 'loony' options by the system as it is at present. To take another example, but using the same broad principles, from the Tsar's point of view in 1916, the Union of the Russian People, the Nationalists and the Octobrists were all parts of the political scene, whereas the Kadets

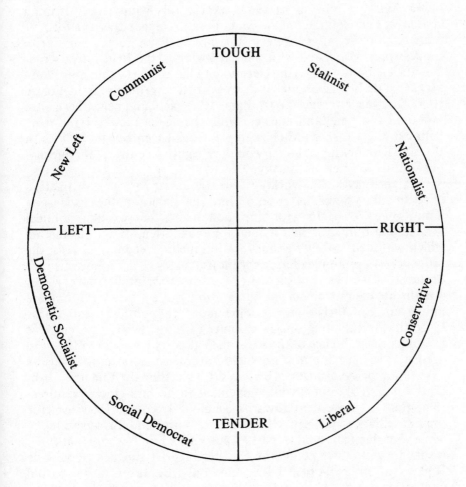

Figure 10.2 The spherical simile

were a regrettable and dissident excrescence: the far Left and the Bolsheviks must have seemed weird, 'loony' extremists, interesting only to the Okhrana.

The position of the economic left–right axis is, of course, crucial and will no doubt arouse considerable debate. My view is that central planning may be associated with the (Brezhnevite) conservative area of the spectrum, since it is generally recognised that after the failure of the Kosygin reforms of 1965, the central 'Ministerial' planning system was consolidated. One could perhaps regard this as a form of 'state capitalism'. In a Western-style political system, free enterprise capitalism is associated with the right wing of the British Conservative Party, or the CDU in Germany. This suggests that the Plan–Market axis lies at about 30 degrees to the vertical axis in Figure 10.3. On this reference axis, Pamyat' is actually near the centre economically and 'anti-market' while being extremely right wing politically. To take another example, Social-Democratic politics in Britain (Kinnockite Labour) would be right of centre economically, but well to the Left politically.

CRS thus gives us a working heuristic device for the investigation of political systems in general, but the device naturally has its limitations. To begin with, the model does not explain political change, but only describes it. The complex, often mysterious factors which will tend to bring about rotation include: economic crisis; the influence of opinion leaders; exogenous factors such as the arms race or the attractiveness and success of rival systems; intellectual currents and the arcane movements of human thought; all these can stimulate movement. Similarly there are some important political actors whose location on the diagram is obscure. In the Soviet system, for example, the influence of the Russian Orthodox Church is difficult to predict, as is the input from such cultural-patriotic individuals as Likhachev or Averintsev. One would have thought that the Orthodox Church should favour movement in an anti-clockwise direction, that is, movement towards religious freedom. However, the present alliance between Gorbachev and the church seems to be somewhat tactical on his part, since the church would naturally associate with such people as Solzhenitsyn or the neo-Slavophile Right. In other words, CRS may only be taken as a partial explanation, and I should warn against too much reliance on computer models and excessive quantification.

We can operate the 'Tough–Tender' Axis of Eysenck with reference to certain variables. The top of the sphere in the Soviet system is one extreme of the one-party state, authoritarianism, ideocracy, centralisation of state power, the planned economy, religious controls and atheist propaganda and control over private associations (sub-group dependence). Conversely, the bottom of the sphere represents multipartyism, democracy, pluralism, devolution of power, the market economy, religious freedom and private associations (sub-group autonomy). Finally, there appear to be three major areas of political discourse: first, Marxism is the language of sectors 1–5, although both sectors 1 and 5 lie outside the realm of the Communist Party of the Soviet Union in strictly political terms; second, nationalism is the language of sectors 5–9, although once again this element will be relatively disguised or muted at the extremes of the range; third, liberal-democracy is the language of sectors 9–12 and 1, although probably politicians attached to sectors 9–12 would question the credentials of sector 1 to be democrats in the Western sense. In other words, we have three overlapping arcs of political discourse. According to this argument, the Ligachev faction in the Soviet Politburo had more in common with the nationalists in 1989 than it did with the democrats and it is thus hardly surprising that a kind of nationalist 'opposition' forming around the journal *Nash Sovremennik* should have been subject to the attentions of Ligachev and even Andreeva towards the end of the 1980s.[8] In contrast, the connections between Gorbachev and the nationalists seemed tenuous, as his 'natural constituency' would seem to lie with the Westernisers and the democrats. In this sense, Gorbachev's overtures towards the Orthodox Church and such moderate 'patriotic' scholars as Likhachev looked tactical, being designed to break the monopoly of nationalism which might otherwise have accrued to the Ligachev faction.

Political change within stable systems can take place within a wide range of options without systemic crisis. The CRS analogy helps to explain why. Slow change across three sectors (90 degrees or so) will not be destabilising. However, rapid change across four sectors (120 degrees), such as occurred early in 1917 in Russia (A–B in Figure 10.3) will tend to be revolutionary, leading to a movement of more than 180 degrees (A–C). Revolutions are exceedingly rare. Political dialogue, even in one-party states, can be sensibly conducted over a wide range of options, and the new institutions of the USSR such as the Congress of Peoples' Deputies, will enable this process to be articulated more clearly. Nevertheless, until political parties other than the Communist Party are allowed, the political debate of the USSR will be conducted obliquely, for example through the traditional Russian 'thick' journals, samizdat publications and the *Sturm und Drang* of the typical Russian *krugovshchina*.[9] Not a little of the necessary input will come from Western experts such as Archie Brown[10] and Michael Tatu[11] and from the Russian *émigré* press. The major difficulty of a one-party system is that the concepts and even the vocabulary of the incumbent General Secretary of the Party (or his equivalent) will dominate all other concepts and languages. It

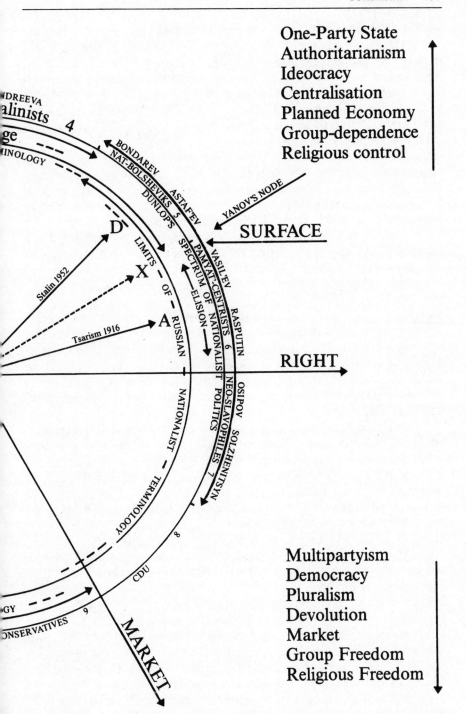

One-Party State
Authoritarianism
Ideocracy
Centralisation
Planned Economy
Group-dependence
Religious control

SURFACE

RIGHT

Multipartyism
Democracy
Pluralism
Devolution
Market
Group Freedom
Religious Freedom

would be a step forward for the Soviet system if it were to recognise the legitimate rights of a 'loyal opposition' to articulate its views clearly. However, it must be admitted that even in a liberal democratic political system, the language and policies of the dominant party of government will set the political agenda. In Great Britain, the tenth year of Thatcherite administration has compelled the Labour Party to adopt a 'new realism', that is, the language (at least) of social democracy.

In the Soviet system, it has been possible to indicate typical adherents of the various sectors only with the help of such researchers as Julia Wishnevsky of Radio Liberty,[12] since a large area of Soviet politics is still arcane or 'Kremlinological', despite the years of *glasnost'* since 1985. For this reason, some of my attributions are open to discussion and I would appreciate any comments from readers. Similarly, the position of many of my points of discussion and illustration on the CRS must be seen as approximate.

My starting point is that of the Russian autocracy in the last year of its existence, point A. In Chapter 2, I argued that the Russian autocracy under Nicholas II became isolated from society and made a crucial mistake in allying itself with the Union of the Russian People, while consistently blocking the Duma and the incipient parliamentarianism which were inherent in the October Manifesto. Thus position A is that of right-wing anti-Semitic, anti-Western and anti-parliamentary authoritarian nationalism: the Tsar's politics were precisely those of Pamyat' today, although some would no doubt argue that the Tsar's powerful and genuine religious faith places him personally nearer to the horizontal axis. After the failure of Prince Lvov's coalition and the resignation of Milyukov and Guchkov, the Provisional Government moved eccentrically but rapidly to the Left under Kerensky. Lenin's 'October Revolution' of 7 November 1917 (position C) completed the transition from A to C, with B being an unstable position. The chronology of events between March and October 1917 may be found in an appendix to John Reed's book, *Ten Days that Shook the World*,[13] and indicates the speed of change within the political system of the Russian Empire during that tumultuous summer.

It should be remembered that Lenin in November of 1917 was still the Lenin of *State and Revolution*,[14] the utopian socialist who believed in internationalism and the 'withering away of the state', and who entered a period of government with the left-socialist revolutionaries. It was only in the following year, 1918, that he signed the Treaty of Brest-Litovsk and then abandoned the coalition. It may be argued that the contours of the future Stalinist one-party state only began to emerge after the xth Party Congress in 1921, and that the Stalinist dictatorship itself cannot be said to have started until 1929 at the earliest. Thus a point such as C adequately represents Leninism in 1917. As I have argued in Chapter 3, the transition from revolutionary Stalinism to National Bolshevism took place only in the post-war period, reaching a position in the region of D just before Stalin's death in 1953.

Khrushchev's innovations were indeed numerous, including the de-Stalinisation process after 1956, and were particularly frenetic after the Khrushchevite 'cult of personality' at the end of the 1950s and early 1960s. However, it should be remembered that although Khrushchev tinkered with central administration and the Party rules, he did not interfere with the Constitution of the USSR as Gorbachev has done and he was certainly a believer in Marxism to the extent of boasting that the 'system' could overtake the Western world by the 1980s. He was also markedly anti-religious, and 'tough-minded' in Communist terms, so that while he was a not a Party conservative, yet he occupied some position close to E on the diagram, that is, further to the Right than either Lenin or Gorbachev.

Under the impact of the events in Czechoslovakia in 1968, which discredited democratisation in the Soviet Party, Brezhnev became a committed 'conservative' in Medvedev's terms during the 1970s. However, with the advent of the neo-Stalinist Constitution of 1977 and the failure of *détente* after 1979, Brezhnev's position seems to have been close to that of neo-Stalinism by the end of the period of 'stagnation' in 1982. That is, given the repression of all dissent under Andropov's KGB and the de facto isolation from the Western world, symbolised perhaps especially by the cutting of telephone communications and the jamming of Western broadcasts, Brezhnev's final position on the diagram approximated to F.

The interregnums of Andropov and Chernenko were too brief in historical terms to be evaluated in the context of the diagram. However, the manifest gerontocracy of the Soviet leadership from 1982–5 both in terms of personnel and policies, seemed to be symptomatic of the gerontocracy of the system itself. The accession of Gorbachev in March 1985 might thus be seen as the last chance of the Soviet régime to avoid a systemic crisis. Gorbachev's *perestroika*, both in terms of the political and the economic systems has been courageous and far-reaching. His bold initiative in terms of foreign policy and his 'new political thinking', his accent on radical changes in thought, policy and action by the Soviet Union, have been dramatic. Quite clearly a shift to the Left, while also involving a dramatic opening to the Western world, Gorbachev's policies have not always been well thought out. His campaign against alcoholism is now admitted to have been a failure, as were the attempts at self-financing (*khozraschet*) in industry without any price reforms, while his failure to see the danger of local nationalisms in conditions of his dramatic de-Stalinisation had created unprecedented crises by the year 1989. Many of his reforms, particularly in the political sphere, have had unpredictable consequences, while *glasnost'* created conditions for a vast national debate throughout the country, particularly after the convocation of the Congress of Peoples' Deputies in 1989, of which the proceedings were televised. Serious miners' strikes in the summer of 1989 threw the leadership into disarray and had to be bought off in an atmosphere of great mistrust between the workforce and the political and managerial élite. In short, the often hasty and ill-considered initiatives of Gorbachev have been radical in the extreme, and he is therefore located at some point to the Left of Khrushchev (whom Gorbachev has incidentally partially rehabilitated) at point G on the diagram.

The logic of Gorbachev's position, although to some extent unacknowledged by him, is one of evolution towards reformist (democratic) socialism and 'Westernisation'. This will ultimately involve free trade unions and multipartyism, together with a slightly expanded role for the free enterprise sector of the economy, and unimpeded communications with the Western world. In other words, the path now being taken by Hungary and Poland seems to be the logical outcome of Gorbachevism, if his policies continue, in the twenty-first century (position Y). However, past Soviet history and in particular the precedent set in 1964 suggest that after Gorbachev there will possibly be a reversion to more conservative position such as F on the diagram. This change will be difficult to effect short of some very serious national crisis, since Gorbachev's legitimacy has been greatly strengthened since 1989 by his formal election to the Presidency of the Supreme Soviet by the Congress of Peoples' Deputies. In other words, he cannot simply be removed from office by his Politburo and Central Committee colleagues, as Khrushchev was in 1964.

Even if a conservative, anti-Gorbachev 'coup' were to become possible, it should be remembered that the CRS is not a static model. As already stated, some exogenous factors and changing variables will need to be taken into account. The first of these is surely that de-Stalinisation has already proceeded far beyond the limits set by Khrushchev: in other words, the neo-Stalinist position may not be at all tenable in the light of the revelations about Stalin which are now common knowledge in the USSR and will become even more widespread with the publication of Solzhenitsyn's electrifying *Gulag Archipelago* in the near future. Another point to bear in mind is the discrediting of the Central Plan. There can be few economists today who believe in what Fidel Castro has called 'rectification' as a means to save the Central Planning system for the purposes of directing a neo-technical economy in the electronic age. In the wake of the

Mezhdurechensk miners' strike of 1989, which spread to the Kuzbass and the Donbass, the Soviet working class is flexing its muscles and protesting about the growing inflation and chronic shortages in practically every area of retail distribution. It remains a moot point whether these kinds of socio-economic developments could be halted by a return to repression. If so, then it could be effected only by a kind of military dictatorship such as that of Poland 1981-3, and greatly extended KGB activity among a population which has recently tasted the fruits of *glasnost'*. Such a military dictatorship would be likely to embrace an ideology to the right of National Bolshevism. Finally, the power of Russian nationalism is not to be underestimated, especially in view of the embryonic moves to secession by the non-Russian republics. The very existence of the Soviet Union as a unified state is threatened, as recent demonstrations in Georgia and elsewhere have shown.[15] These independence or secession movements have a dimension which may not yet have been appreciated sufficiently in the West: many non-Russian republics such as Estonia have large Russian populations who have made their homes outside the RSFSR and believe they have every right to them. They have been schooled in the ideas of Soviet great-power hegemonism and a membership of a nation whose culture and language are those of the 'older brother' of the Federation. Now, they are being compelled to learn non-Russian languages and to have their voting rights curtailed by republican legislation which they thought was inferior to All-Union legislation. In Estonia and elsewhere, a pragmatic Russian nationalism has given rise to 'Intermovement' formations with very real interests to protect. In 1989 Russian workers in Estonia have already staged a significant strike against the legislation of the Estonian parliament. How will the Supreme Soviet react? The new guidelines for Soviet nationalities policy, formulated at a special Central Committee Plenum in 1989, had some very urgent and complex matters to decide.[16]

The ideology of these 'Intermovements' in non-Russian republics bears some close scrutiny. It is highly likely to be the resentful, powerful nationalism of a *pied noir* variety, reminiscent of the nationalism of French settlers in Algeria. It would be surprising if that in its turn does not have some repercussions for membership and policy within the Russian Popular Front Pamyat'. By embracing the support of the nationalists, Ligachev or any similar conservative/neo-Stalinist such as Andreeva may be clutching at a Frankenstein's monster. The imposition of martial law in any significant part of the Soviet Union and above all the invasion of a national republic by Soviet forces, would signal the end of *perestroika*, but it might not thereby install the status quo ante. Instead, a potentially revolutionary situation such as X could conceivably occur. It is no exaggeration to say that the very survival of the Soviet Union as a state is threatened in the 1990s in a way in which it has not been since 1941–2. In other words, contrary to the claims of the conservatives, a reversion to the 'good old days' seems on the basis of the above argument, to be potentially revolutionary.

A movement to a position close to X on the diagram is certainly a possibility, but to assume that it is the only alternative for the political development or change in the Soviet system is to accept uncritically the prophecies of Yanov.[17] Reference to the CRS will indicate that within the so-called Dunlop Spectrum there are two points which I have marked respectively as the 'Yanov Node' and the 'Dunlop Elision'. The Yanov Node is marked because it seems to me that he is saying that all Russian nationalism today tends towards the ideology of Pamyat', so that this sector of the spectrum will exert a kind of magnetic force within the Russian nationalist arc, inevitably resulting in a revolutionary position such as X. However, this analysis of nationalist thought is analogous to the position taken up by former anti-Communists, who frequently stated that 'all Communists are the same', thus blurring any distinctions between shades of opinion within the CPSU, and indeed making all Kremlinology impossible and the study of comparative Communism practically meaningless. Statements of the kind 'All ——ists are the same' are significant as a statement about the political allegiance of the speaker, but do not always help to clarify or predict political outcomes.

Similarly, the Dunlop Elision contains the implicit belief that centrists and Pamyat' occupy common ground on the spectrum. I think this may be an oversimplification. To be concerned about the loss of one's national culture and monuments, as many who joined VOOPIK have been, and as Rasputin and others have indicated in their writings, does not automatically mean that one believes in the *Protocols of the Elders of Zion*, or that aggressive street politics of a Black Hundred variety will become a mass movement. Moreover, the emergence of a Black Hundred mass movement will not immediately in itself lead to a powerfully aggressive militarism. Instead it could lead to the break-up of the Soviet Union, or to what the Western press in 1989 has called the 'Soviet Disunion'.[18]

The reader will also note that the axis which lies along the points X–Y is an axis which divides anti-Westernism and national isolation from Westernisation and reintegration into the World economy. Which Soviet citizen in his right mind would choose the former alternative? It is therefore in the interests of most Soviet citizens, as well as those of the West, that Gorbachev's *perestroika* should succeed. It has already been said many times in 1989 in the Western press that 'Communism is dead', but few people have yet considered the implications of that statement. A transition of the CRS from sectors 2 and 1 towards 12 and 11 (or the transition from the one-party state to a multiparty socialist reformism) is so far unexplored and has no historical precedents. However, if the precedent being set in Poland and Hungary continues to develop into the 1990s, such a transition will occur. A very valuable supplement published by *The Economist* in August 1989 indicated that transition in the direction of Y on the diagram might be possible.[19]

Nations and states are not laboratories and the situation at the end of the 1980s has indicated that Communist systems can undergo change in either direction. The repression of the democracy movement in Tiananmen Square seems to indicate that the People's Republic of China has temporarily chosen the path of military authoritarianism and xenophobic reaction, while the fissiparous nations of Yugoslavia may yet face an attempt to impose military rule and Serb hegemonism. However, political change in Poland, which has already held partially free elections, and in Hungary, where free elections are promised in the 1990s, have been in the direction of 'Y'. Finally it should be noted that the exogenous influence of other political systems on the CRS in question has not been taken into account. Presumably Western European and American interests will influence developments in Hungary and Poland, while any newly reactionary regime in the USSR might halt the socialist or liberal reformism in Eastern Europe.

In conclusion, it will be seen that Russian nationalism has become a very significant factor in Soviet politics in the last decade of the twentieth century. It is possible that Russian nationalism will decide the direction in which the Soviet 'sphere' will move, and might contribute, with other local nationalisms to the break-up of the Soviet Union as a state. Russian nationalism deserves our closest attention and I suggest that certain aspects of this subject should now be investigated with special care. First, the evolution of the Ligachev–Andreeva coalition or their successors towards closer co-operation with National Bolshevism and Russian nationalism proper. Second, the ideology of the new Russian dominated Intermovements in the Baltic states and elsewhere, and their connections with Pamyat: in this connection, the proposals of Moscow with respect to the future of the Baltic States within the Federation will play a crucial role, as will the deliberations of the Central Committee on the future direction of nationalities policy in general. Third, the reaction of Moscow to the newly emerging militancy of Georgian nationalism will be of particular importance. Fourth, the growing mood of Islamic fundamentalism in the Central Asian republics and the reaction of Russian nationalism and the Soviet military should be studied separately. Fifth, the future development of Pamyat' should be watched closely. Successful prosecution of Pamyat' under Article 74 of the RSFSR Criminal Code will prove to be difficult as it will tend to create martyrs and opposition to the regime. As the example of the Weimar Republic shows, prosecution of extreme nationalists by a weak and newly domocratic regime may prove to be ultimately unsuccessful. However, the successful prosecution of Pamyat' and the continuation of reform towards federation would be steps in the right direction.

NOTES

1. S. Carter, 'The political and social thought of F. M. Dostoevsky' (unpublished PhD thesis, London University, 1987).
2. Andrei Amalrik, *Will the Soviet Union Survive until 1984?* (London, Allen Lane, 1970), pp. 174–87. First published in *Survey*, 99 (1976).
3. H. J. Eysenck, *Sense and Nonsense in Psychology* (London, Pelican, 1964), Chapter 7.
4. J. Dunlop, *Radio Liberty Research Bulletin*, Special Edition, 'Russian nationalism today' (19 December 1988), p. 2.
5. R. Medvedev, *On Socialist Democracy* (London, Macmillan, 1975), Chapter III.
6. Carter's Rotating Sphere (CRS) has already been dubbed by some 'Carter's Crystal Ball'.
7. The appellation Pamyat' Centrists is taken from the work of John Dunlop and I have called it 'The Dunlop Elision'. I have suggested that this elision may be something of an oversimplified view.
8. See Julia Wishnevsky, 'Ligachev, Pamyat and conservative writers' *Radio Liberty Research Bulletin*, RL113/89 (28 February 1989).
9. *Krugovshchina* is related to the Russian word *krug* (circle) and refers to the tendency for political and social discussion to take place among Russians within tightly closed circles with a penchant for discussion and splits rather than action.
10. A. Brown (ed.), *Political Leadership in the Soviet Union* (London, Macmillan, 1989).
11. M. Tatu, *Gorbachev: L'URSS va-t-elle changer?* (Paris, Editions du Centurion, 1987), *passim*.
12. Julia Wishnevsky, 'A guide to some major Soviet journals', *Radio Liberty Research Bulletin*, RL Supplement 2/88 (20 July 1988).
13. J. Reed, *Ten Days that Shook The World* (London, Penguin, 1977), pp. 15–17.
14. V. I. Lenin, *State and Revolution* (Moscow, Progress Publishers, 1965; first published 1917).
15. *The Independent* 25 July 1989, p. 10. Reuter's Report from Tbilisi stated: 'At least 20,000 Georgians, waving flags and shouting "Down with the Russian Empire", marched through the capital of Georgia yesterday while all big enterprises in the city stopped work.'
16. C. C. Plenum on Nationalities Policy, 1989.
17. A. Yanov, *The Russian Challenge and the Year 2000* (New York, Basil Blackwell, 1987), *passim*.
18. e.g. Norman MacRae in *The Sunday Times*, 23 July 1989, p. B5.
19. *The Economist* (12–18 August 1989), Eastern Europe Survey.

Conclusion

Russian nationalism has had a sporadic and not altogether benign influence on politics at least since the middle of the nineteenth century. The utopian conservatism of Slavophile thought arose in answer to the criticisms of the Westerners in the 'remarkable decade', but in the following generation both Panslavism and the doctrines of official autocracy severely retarded the political development of tsarism and gave it a millennial and even racist character. In the regime crisis of 1905–7, an anti-Semitic protofascism emerged which helped to undermine the embryonic parliamentarianism of the Duma period and to discredit Russia in the eyes of the international community. In 1917, the extreme Right evolved into a full-blown fascism, which later provided inputs for the development of German Nazi doctrines.

After a relatively brief period of Leninist internationalism, the Soviet Union embraced the policy of 'socialism in one country' in 1924, while the Comintern became the instrument of Soviet foreign policy and domination by the CPSU. The 1920s also saw the rise of the influence of Smenavekhism and National Bolshevism. Stalinism, particularly during and after the Great Patriotic War, evolved into a weird mixture of Marxist-Leninist terminology and Russian nationalist ideology, while late Stalinist nationalities policy implied superiority of the Russians as 'elder brothers' of the Soviet national-ities with Russian as the dominant language of the federation. Khrushchev's frenetic reformism failed to re-establish the reputa-tion of Soviet socialism, but instead discredited much of the Soviet past and helped to undermine the credibility of Marxism-Leninism as an ideology. It is hardly surprising that many sincere Russian patriots should have embraced a dissident (neo-Slavophile) Rusian nationalism during the Brezhnev years, while the regime itself flirted with Russian national values as a potential ideological ally. Once again a regime crisis in the new Russian Empire saw the emergence of Russian nationalists whose relationship with the Soviet leaders was, to say the least, ambiguous. The crisis of the Soviet system itself in the 1980s has once more seen the emergence of protofascist organisations such as the Russian Popular Front

Pamyat', Otechestvo and others, which apparently have a considerable following and a street presence.

As I have already said, history is by no means compelled to repeat itself; nevertheless, any reversion to the neo-Stalinist wing of the Party would presumably involve an alliance with Russian nationalists at an official level. There is a precedent in Soviet history for a 'clockwise' movement of the CRS, and as Yanov has argued, rotation towards some point such as 'X' on the diagram might become a rapid social movement, leading to civil war and military dictatorship. However, in 1989 the future political development of the Soviet system cannot be predicted with certainty.

More than two decades ago, I personally witnessed the military oppression of the 'Prague Spring', Czechoslovakia's embryonic socialist democracy, by Warsaw Pact forces led by the USSR. It was then that I decided to devote my career to the study of this formidable Soviet power which seemed at that time so alien to every Western value, such as democracy, human rights, national self-determination, pluralism and even European culture itself.

By 1990 the doctrines of 'socialism with a human face' have at last reached Moscow itself. Can these doctrines survive and develop in the USSR at the end of this millennium and beyond? Or will the USSR revert to a neo-Stalinist or Russian nationalist anti-Westernism which might conceivably bring with it the threat of war? Unfortunately political science is not futurology because societies and state systems are not laboratories. By the same token, the study of politics is not historicism and past patterns do not necessarily repeat themselves. However, every state has its own particular traditions, its own evolution and political spectrum. In particular, as the Slavophiles once said, Russia has its 'own way of being' (*Samobytnost*). The foreigner, if he is sensible, pauses thoughtfully before pronouncing on Russian affairs and it is in any case for the Soviet peoples and the Russian people to decide their own futures. There is very little that Westerners can do to influence events in the Soviet Union and I am not convinced that any such attempts, up to and including a new 'Marshall Aid' programme, would be welcomed. At the same time, we cannot be entirely indifferent to the political future of such a significant state. We have often been told that the post-war balance of power in Europe has preserved the peace since 1945. If that balance in Europe is now disturbed by political turmoil in Eastern bloc countries or the USSR, the consequences for continuing peace will become incalculable.

Gorbachev's *perestroika* is a relatively recent phenomenon and its consequences are impossible to predict. While a great deal has become clearer as a result of greater openness (*glasnost'*) within the Soviet political process, *perestroika* has undoubtedly unleashed a veritable Pandora's Box of new aspirations, in particular nationalist movements among non-Russians and a powerfully reactive Russian nationalism. There has also been a tendency for progressive, democratic, cultural and linguistic nationalism to change its character towards movements which are assertive, authoritarian and even hegemonistic. Many would argue that the emergence of nationalist movements within the Soviet system is a symptom of the terminal decline of Marxist-Leninist ideology. However, it is not the purpose of this book to indulge in ideological triumphalism. It is enough to point out that the Soviet political scene now involves three 'strong' players, namely reformers, conservatives and nationalists. At present (1989) the Russian nationalists are only significant in the context of a power struggle between party reformers and 'Brezhnevite' conservatives, but Russian nationalism could conceivably acquire a momentum of its own in the immediate future, particularly if it develops in reaction to the newly emerging local nationalism, the endemic ethnic chaos of such areas as the disputed enclave of Nagorno-Karabakh, Georgia and elsewhere, or in answer to the incipient socio-economic crisis of the Soviet system as a whole. The national aspirations and disappointments of the non-Russian republics can be focused against the Russians and Moscow, but the Russians themselves will have to find other scapegoats for the poor conditions in which they find themselves. In this context, the plots of 'Western imperialism' can sometimes merge in the popular imagination with the supposed machinations of the international Judaeo-Masonic conspiracy.

While it is impossible to explain the motive forces for change within the Soviet political system, nevertheless I suggest that certain factors appear to predict development towards socialist reformism (an 'anti-clockwise movement' of the CRS), while others would stimulate change towards neo-Stalinism and Russian nationalism (a 'clockwise movement'). Observation of these trends over the next few years will enable us to read the Soviet political barometer, hopefully in advance of dramatic change, and will thereby enable us to adjust policy accordingly. I have called an anti-clockwise movement 'The Prague 1968 Syndrome', while a clockwise movement is termed 'The Tiananmen 1989 Syndrome'.

THE PRAGUE 1968 SYNDROME

1. The successful prosecution of Pamyat' leaders under article 74 of the RSFSR Criminal Code and a declining circulation and readership of *Nash Sovremennik* and *Molodaya Gvardiya*.
2. The continuation of *glasnost'* and improved communications with

the West in general.

3. The consolidation of Gorbachev's institutional reforms and the rule of law (*zakonnost'*) including the regular convocation of the Congress of People's Deputies, open reporting/televising of sessions of the Supreme Soviet and the accurate publication of Central Committee Plena. The re-election of Gorbachev by a new Congress of People's Deputies in a contested election for President in 1994 would be particularly significant, especially if he abandoned the General Secretaryship of the Party but retained the Presidency.

4. The clarification of the Party's role within Soviet society along the lines of the resolutions of the xIxth Party Conference, and the convocation of the xxvIIIth Congress at the expected time (1991) would be significant, while the removal of Ligachev from the Politburo at any Central Committee Plenum would be of crucial importance. The continuing subordination of the military, as shown by Central Committee membership or the Politburo status of the Defence Minister would be significant.

5. The adoption of a more pragmatic nationalities policy is essential to Gorbachev, and must ensure that no Union Republic secedes from the USSR. The re-establishment of law and order in Nagorno-Karabakh, Abkhazia and other trouble spots is essential.

6. In the long term, there must be improvement in certain crucial economic indicators such as: price reform; containment of the rate of increase of inflation; solution of the problem of excess money supply and the budget deficit; partial elimination of rationing and shortening of queues; and the revitalisation of the agricultural sector.

7. A notable success in foreign policy is required, such as successful mediation in the Middle East or significant arms agreements in the field of conventional weapons. Intervention in Eastern Europe would be particularly disastrous.

8. Toleration of steady democratisation of social life should include: clarification of the limits of the right to strike; the formation of free trade unions; legalisation of opposition groups within the Congress of People's Deputies; recognition of the Democratic Union; increasing cultural and religious freedoms; clarification and observance of emigration rights; liberal laws on the formation of private associations and ultimately the legalisation of political parties other than the Communist Party.

One might add in parenthesis that the teaching of political science as a discipline in institutions of higher education in the USSR and the award of higher degrees up to and including Doctor of Political Science would be a hopeful sign of growing political maturity in

Soviet society as a whole.

THE TIANANMEN 1989 SYNDROME

1. The spreading of Pamyat' and particularly its support within the Soviet armed forces, combined with significant intelligentsia support among important cultural figures.
2. Legal limitations on *glasnost'*, the persecution of investigative journalism and restrictions on contacts with the West, such as attempted jamming of radio broadcasts.
3. The reversal or irregular constriction of the new institutions, such as closed sessions of the Congress of People's Deputies, control of media reporting and a general rise of administrative arbitrariness (*administrativnyi proizvol*) such as the declaration of martial law in significant areas of the country. The defeat of Gorbachev electorally before 1999 would be extremely significant, as would the removal of Gorbachev from the political scene by unorthodox means.
4. The continuation of *podmena* in Party life, and the convocation of an extraordinary Congress of the Party. This latter might well occur at Gorbachev's behest, but it would be a sign of unusual political pressure on Politburo activity. Retention of long-term political office by Ligachev, combined with demotion of Gorbachev supporters such as Yakovlev or Luk'yanov would be meaningful. A significant or sudden rise in the profile of the military within the political system should be closely watched.
5. The secession of a Union Republic, especially if countered by force, would be catastrophic for *perestroika*. Continuing ethnic flare-ups would be damaging, especially if they involved substantial loss of life. Continuing decline of important economic indicators, particularly agricultural production, would be extremely destabilising. Some economic problems, particularly those connected with the retail distribution system, must be solved in the short term.
7. Stagnation in foreign affairs and overweening political or, particularly, military pressure in Eastern Europe would be disastrous for *perestroika*.
8. Restrictions on trade union activity or the right to strike, demonstrate and associate, combined with ideological conformism and religious or cultural restriction (such as the reintroduction of *glavlit*) would be retrogressive. Restrictions on foreign travel and particularly on Jewish emigration would be extremely significant.

Some of the above points may seem to be a statement of the

obvious, but one should bear in mind that short of a sudden and dramatic change which would be evident, the Tiananmen 1989 Syndrome can occur gradually and cumulatively, since Gorbachev's formal political power has been secured with some care so that it would be possible for Gorbachev to retain nominally the reins of power within his grasp, while *perestroika* was eroded from within. Most particularly, it is the sphere of socio-economic reality which appears adverse to *perestroika*, and the effects of this will take time to work their way through into the political system.

What will happen if *perestroika* fails? Some commentators such as Alexander Yanov have predicted the collapse of *perestroika* and a systemic crisis, and go as far as to forecast a fascist dictatorship, armed with nuclear weapons and Armageddon by the year 2000. Gennady Shimanov does not go this far but has predicted instead a state of anarchy and international disequilibrium:

What will the furthest liberalisation of the Soviet Union lead to? Only to its failure. Why? Because the fund of contradictions in it – national, religious and all others – is so great that emancipation will lead to an explosion which will destroy the regime, bringing the country to bloody chaos, forming a huge political vacuum in its place. Having destroyed the world balance of forces it will provoke a collision of the world powers. This outburst will eventually detonate conflicts between America and China, which one way or another will draw in all the rest of the countries.[1]

May I suggest that neither of these predictions need necessarily come to pass? Stalinism is widely discredited, and Russian nationalism (except the CDU) is hardly a force for progress. But the latest manifestation, Pamyat', has taken care to appeal to that deep-seated patriotism which has been a fundamental part of the make-up of Russians of almost every political complexion, both past and present. Therefore its potential as a political force cannot be ignored or underrated. However, the true path of Russian patriotism surely cannot lie along the road signposted by Pamyat'. For *perestroika* offers to Russia and to the world the first real possibility of a lasting and effective *détente* between the superpowers since the beginning of the Cold War more than forty years ago. There may not be another chance. If Gorbachev fails and a regime sympathetic to Pamyat' succeeds him in power, Armageddon may be much nearer than we think.

NOTE

1. D. K. Shipler, *Russia: Broken idols, solemn dreams* (London, Macdonald, 1983), p. 345.

Postscript

In 1989 a number of Russian nationalist organisations entered the political and cultural arena, including the Russian Workers' United Front. The organisations connected with Pamyat', seemed to be fragmenting, but their influence remained strong, as will be seen from the document below. At the end of 1989 a 'bloc' of Russian nationalist groups published an electoral manifesto in *Sovietskaya Rossiya;* they intend to fight the Republic and local elections in the RSFSR on the basis of this programme. I have translated the programme from *Sovietskaya Rossiya* where it was published in summary form. Any omissions are indicated in the usual way with ellipses in the text.

As I hope I have explained in this book, the election platform of the ten/twelve 'social-patriotic movements' may seem to Westerners to be excessively hard-line, atavistic, anticapitalist and authoritarian, but the bloc will probably have a considerable following in the Russian Republic. Only the election results will confirm or disconfirm this opinion. However, electoral, social or political confusion will also tend to advance the nationalist cause.

SOVIETSKAYA ROSSIYA, 30 DECEMBER 1989
'TOWARDS A NATIONAL AGREEMENT'

For the first time representatives of ten social-patriotic movements in our Republic have gathered together, so to speak, under one umbrella. They consist of: the United Council of Russia; *Unity;* Club of Peoples' Deputies and the electors of *Rossiya;* the All Russian Cultural Foundation VOOPIiK; the Russian Workers' United Front; the Social Committee for the Volga; the Fraternity of Russian Artists; the Russian Section of the International Foundation for Slavonic Letters and Culture; and the Union for the Spiritual Renewal of the Fatherland. Of course, all these groups have their own viewpoints, but in the forthcoming elections for the peoples' deputies of the RSFSR and the local Soviets they have decided to act as a united bloc. In the course of some intense and interesting discussions they have worked out a single electoral programme. The original document is extensive and only its essential points are outlined here.

The bloc is seriously concerned about the economic crisis, and considers that the existing basic structures of our national economy are being dismantled recklessly, even though there are some that could be modernised, the sole aim being to exchange our present structure for an anarchic market mechanism. [The market mechanism] does not possess sufficient power for the consolidation of society; concessions are being made to separatists and every kind of 'leftist radical' who are already planning to dismember the USSR and to sell off our national riches to Western 'partners'. It is to be viewed with concern that the 'blank pages' of our history are being filled in to the extent that they are becoming 'black holes'. This process, which is being undertaken by certain circles, is in fact instilling a persistent inferiority complex into the Soviet people.

We now turn to the many negative processes which are developing in society, especially those which are creating social unrest, encouraging the collapse of moral standards, and which will impoverish education. The growing campaign for the legislation of private property under the false slogan of 'popularisation' ('narodizatsiya') of the means of production is cause for concern. . . .

The bloc of Russian social-patriotic movements proposes a way out of the crisis, a renewal of the national life of the Russian and other fraternal peoples of the Republic, a regeneration of their self-esteem. Soviet Russia is a self-sufficient socialist republic, a member of the USSR, but has the ability to exercise those rights which define the basis of state sovereignty.

And for this [state sovereignty] it is necessary to create or recreate our own administratively controlled economy, which will end the present interference by Union organs in the affairs of the Republic. . . . The primary task will be the creation of political and social structures. . . .

The territorial boundaries of Soviet Russia were set up arbitrarily in the 1920s and were arbitrarily changed again during the following decade. In the event of any Republic leaving the USSR, Russia would strive to spread the sovereignty of the Republic to all her many peoples. . . . An objective and fair consideration of this question and its resolution are essential. Soviet Russia must take complete control of her economic potential, her land, waters and natural resources, and must end the uncontrolled exploitation by All-Union institutions of [Russia's] territory, which has not been sanctioned by her Supreme Soviet. A full Russian Academy of Sciences should be set up for the purpose of realising our actual potential and achieving a modern level of economic and social development. Soviet Russia should have normal relations with other Union Republics and equal, proportional, political, juridical and economic representation in the Union government, administration and planning bodies. From 1991 Soviet Russia must cease the present practice of transferring to the Union budget tens of millions of roubles, which go towards, subsidies and artificial increases in the standard of living of other regions, and which are not earned by their own labour. We must observe the principle of proportionality of fiscal resources among the members of the USSR. Budgetary and pricing policies should not create disproportionality in the material security of workers of various nationalities. The transition to cost-accounting (*khozraschet*) in the Union Republics can produce the desired result if this transition is equitable. [The price of] any product should correspond to the costs of production, materials and energy which are relevant to Union Republics apart from Russia.

The economy and industry of Soviet Russia should be directed towards the needs of the Republic and the needs of the people. This is a prospective strategic plan and the future bloc of deputies propose to work towards its realisation. [The bloc] will work out a general plan for the scientific-technical and industrial-economic development of Russia which will eliminate further wastage of her land and resources.

The country must stop extensive development which condemns her to chronic backwardness in relation to many other countries of the world. Modernisation is the chief goal of industrial development, that will solve ecological problems and create better conditions of work. Modernisation is the contemporary way towards improving the method of production and the realisation of labour resources for human needs. This is the way to liberate woman from unwanted emancipation and to allow her return to the family, where she can fulfil her role as mother, the protectress of the home and the support of the nation.

The peasant must be a legal guardian of the land which he works, of the products of his labour. Only the peasants themselves can decide which methods of production are best for them. The land must be leased on undated terms to the peasant, his family and his heirs, and not leased by others for their exploitation. We must take account of the freedom-loving traditions of the Russian peasant and his liking for collective principles. We have had enough of experiments with the Russian soil and the peasant – its sower and protector.

A significant part of the programme concerned the resolution of worsening ecological problems.

The national economy of Soviet Russia, the document emphasised, is founded on social property. This choice was made in

1917 by the people themselves and no parliament, no government has the right to change it. Our deputies will ensure that this property issue will be decided only by a universal referendum.

The people have the right to demand from the government a legal way to recover from the second economy (*u tenevoi ekonomiki*) those milliards of roubles and other material wealth accumulated for decades at the expense of state and workers. With this aim in view it is urgently necessary to carry out financial reforms or more precisely the exchange of monetary tokens up to 10,000–15,000 roubles per capita. The remaining money should be validated only on condition that a declaration of income proves its honest origin in labour. Let the flames of popular anger and justice consume the sharp operators of the corrupt black market, speculators, second-hand dealers, cooperatives, racketeers, swindlers, bureaucratic grafters, everyone who got rich or who gets rich by dishonest, thieving means. Let social justice triumph.

It is essential to introduce a progressive tax on inheritance. These measures will enable us to remove the threatening influence of the second economy and the mafia upon society . . . . Corruption precedes crisis to a considerable extent. We demand – say the authors of the programme – a purge of the administrative apparatus and the bringing to justice of all those who have used their responsible positions for the purpose of gain or the flouting of workers' rights. We demand the calling to account of all those who destroy the country, who conclude international agreements in the interests of foreign 'partners'. Foreign policy and external trade must be in the interests of the people and under the control of the people.

Our country has been created by the blood and toil of many generations, and no one has the right to trade our territory, displacing her economic occupants. The bloc is against the creation of 'free trade zones', concessions, joint enterprises of a neo-colonial type which will act on the principle of 'to them – income; to us – the leavings'.

Soviet Russia is a multi-national state. Not one of its nations has privileges, and the principle of equality of citizens applies to the whole territory of the Russian Republic. Separatism is antithetical to its state integrity. This does not prevent the development, preservation, strengthening of the autonomous education and national particularism of the peoples who are part of the one and indivisible Soviet Russia. Russians have equal rights over the whole territory of the RSFSR; and moreover nations and nationalities within the RSFSR are represented proportionately in the legislative and executive organs.

Ethnic *émigrés* from Soviet Russia live in all the Republics of the Union and are often grouped together. We propose that representatives of the RSFSR should be appointed in these Republics to create a link with their compatriots. In cases of discrimination, Russia would undertake all measures compatible with international practice for the defence of human rights.

The need for a committee on refugees and for the definition of their status has been growing for some time in this country. The juridical definition and proven status of the refugee should be the political, economic and moral responsibility of that republic which he has been obliged to leave. A person of any nationality must be certain of the future and his security from attacks against his peace, his rights and honour.

For a way out of the crisis, the overcoming of crime and the preservation of the independence and rights of Soviet Russia, a modern national army, a strong officer corps and powerful and authoritative law-enforcement agencies are necessary. Against the background of the fulfilment of all its military programmes by the United States, the judgement of politicians and journalists as to a reasonable level of defence is seen as naïve. We must not reduce the army, the militia, or the KGB [who are seen as] scapegoats for the failures of foreign policy and the economy, corruption and waste. The military – patriotic training of the young should be an integral part of the healthy national education of those who will inherit the Russia of the future.

The resolution of political, economic and ecological problems is not an end in itself. It is only a means of enriching national life, the morality, spirituality and culture of the people. Schools should teach citizenship and patriotism to produce a worthy, honest worker and not a semi-educated dilettante. The development of the school system is a responsible national task and the highest authority in the state should undertake it in the name of a secure future for our people.

The mass media actively influence the consciousness of people today, especially the young. A popularisation of 'mass culture' is occurring, an unrestrained propaganda in favour of amoralism and individualism, pornography and violence. The All-Union television channels are non-national, and it is time to put a stop to the belittling of the peoples of Russia. For this purpose it is necessary to limit Union broadcasting to Russian territory, to leave time for informational programmes and to create a state television/radio for the RSFSR. Russia and her great culture is antithetical to the pro-Western propaganda complex. The peoples of the RSFSR need a national mass media! They should broadcast better examples of national culture and world classics. Only on this basis can we affirm truly universal values and mutual understanding between nations. In conditions of all-pervasive permissiveness, profitable for some, the deputies of the bloc will demand the adoption by the Supreme Soviet of the RSFSR of a law on morality, which will protect us against the defilement of the spiritual environment and punish the propagandists of shamelessness and relativism. We are against the so-called 'private' mass media, the true owners of which will be the smart operators of a corrupt second economy, of comprador capital.

The traditional religions of the peoples of the country defined to a considerable extent our national and cultural-historical character, our moral and spiritual experience. We consider, write the authors of the programme, that the Russian Orthodox Church and other religious organisations could take an active part in the development of the spiritual life of the peoples of Soviet Russia. For this purpose, legislation is essential concerning the freedom of conscience both for believers and atheists, linking historical tradition with the social-cultural realities of our time.

A political and administrative centre is necessary for the full state definition of Soviet Russia. A concentration of the political and spiritual life of the Russians is centred, historically, in Moscow. The programme emphasises that our deputies will demand the creation of a USSR administrative centre *outside* Moscow, so as to free her (Russia) from the pervasive power of all-Union administrative structures.

The bloc of social-patriotic movements calls for the achievement of national unity in the struggle for the genuine renaissance of Russia.

Sovietskaya Rossiya
30 December 1989, p. 3

Bibliography

BOOKS IN ENGLISH, FRENCH OR RUSSIAN

Abramov, F. (1987), *Brat'ya i Sestry*, Moscow, Sovietskaya Rossiya.

Abramov, F. (1963), *The New Life: A day on a collective farm*, New York, Grove.

Alexeyeva, L. (1987), *Soviet Dissent*, Conn., Wesleyan University Press.

Agursky, M. (1987), *The Third Rome: National Bolshevism in the USSR*, Boulder and London, Westview Press.

Amalrik, A. (1970), *Will the Soviet Union Survive until 1984?*, London, Allen Lane, Penguin Books.

Astaf'ev, V. (1986), 'Catching Gudgeons in Georgia', *Nash Sovremennik*, No. 5, 1986, 123–41.

Astaf'ev, V. (1979), *Sobranie Sochinenii v Chetyrekh Tomakh*, Moscow, Molodaya Gvardiya.

Baron, S. W. (1976), *The Russian Jews under the Tsars and Soviets*, London, Macmillan.

Belov, V. (1987), *Vse vperedi* (*Everything is still to come*), Moscow, Sovietsky Pisatel'.

Belov, V. (1983), *Morning Rendezvous*, Moscow, Raduga.

Berdyaiev, N. (1947), *The Russian Idea*, London, Geoffrey Bles.

Berdyaiev, N. et al. (1967), *Vekhi* (*Signposts*), Frankfurt, Possev.

Berlin, Sir I. (1979), *Russian Thinkers*, London, Pelican Books.

Brown, A. (ed.) (1989), *Political Leadership in the Soviet Union*, London, Macmillan.

Bulgakov, M. (1973), *The White Guard*, London, Fontana Paperbacks.

Carr, E. H. (1954), *A History of Soviet Russia*, Vol. IV: *The Interregnum*, London, Macmillan

Carr, E. H. (1958), *A History of Soviet Russia*, Vols V–VIII, *Socialism in One Country*, London, Macmillan.

Carrère d'Encausse, H. (1978), *Decline of an Empire*, New York, Harper Colophon Books.

Carter, S. (1977), *The Politics of Solzhenitsyn*, London, Macmillan.

Carter, S. (1987), 'The political thought of F. M. Dostoevsky', London University, unpublished PhD thesis.

Chernyshevsky, N. G. (1961), *What is to be done?*, New York, Vintage.

Chernovsky, A. (ed.) (1929), *Soyuz Russkogo Naroda*, Moskva, Leningrad.

Conquest, R. (1967), *Soviet Nationalities Policy in Practice*, London, The

Bodley Head, Soviet Studies Series.
Crankshaw, E. (1966), *Political Leaders of the Twentieth Century: Khrushchev*, London, Pelican Original.
Custine, Marquis de (1843), *La Russie en 1839*, Paris.
Danil'evsky, N. Ya. (1871), *Russia and Europe: An inquiry into the cultural and political relations of the Slav to the Germano-Latin world (Rossiya i Yevropa)*, St Petersburg.
Dolinin, A. S. (1928), *F. M. Dostoevsky: Pis'ma*, Vol. i, Moscow.
Dostoevsky, F. M. (1953), *Crime and Punishment*, Oxford, Oxford University Press.
Dostoevsky, F. M. (1953), *The Devils*, London, Penguin Classics.
Dostoevsky, F. M. (1979), *The Diary of a Writer*, London, Peregrine Smith.
Dostoevsky, F. M. (1978), *The Gambler*, London, Everyman.
Dostoevsky, F. M. (1927), *The Idiot*, London, Everyman.
Dostoevsky, F. M. (1955), *Winter Notes on Summer Impressions*, London, J. Calder.
Dudintsev, V. (1957), *Ne Khlebom Edinym (Not by Bread Alone)*, London, Hutchinson.
Dunlop, J. B. (1985), *The New Russian Nationalism*, New York, Praeger.
Dunlop, J. B. (1976), *The New Russian Revolutionaries*, Mass., Nordland.
Edelman, R. (1980), *Gentry Politics on the Eve of the Russian Revolution: The Nationalist Party 1907-1917*, New Brunswick, NJ, Rutgers University Press.
Ehrenburg, I. (1954), *Ottepel' (The Thaw)*, Moscow.
Eysenck, H. J. (1964), *Sense and Nonsense in Psychology*, London, Pelican.
Freeborn, R., Milner-Gulland, R. and Ward, C. (eds) (1976), *Russian and Soviet Literature*, Cambridge, Mass., Columbus Slavic Publishers.
Gillespie, D. C. (1986), *Valentin Rasputin and Soviet Russian Village Prose*, London, Modern Humanities Research Association.
Goedsche, H. (Retcliffe, Sir J.) (1868-70), *Biarritz*, 3 Vols, Berlin.
Gorbachev, M. S. (1988), *Perestroika: New thinking for our country and the world*, London, Collins Harvill.
Hallas, D. (1985), *The Comintern*, London, Bookmarks.
Hammer, D. P. (1984), 'Vladimir Osipov and the Veche Group 1971-74', *The Russian Review*, USA, No. 43.
Hammer, D. P. (1989), *Russian Nationalism and Soviet Politics*, Boulder and London, Westview Press.
Handman, S. (1921), 'The sentiment of nationalism', *Political Science Quarterly*, UK, No. 36.
Harper, S. (1908), *The New Electoral Law for the Russian Duma*, Chicago.
Heller, M., Nekrich, A. (1986), *Utopia in Power: A history of the USSR from 1917 to the present*, London, Hutchinson.
Hosking, G. (1980), *Beyond Socialist Realism*, London, Granada.
Hosking, G. (1985), *A History of the Soviet Union*, London, Fontana.
Hosking, G. (1973), *The Russian Constitutional Experiment: Government and Duma, 1907-1914*, Cambridge, Cambridge University Press.
Kagarlitsky, B. (1988), *The Thinking Reed*, London, Verso.
Karklins, R. (1986), *Ethnic Relations in the USSR: The perspective from*

below, Boston, Mass., Allen and Unwin.
Katkov, G. (1967), *Russia: February 1917*, London, Fontana.
Katkov, G. et al. (1973), *Russia enters the Twentieth Century*, London, Methuen University Paperbacks.
Kazakov, Yu. (1965), *Zapakh Khleba (The Smell of Bread)*, London, Harvill Press.
Kedourie, E. (1966), *Nationalism*, London, Hutchinson University Library, 3rd edn.
Khrushchev, N. S. (1971), *Khrushchev Remembers*, London, Sphere Books.
Kichko, T. (1964). *Iyudaizm bez prikras (Judaism without embellishment)* UkSSR., Akademiya Nauk.
Kohn, H. (1967), *The Idea of Nationalism*, New York, Macmillan.
Kohn, H. (1953), *Panslavism: Its history and ideology*, Ind., University of Notre Dame Press.
Labedz, L. (ed.) (1974), *Solzhenitsyn: A documentary record*, London, Pelican.
Lapidus, G. (1984), 'Ethnonationalism and political stability: the Soviet case', *World Politics*, Vol. 4 (July).
Laqueur, W. (1965), *Russia and Germany: A Century of Conflict*, London, Weidenfeld and Nicolson.
Lenin, V. I. (1963–70), *Collected Works*, Moscow, Politizdat.
Leskov, N. S. (1984), *Five Tales*, London, Angel Books.
Levitsky, V. (1914), 'Pravye Partii', in L. Martov, P. Maslov, A. Potresov, *Obshchestvennoe dvizhenie v Rossii v nachale xx veka*, Vol. iii, Book 5, St Petersburg.
Lieven, D. C. B. (1983), *Russia and the Origins of the First World War*, London, Macmillan.
Linden, C. A. and Simes, D. K. (eds) (1977), *Nationalities and Nationalism in the USSR: A Soviet dilemma*, Washington, Center for Strategic and International Studies.
McAuley, M. (1984), 'Nationalism and the Soviet multi-ethnic state', in N. Harding (ed.), *The State in Socialist Society*, London, Macmillan.
McCauley, M. (1984), *Octobrists to Bolsheviks*, London, E. Arnold.
McCauley, M. (1987), *The Soviet Union under Gorbachev*, London, Macmillan.
McCauley, M., Carter, S. (1986), *Leadership and Succession in the Soviet Union, Eastern Europe, and China*, London, Macmillan.
Masaryk, T. G. (1968), *The Spirit of Russia*, Vol. ii, London, George Allen & Unwin.
Materialy xxii-ogo S'yezda KPSS (1961), *The Road to Communism*, Moscow, Politizdat.
Medvedev, R. (1986), *Khrushchev*, London, Chalidze Publications.
Medvedev, R. (1975), *On Socialist Democracy*, London, Macmillan.
Nahaylo, B. (1987), '*Nationalities Policy*', in M. McCauley (ed.), *The Soviet Union under Gorbachev*, London, Macmillan.
Nechaeva, V. S. (1975), *Zhurnal M. M. i F. M. Dostoevskikh' Epokha, 1864–65*, Moscow, Izdatel'stvo Nauka.
Nilus, S. A. (1952), *Protocols of the learned elders of Zion*, Los Angeles,

Christian Nationalist Crusade.

Oberländer, E. (1973), 'The role of the political parties', in G. Katkov et al. (eds), *Russian enters the Twentieth Century*, London, Methuen University Paperbacks.

Pasternak, B. (1989), *Doktor Zhivago*, Moscow, Sovietskaya Rossiya.

Pearson, R. (1977), *The Russian Moderates and the Crisis of Tsarism, 1914-1917*, London, Macmillan.

Programma Kommunisticheskoi Partii Sovietskogo Soyuza (1961) (*Programme of the Communist Party of the Soviet Union*), Moscow, Politizdat.

Pushkin, A. (1980), 'Yevgeny Onegin', in *Izbrannye Sochineniya*, Vol. II, Moscow, Khudozhestvennaya Literatura.

Rasputin, V. (1971), *Poslednyi Srok* (*Borrowed Time*), Novosibirsk, Zapadno-Sibirskoe Knizhno Izdatelstvo.

Rasputin, V. (1972), *Vverkh i vniz po techeniyu* (*Downstream, Upstream*), Moscow, Sovietskaya Rossiya.

Rasputin, V. (1976), *Proshchanie s Materoi* (*Farewell to Matyora*) in *Nash Sovremennik*, Nos. 10-11,

Rasputin, V. (1985), *Pozhar'* (*Fire*), in *Nash Sovremennik*, No. 7.

Rasputin, V. (1975), *Zhivi i Pomni* (*Live and Remember*), Moscow, Sovremennik.

Rasputin, V. (1968), *Den'gi dlya Marii* (*Money for Maria*), Moscow, Molodaya Gvardiya.

Reddaway, P. (ed.) (1972), *Uncensored Russia*, London, Jonathan Cape.

Reed, J. (1977), *Ten Days That Shook The World*, London, Penguin.

Riha, T. (1969), 'Constitutional Developments in Russia', in T. Stavrou (ed.), *Russia under the last Tsar*, Minn., University of Minnesota Press.

Rogger, H. (1986), *Jewish Policies and Right-Wing Politics in Imperial Russia*, Calif., University of California Press.

Rogger, H. (1983), *Russia in the age of modernisation and revolution 1881-1917*, London, Longman.

R.I.I.A. (1939), *Nationalism*, Oxford, Oxford University Press.

Rutland, P. (1984), 'The Nationality Problem and the Soviet State', in N. Harding (ed.), *The State in Socialist Society*, London, Macmillan.

Rybakov, A. (1987), *Deti Arbata* (*Children of the Arbat*), Moscow, Druzhba Narodov.

Scammell, M. (1985), *Solzhenitsyn: A biography*, London, Hutchinson.

Shipler, D. K. (1983), *Russia: Broken Idols, Solemn Dreams*, London, MacDonald.

Shmakov, A. S. (1912), *Mezhdunarodnoe Tainoe Pravitel'stvo* (*The International Secret Government*), Moscow.

Sholokhov, M. (1967), *And Quiet Flows the Don*, London, Penguin Classics.

Sholokhov, M. (1979), *Virgin Soil Upturned*, 2 Vols, Moscow, Progress.

Shukshin, V. (1986), *Articles*, Moscow, Raduga.

Silver, B. (1979), 'Soviet nationality problems: analytic approaches', *Problems of Communism* (July-August).

Slonim, M. (1969), *The Epic of Russian Literature*, Oxford, Oxford

University Press.

Smith, A. D. (1983), *Theories of Nationalism*, London, Duckworth.

Snyder, L. L. (1984), *Macro-nationalisms: A history of the Pan-Slav movements*, Westport, Conn., Greenwood Press.

Soloukhin, V. (1971), *Searching for Icons in Russia*, London, Harvill.

Soloukhin, V. (1988), 'The guests were arriving at the dacha', *Scenes from Russian Life*, London, Peter Owen.

Soloukhin, V. (1967), *Pis'ma iz Russkogo Muzeya*, Moscow, Sovietskaya Rossiya.

Soloukhin, V. (1966), *A Walk in Rural Russia*, London, Hodder and Stoughton.

Solzhenitsyn, A. (1974), *Arkhipelag GULag*, III-IV, Paris, YMCA Press.

Solzhenitsyn, A. (1976), *Arkhipelag GULag*, V-VII, Paris, YMCA Press.

Solzhenitsyn, A. (1972), *August 1914*, London, The Bodley Head.

Solzhenitsyn, A. (1970), *The First Circle*, London, Fontana Books.

Solzhenitsyn, A. et al. (1975), *From Under The Rubble*, London, Harvill.

Solzhenitsyn, A. (1984, 1986), *Krasnoe Koleso*, Vols II, III, Paris, YMCA.

Solzhenitsyn, A. (1976), *Lenin in Zurich*, London, The Bodley Head.

Solzhenitsyn, A. (1974), *Pismo Vozhdyam Sovietskogo Soyuza* (*Letter to Soviet Leaders*), Paris, YMCA Press.

Solzhenitsyn, A. (1971), 'Matryona's Home' in *Stories and Prose Poems*, London, The Bodley Head.

Solzhenitsyn, A. (1981), *Publitsistika. Stat'i i Rechi*, Paris, YMCA.

Solzhenitsyn, A. (1973), *Nobel Prize Lecture*, London, Stenvalley Press.

Solzhenitsyn, A. (1962), *Odin Den'Ivana Denisovicha* (*One Day in the Life of Ivan Denisovich*), London, Flegon Press.

Solzhenitsyn A. (1976), 'Warning to the Western World' in *The Listener*, 4 March 1976 and 25 March 1976, London, BBC.

Stavrou, T. G. (1969), *Russia under the last Tsar*, Minn., University of Minnesota Press.

Tatu, M. (1987), *Gorbatchevi: l'URSS va-t-elle changer?*, Paris, Editions du Centurion.

Tolstoy, L. N. (1972), *War and Peace*, London, Pan Books.

Ustryalov N. (1921), *Smena Vekh* (Change of Landmarks), Prague.

Walicki, A. (1975), *The Slavophile Controversy*, Oxford, Oxford University Press.

Westwood, J. N. (1987), *Endurance and Endeavour: Russian history 1812–1986*, Oxford, Oxford University Press.

Yanov, A. (1987), *The Russian Challenge and the Year 2000*, New York, Basil Blackwell.

Zinoviev, A. (1979), *The Yawning Heights*, London, The Bodley Head.

JOURNALS AND NEWSPAPERS

Arkhiv Samizdata, AS Nos. 1132, 1801, 1846, 2045, 2086, 2218, 2466, 6138.

Dagens Nyheter, 21 August 1987.

The Daily Telegraph, 8 August 1988.

Détente, Winter 1987.
Druzhba Narodov, No. 6, 1988.
The Economist, 12–18 August 1989
The Independent, 28 December 1988, 31 October 1988, 25 July 1989.
Izvestiya, 27 January 1988.
Jews and Jewish Topics in Soviet and East European Publications, No. 4 (Winter 1986–7).
Kommunist, No. 2, 1982.
Komsomolskaya Pravda, 22 May 1987, 19 December 1987.
Leningradskaya Pravda, 9 October, 1988.
Literaturnaya Gazeta, 15 November 1972.
Molodaya Gvardiya, No. 4, 1968; No. 9, 1968; No. 3, 1987.
Moscow News, February 1988, August 1988.
Moscow Patriarchate Press Release, 4 June 1988.
Nash Sovremennik, No. 11, 1976; No. 3, 1981; No. 7, 1981; No. 11, 1981; No. 7, 1985; No. 10, 1987; No. 1, 1988.
Nauka i Religiya, No. 3, 1988.
Novoe Russkoye Slovo, 14 June 1989.
Pravda, 28 January 1949, 17 October 1964, 1 July 1988.
Russkaya Mysl', 27 March 1987, 31 July 1987.
Sovietskaya Kul'tura, 28 June 1987, 23 July 1987.
Sovietskaya Rossiya, 13 March 1988, 30 December 1989.
The Sunday Times, 23 July 1989.
Survey, No. 99, 1976.
Voprosy Literatury, No. 9, 1976.

RADIO LIBERTY RESEARCH BULLETINS

J. Dunlop, Special Edition 19 December 1988 'Russian nationalism today'
V. Konovalov, RL 394/88.
Elizabeth Teague, RL 556/88.
Julia Wishnevsky, RL 341/87.
Julia Wishnevsky, Supplement 2/88 (20 April 1988).
Julia Wishnevsky, RL 113/89.

Index

Bolshoi Theatre, 124
Bonch-Bruevich, V., 68
Bondarchuk, S., 126
Bondarenko, V., 122
Bondarev, Yu., 111, 125, 126
Borodin, L., 79, 84, 107, 127
Borodino (Battle), 114
Borrowed Time (Rasputin), 94
Bosh, Ye, 67
Bratsk, 94
Brest-Litovsk (Treaty), 8, 45, 47,
  66, 140
Brezhnev, L., 7, 8, 52, 58, 75–102,
  109, 132, 141, 147
Brown (Professor A.), 137
Büchner, L. 18
Bukharin, N., 8, 44, 48, 50, 125
Bulastel', P., 29
Bulgakov, M., 49, 50
Bulygin Imperial Rescript, 30
Bunin, I., 46, 94
Burlatsky, F., 111
Buryats, 117
Butmi, G., 32, 33
Byelorussia, 123
Byelorussian Jews, 123
Byzantium, 14, 21

Canada, 85
Carr, E., 43, 44, 45
Carrère d'Encausse, H., 10
Carter, D. (CB), 9
Carter, (Mrs J.), 9
Carter, (Dr S), 62
CRS (Carter's Rotating Sphere),
  133, 136, 138–46, 148
Castro, F., 59, 142
'Catching Gudgeons in Georgia'
  (Astaf'ev), 117
CDU, 136, 152
Central Asia, 145
Chaadayev, P., 16
'Chalmaevism', 83–4, 103
Chebrikov, V., 124, 132
Cheka, 68
Chernenko, K., 1, 141
Chernobyl, 92, 114
Chernyshevsky, N., 22, 24, 85

Chicherin, G., 44
Chikin, V., 126
China, 62, 76, 145, 152
Christianity, 46
Christian-Democracy, 133
Christian Science Monitor, The
  115
Chronicle of Current Events, 75
City of London Polytechnic, 9
City University of New York, 124
Clausewitz, 66
Club of Peoples' Deputies, 153
Cold War, 52, 60
Collectivisation, 73, 107
Comintern:
  Second World Congress, 44
  Third World Congress, 44
  Fourth World Congress, 44
  Fifth World Congress, 45
Commissar for War, 49
Communism, 50, 58
Communist Party of the Soviet
  Union:
  Xth Congress, 44, 140
  XXth Congress, 5, 55, 58, 104
  XXIIth Congress, 49, 57, 60
  XXIIIth Congress, 75
  XXVIIth Congress, 1
  XXVIII Congress, 150
  XIXth Conference, 1, 126, 150
  RKP (b), 44, 45
Congress of Peoples' Deputies,
  103, 137, 142, 150, 151
Conquest, R., 10
Conservative Party, 136
Constantinople, 14, 19
Council of Florence, 14
Crankshaw, E., 55
Crime and Punishment
  (Dostoevsky), 23
Crimean Tatars, 52, 55, 68, 117
Cuba, 59
Custine (Marquis de), 16
Czechoslovakia, 76, 83, 115, 141,
  148

Daghestan, 53
Daily Telegraph, 164